Local Area Networks

2nd Edition

M Devargas

MANCHESTER · OXFORD

British Library Cataloguing in Publication Data

Devargas, M
  Local Area Networks — 2nd ed
  I. Title
  004.68

ISBN 1-85554-160-2

© M Devargas, 1992

All rights reserved. No part of this publication may be reproduced, stored in a retrieval system, or transmitted, in any form by electronic or mechanical means without the prior permission of NCC Blackwell Limited.

First published in 1992 by:

NCC Blackwell Ltd, 108 Cowley Road, Oxford OX4 1JF, England.

Editorial Office: The National Computing Centre Limited, Oxford House, Oxford Road, Manchester M1 7ED, England.

Typeset in 10pt Times Roman by M Wilson, The National Computing Centre Limited, Oxford Road, Manchester M1 7ED and printed by Hobbs the Printers of Southampton.

ISBN 1-85554-160-2

For Michelle, my wife — my inspirer and long-suffering supporter. I am indebted to you for your constant and invaluable guidance during this interminable task and most of all for your patience and love.

Preface

Local Area Networks (LANs) are currently part and parcel of everyday business life, without them many businesses would not be able to function or, in some cases, survive. The evolution of LANs has been the most outstanding success story in Information Technology in recent years, very few could have imagined in the early days of Personal Computers, that today, PCs are one of the most important strategic tools within many organisations and in conjunction with this the obvious need for LANs.

This second edition of the NCC's LAN book brings together all the relevant topics within LAN technology that have emerged in the past two decades of IT and personal computing.

The author has taken the previous edition and has expanded each topic and added new information on state-of-the-art LAN technology, issues and techniques. Following the same content-criteria as the previous edition, this book gives the reader a complete picture of LANs, from the basics of what LANs are to the technologies available, including inter-networking; sharing techniques, from its origins of ALOHA to Token Passing (plus two case studies - Ethernet and Token Ring); the most popular LAN applications; client-server methodology and its influence on LANs; network security; standards; and future LAN technologies, for example, cordless LANs, FDDI and ISDN.

Additionally, this edition has a chapter explaining the basics on how to choose a LAN, giving the reader a step-by-step method and a chapter describing the most popular LAN to date, Novell.

This edition would be of interest to any individual (whether a novice or an expert) who wishes to enhance their knowledge of LANs. If they are a novice the book guides them step-by-step from first principles. At each chapter ending, the novice is given the opportunity to revise the most important terms within that chapter.

If the reader is already LAN literate, then they could use this edition as basic reference material in terms of technologies available, security, application areas, client-server and standards. Furthermore, it would also give them some insight into what the future may hold for LANs, indicating areas which should be further investigated, for example, ISDN.

This edition of NCC's LANs publication is the most up-to-date publication of its kind to date, obviously, as technology advances numerous new and important features will be developed for LANs. However, this book will still be an important asset to any serious IT professional, since its contents will not be out-dated as any addition or change within this technology will still need to be based on what now exist.

Contents

Page

Preface

1	**What are Local Area Networks?**	1
	Introduction	1
	Types of Networks	2
	History	11
	Terms to Review	13
2	**Technologies Available**	15
	Introduction	15
	Main requirements	15
	Classification of Technologies	18
	Transmission Media	22
	Topologies	44
	Signalling Techniques	51
	The use of LAN Servers	58
	Inter-Networking	61
	Terms to Review	69
3	**Network Sharing Techniques**	73
	Introduction	73
	Multiplexing Techniques	73
	Broadband Bus-Sharing Techniques	77
	Ring Access Techniques	90
	PABX Approach	97
	Which Access Method Should I use?	106
	Case Studies	107
	Terms to Review	112

4	**Application Areas**	115
	Introduction	115
	Computer Networks	117
	Terminal Networks	127
	Office Systems	130
	Document Imaging	133
	Other Applications	134
	Conclusions	148
	Terms to Review	149
5	**Client-Server Methodology**	151
	Introduction	151
	Extending the Workgroup's Capacity	152
	The use of Networking and Relational Database - an example	155
	Terms to Review	157
6	**Local Area Network Security**	159
	Introduction	159
	Security Theory	159
	Network Security	161
	Risk Analysis	167
	Conclusions	171
	Terms to Review	171
7	**The Standards Situation**	173
	Introduction	173
	LAN Standards Making Bodies	174
	IEEE Standards Work	175
	Open Systems Interconnection	182
	ISO work on Local Area Networks	194
	Terms to Review	196
8	**Choosing a Local Area Network**	197
	Introduction	197
	Options for Local Networks	197
	Performance	199
	Planning and Designing your Network	202
	Carrying out the Installation	208
	Terms to Review	209

9	**Case Study**	211
	Introduction	211
	Novell Networking Environment	211
	Terms to Review	216
10	**The Future of LANs**	217
	Introduction	217
	FDDI and LANs	218
	Cordless LANs	220
	ISDN and LANs	220
	Terms to Review	225
Glossary		227
Index		239

1
What are Local Area Networks?

INTRODUCTION

For most businesses their main goals are maintaining as high a profit margin as possible and also establishing an unbeatable competitive advantage. To succeed in today's highly competitive environment, companies need to be able to use their existing resources and investments in the most cost effective manner. This means that ever greater pressure is placed on increasing the productivity of the workgroup.

The use of information technology (IT) has become synonymous with greater productivity and effectiveness. Most businesses and organisations rely heavily on their IT systems, to the extent that if the systems are not available the business grinds to a halt: bills are not sent, orders are not processed, etc. This increasing dependency on IT means that rapid change in commercial practices comes hand-in-hand with technological advances. The management of such change is the most critical challenge open to the business executive.

Since the early 1980s management have come to realise that without IT a business has little chance of survival. IT has become part and parcel of their everyday business requirements. This became apparent when the first PC (personal computer) was introduced. The PC was the forerunner to a decade of innovation and changes in IT throughout the world. PCs were the low-cost tool that introduced many businesses to computers. This introduction into IT was only the beginning of a transformation in the whole make-up of the business workgroup.

Once businesses saw the impact these machines had on their accounts, letter writing, etc., the next step was obvious — how could they share their most valuable asset — information? Networking meant that a person's information was not locked away on one PC, it could be transmitted across a wire to a colleague. Furthermore, by connecting several PCs management saw a way of improving the workgroup's productivity many times over. The Local Area Network (LAN) was born.

Initially the introduction of LANs was based on the prime philosophy of sharing information and resources (for example, a resource could be a printer or a disk storage device) across a local workgroup or department.

2 *What are Local Area Networks?*

A LAN is best defined as follows:

> *A Local Area Network (LAN) is primarily a data transmission system that aids the intercommunication between people or applications, by the use of terminals or personal computers and their peripherals within the confines of a restricted geographical area.*

While this is still the main objective and definition of a LAN, today's LANs can also be viewed as a layered system of interconnected workgroups. For example, within a company different departments could have their own LANs. If they wish to pass information between themselves a 'backbone' LAN could be used to link them. This backbone could be used to link multiple LANs and even provide a link into a central computer.

This means that intercommunication is the key to the future of LANs, and these are likely to become confused with Wide Area Networks (WANs). The growth in the use of LANs has been phenomenal. LANs are being used in numerous environments, from the typical office to the process control system of a manufacturer. In 1990, more than 2.8 million new LAN connections were sold in Europe, the future growth of LANs seems to be assured.

TYPES OF NETWORKS

The simplest form of communication takes place between two entities that are directly connected by some form of point-to-point transmission medium. Often however, this is impractical since the communicating devices are either too far away from each other and hence too costly to connect or because there are more than two devices trying to communicate.

Point-to-Point Communications

In a point-to-point network each terminal is connected to a main computer via a dedicated link. It may be transitory and exist only for the duration of a call as with a Public Switched Telephone Network (PSTN), or may exist permanently as a leased circuit or direct link. *See* Figure 1.1.

Point-to-point configurations are commonly used where only a limited number of physically distinct routes are needed. This type of connection could be viewed as the ideal situation since your terminal has immediate access to the computer at any time. Furthermore, the speed of response is maximised, as the capacity of the line is wholly dedicated to your transmission. However, point-to-point operation usually has a high level of redundancy because the line is not fully utilised, ie during the time spent by the user in typing, thinking, etc.

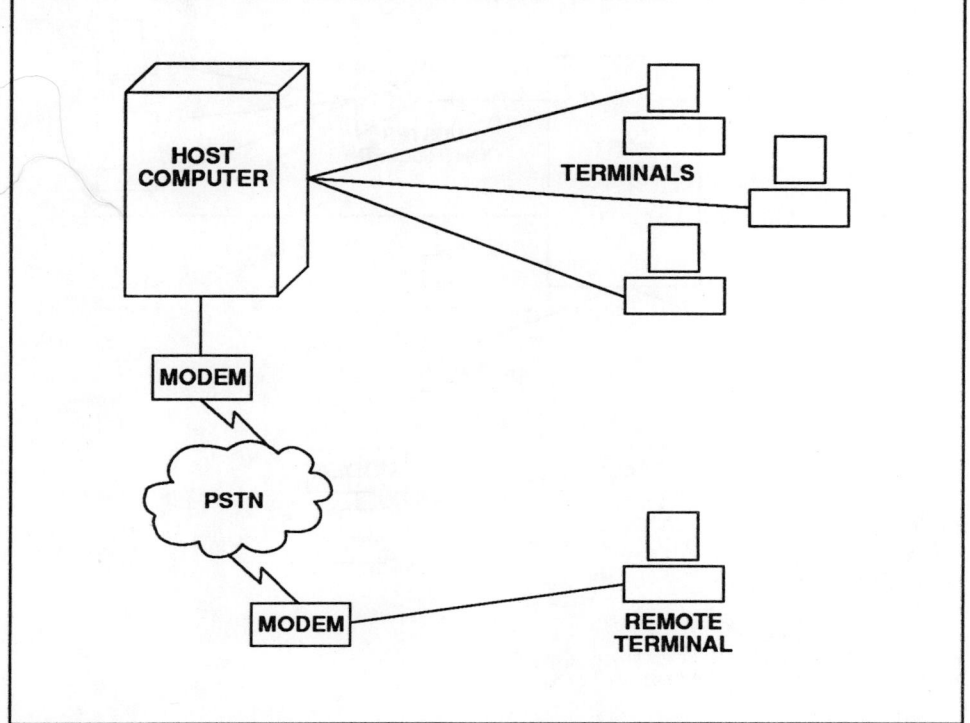

Figure 1.1 Point-to-point communications

Multi-Point Communications

Where a large number of locations (or devices) need to be connected and can be broken down into physical clusters the multi-point form of configuration can be more cost effective. In this configuration two or more devices share the same medium.

Although there is a cost saving in its physical layout (ie line utilisation is increased), the software required to run such a network needs to determine when each terminal is allowed to transmit (ie avoid contention) and also distinguish each terminal uniquely in order to be able to reply to a request. This technique is called polling.

Polling means that each terminal gets the opportunity to transmit and the full speed of the line is available (*See* Chapter 3 for further information on polling). However the bigger the network and the greater the number of terminals, the greater the amount of wait-time a terminal will be subjected to. This is obvious as the polling computer must give every terminal a chance to transmit and hence it will take the central computer a while to return to the first terminal.

4 What are Local Area Networks?

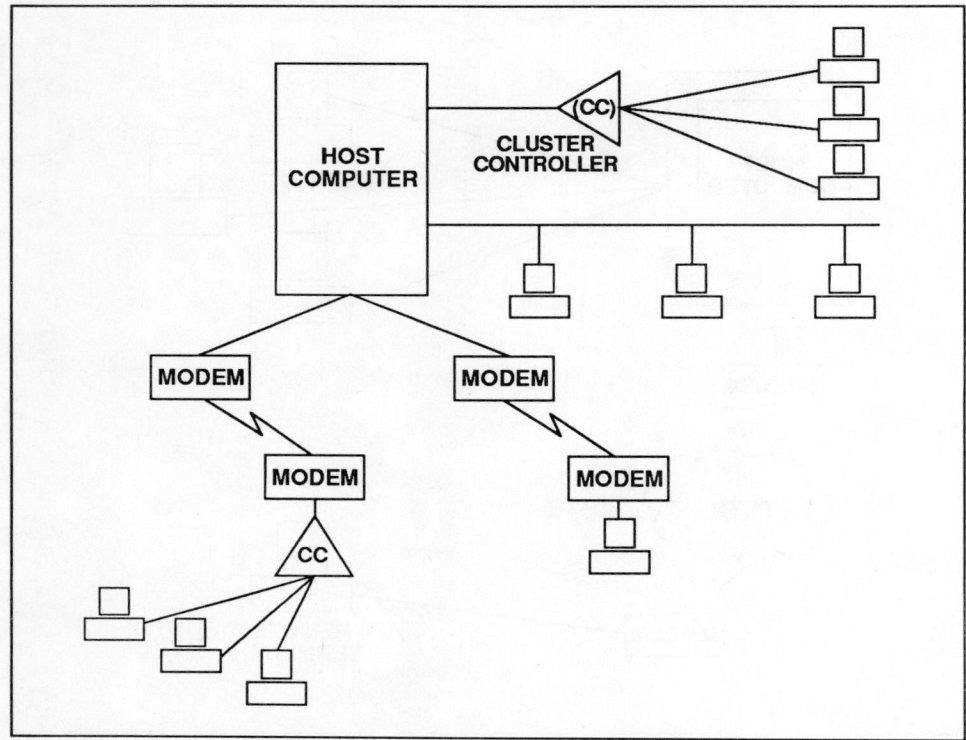

Figure 1.2 Multi-point communications

Multiplexing Communications

Following on from the multi-point network, this type of network can be viewed as the simplest type of multiplexing mechanism. Multiplexing is a generic term for sharing a line. The two main advantages associated with this technique are that a host computer needs only one Input/Output (I/O) port for multiple terminals and that only one transmission line is required.

Multiplexing can be divided into three types of technique. The first, Frequency-Division Multiplexing (FDM), is the most widespread and is familiar to anyone who has ever used a radio or television set. The second is a particular case of Time-Division Multiplexing (TDM) often known as synchronous TDM. This is commonly used for multiplexing digitised voice streams. The third type seeks to improve on the efficiency of synchronous TDM by adding complexity to the multiplexer. These techniques will be discussed further in Chapter 3.

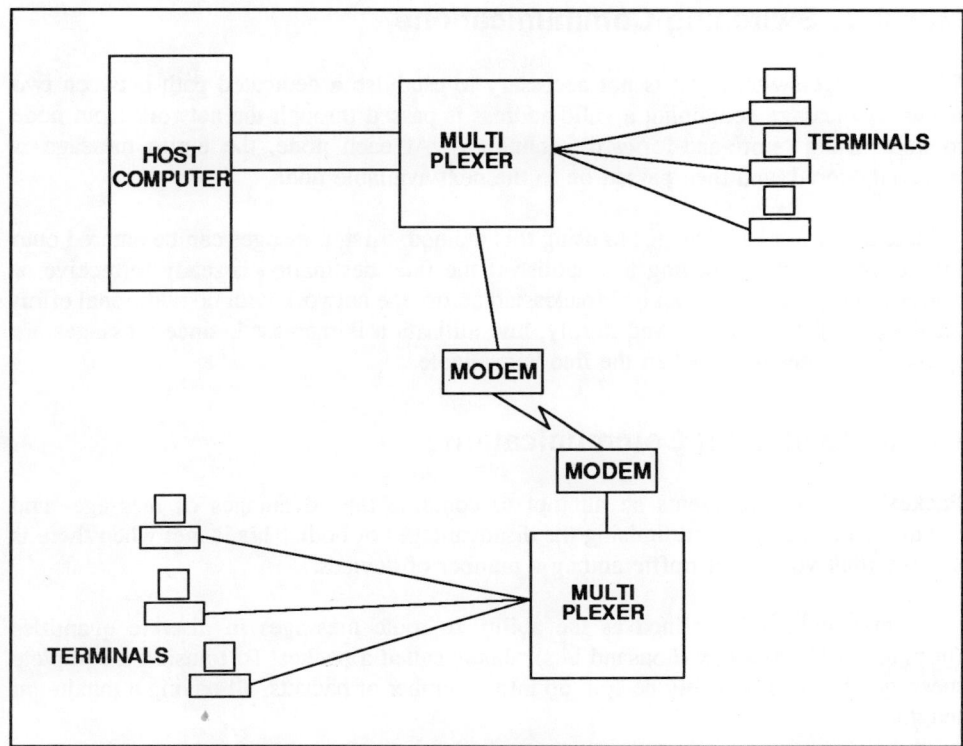

Figure 1.3 Multiplexing communications

In this early introduction to types of networks it is enough to appreciate that simple multiplexing techniques generally provide a transparent connection between terminals located remotely or locally from a host computer and the computer's I/O ports and its terminals. *See* Figure 1.3.

Circuit-Switching Communications

Communications via circuit-switching means that there is an assigned communications path between two transmitting devices. The path is a connected series of links between terminals or switching-centres or exchanges. On each physical link, a channel is dedicated to the connection. Once the transmission is terminated, the circuit is released. An example of circuit-switching is the traditional analogue telephone network.

Circuit-switching can be rather inefficient as the channel capacity is dedicated for the duration of the transmission, even if no data is transmitted — much like the point-to-point link.

Message-Switching Communications

With message-switching it is not necessary to establish a dedicated path between two nodes. A message containing a valid address is passed through the network from node to node using 'store-and-forward' techniques. At each node, the entire message is received, stored, and then passed on to the next available node.

There are several advantages to using this method. First, messages can be entered onto the network without needing to establish if the final destination is ready to receive or not. Secondly, messages can be broadcasted across the network with no additional effort on the part of the sender. And thirdly, line utilisation is increased, since messages are queued and transmitted when the line is available.

Packet-Switching Communications

Packet-switching represents an attempt to combine the advantages of message- and circuit-switching while minimising the disadvantages of both. This is met when there is a substantial volume of traffic among a number of devices.

Packet-switching is defined as the ability to route messages in discrete quantities (normally 1000 to a few thousand bits); this is called a packet. To transmit a complete message, it would probably be split up into a number of packets, all having a maximum length.

Each packet has a controlled format and a maximum size. It contains data, destination address and checking information. Terminal A transmits the packet to Terminal B via intermediate stations/exchanges which store it briefly and then pass it onto the next node on the line. *See* Figure 1.4.

Packets can be transported around the network in two ways. The first is what is called the *datagram* approach. Here each packet is treated independently and addressed individually - just as messages are treated independently in a message-switching network. Although, every packet is delivered to a particular destination, the route utilised for individual packets could be different, depending on the availability of the lines. The second approach is called the *virtual circuit*. Here a logical connection is established before any packets are sent. Note, that this does not mean that there is a dedicated path, a packet is still buffered at each node and queued for output over a line. The difference from the previous approach is that a node need not make a routeing decision for each packet. It is made once for each connection.

The most commonly known packet-switching protocol is X.25. This has been established as the interface standard between terminals and packet-switching networks. X.25 is compatible with the bottom three layers of the International Standards Organisation (ISO) Open Systems Interconnection (OSI) seven layer model. (*See* Chapter 7 for

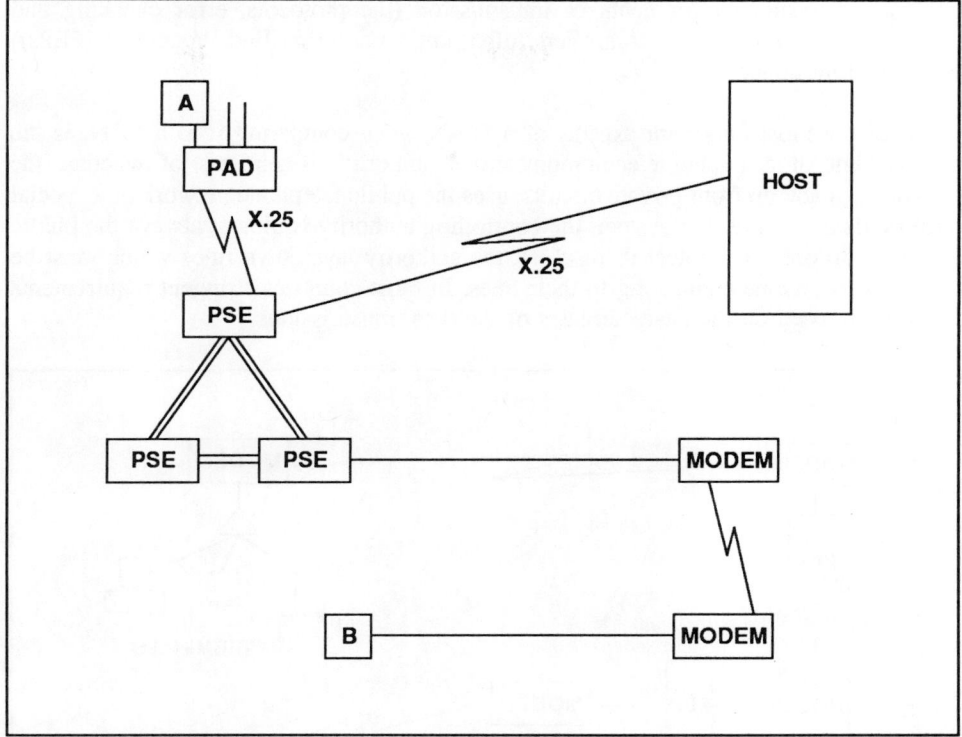

Figure 1.4 Packet-switching communications

PAD = Packet-Switching Disassembly
PSE = Packet-Switching Exchange

further information on OSI.) This means that many private and public network providers are standardising on X.25 packet-switching techniques.

Wide Area Communications

Wide Area Networks (WANs) include all the networks which are involved in transporting information from one location to another. A WAN will almost always be used whenever the information needs to be transmitted across a wide geographic area, with distances from several to thousands of kilometres. The error rate will be far from negligible and error detection procedures are essential for almost every situation. The technique used could be any one of those already described from packet-switching to point-to-point networking.

In contrast to LANs which have only a few components, WANs involve a large number of devices between source and destination. As more lines are needed and

8 What are Local Area Networks?

because of special requirements of transmission (the protocols, error checking and correction) communications controllers (often known as Front End Processors (FEPs)) have to be introduced.

One of the most important aspects of a WAN when comparing it to a LAN, is the involvement of a public telecommunications authority. Regardless of whether the network is made up from private circuits, uses the public telephone network or a special purpose data transmission system, the controlling authority is almost always the public authority. In order to protect themselves, the authority lays down rules which must be observed by anyone connecting to their lines. In most countries stringent requirements are also imposed on the characteristics of the data transmissions.

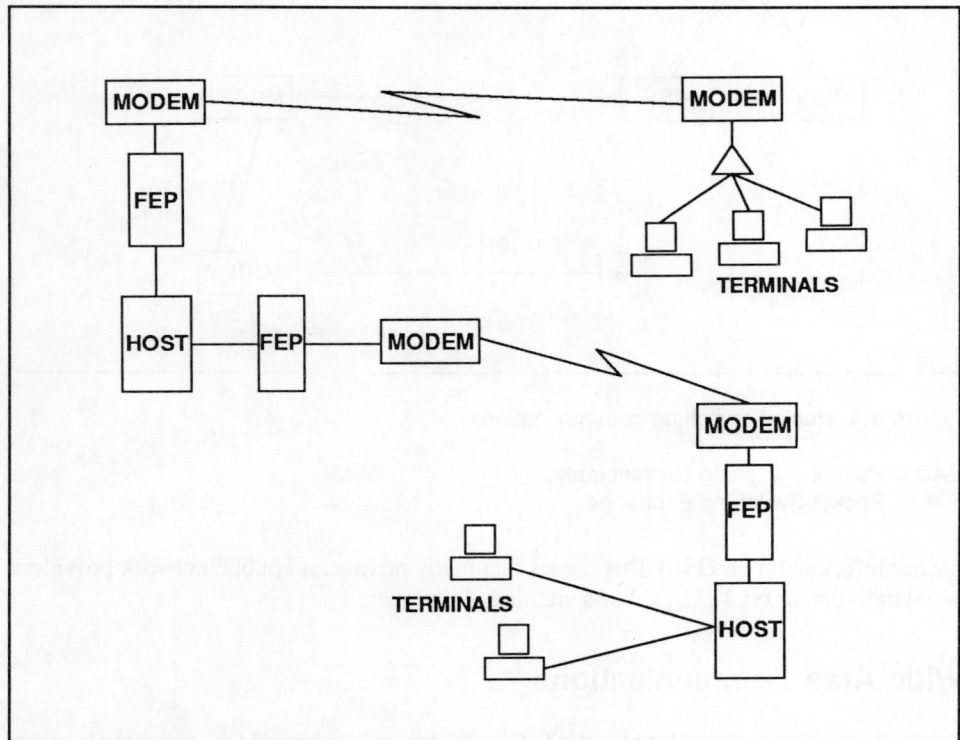

Figure 1.5 WAN communications

Local Area Networks

LAN is not an explicit term but is usually referred to within the IT world as an inexpensive business information network, which can transmit data, graphics and *speech*.

Types of Network 9

The key characteristic of a LAN is the fact that the whole of the network, confined to one site or over distances of up to a couple of kilometres, is completely under the control of one organisation. This does not prevent communication taking place between users of the LAN on one site and others elsewhere. This would be achieved using WANs with special bridging equipment common to both the local and wide area network to perform the function of taking messages from one network and putting them on the other. LANs could be used as device concentrators for a WAN.

Similar to all the previous communications configurations already described, a LAN connects together terminals and computers and other devices. The network can have many shapes (topologies), and many methods of transmitting the information can be employed. Coaxial cables, multi-core cables, twisted pairs, fibre optic cables or even telephone wiring could be used. For further information on cables *see* Chapter 2.

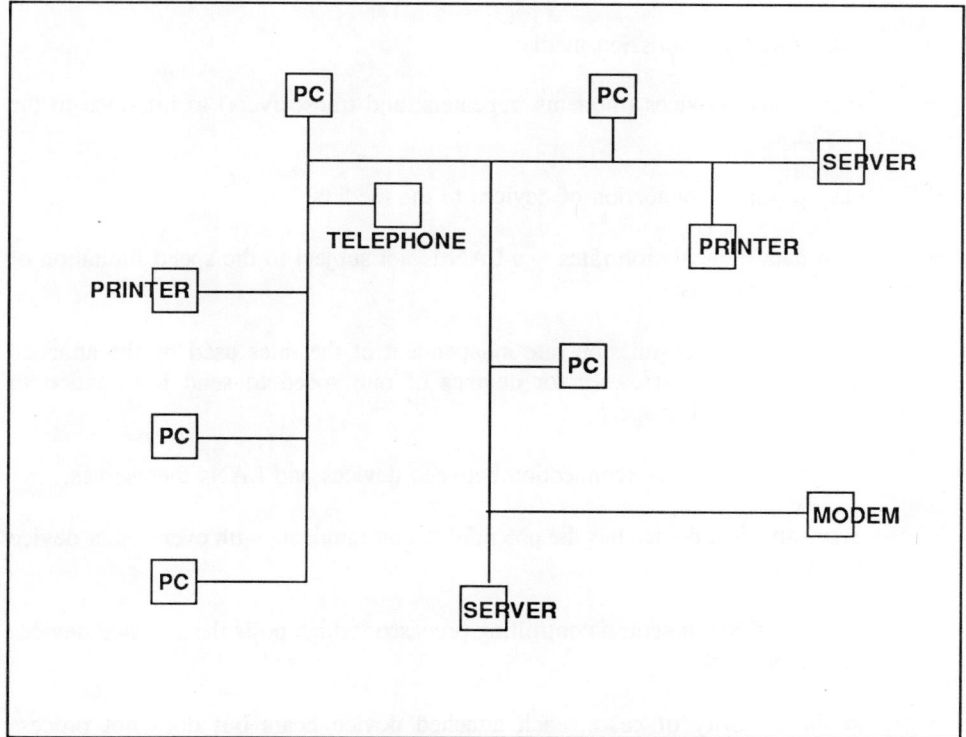

Figure 1.6 LAN communications

In terms of speed, LANs can normally operate at much higher rates than WANs, for example, using a standard telephone line with modems the limit is usually about 19.2 Kbps, while a LAN could function at 10 Mbps or more. These higher speeds are ideal for connection of computer-to-computer applications, for example, Electronic Data Interchange (EDI). High speed is also needed to handle speech in digital form. These high speeds are still, to date (1992), being investigated and developed by the major LAN manufacturers, but due to costs, complexity and the lack of reliable standards, the findings have not yet been produced.

It is unrealistic to attempt to define LANs in terms of their topology or transmission capability as these can have much wider applicability, as will be seen later. LANs can be used in the manner suited to the organisation which own them, and can be completely independent of the constraints imposed by public telephone authorities, the Européen Comité Consultatif International de Télégraphique et Téléfonique (CCITT) or other public services.

The main attributes of present-day LANs can be summarised as follows:

— economical transmission media;

— inexpensive devices (modems, repeaters, and transceivers) to interface to the media;

— easy physical connection of devices to the media;

— high data transmission rates — a LAN is not subject to the speed limitation of common carriers;

— network data transmission rate independent of the rates used by the attached devices, making it easier for devices of one speed to send information to devices of another speed;

— a high degree of interconnection between devices and LANs themselves;

— every attached device has the potential to communicate with every other device on the network;

— there is seldom a central controlling processor which polls the attached devices on the network;

— in the majority of cases, each attached device hears but does not process messages intended for other devices;

— expensive peripherals like laser printers and hard disk storage devices may be shared among all the network users, thereby reducing the effective unit cost;

— single networked versions of software may be held centrally and accessed by user's stations when the application needs to be run. The most popular LAN applications to date are word processing, spreadsheets, file transfer, electronic mail and database sharing;

— limited geographical scope - usually confined to a business office building, although a maximum distance limitation, depending upon the technology, of 80 kilometres can be achieved;

— may serve a department, an entire building or a cluster of buildings.

It is important to note the actual data transmission rate used, the access method nor the topology of the network are essential characteristics.

Metropolitan Area Network (MAN) Communications

Metropolitan Area Networks (MANs) fall between LANs and WANs in geographical scope. This type of network consists of two contra-directional data buses (a bus is a signal route to which several parallel devices can be attached so that the signals can be passed between them — for further information on bus refer to Chapter 2) up to 150km long, with uni-directional read and write functions for each bus. They may take the form of a point-to-point, an open-ended bus or a looped bus.

MANs are still being developed and investigated. Their topologies, data transmission rates and protocols are still to be fully standardised. The only standard to be produced so far is its protocol — Distributed-Queued Dual-Bus (DQDB). DQDB was developed by the Institute of Electical and Electronic Engineers (IEEE) 802.6 Working Group and is a generic name for a high speed, shared-medium-access protocol consisting of pairs of buses funnelling data in opposite directions. DQDB uses Queued Packet-Switching Exchanges (QPSX).

In terms of topology and data rates, at the time of writing the topologies that are being used are adaptations of either the star (for further information on star topology read Chapter 2) or tree-and-branch topologies. The data rates can transmit up to 2.048 Mbps.

Some of the applications that most frequently use MAN technology are:

— interconnecting LANs;
— high-resolution graphics, image and compressed video transmission;
— interconnecting PBXs.

HISTORY

The history of LANs has brought together many separate developments. By the first half of the 1970s LANs were more a topic of discussion and development in research laboratories than commercial products. This experimental work was designed to carry digital information across computer devices. Until that time most computer networks had been built around traditional telecommunications systems designed to transport analogue speech signals. Digital information was translated into an analogue stream of tones which represented the bit pattern being transmitted. The various analogue signals were translated back by the recipient into the corresponding digital information.

This methodology of transmission has been used not only for connecting terminals to a local central processor, but is still used currently in the public telephone network to connect to a remote device. This type of connection uses the modem to translate the digital signals to analogue signals and vice versa, so that the carrier can transmit the signal.

The advent of packet-switching transmission was one of the determinant factors influencing the design of Local Area Networks, as this method shares a single transmission system across multiple users.

The development of packet-switching brought about the first implementation of a LAN, although this might be seen as a WAN implementation due to its geographical distribution.

The University of Hawaii adapted this method to connect remote users to its computer centre. The Hawaiian Islands, at the time had an unreliable telephone system, distributed across a very difficult geographical archipelago. The University implemented a radio broadcasting system called ALOHA, where every device broadcasted a packet of information whenever it had one to transmit. All the devices continuously listened to the radio channel and read into storage packets addressed to them. They then acknowledged receipt by sending back another packet. If any packets collided then this would be detected as no acknowledgement would be received.

ALOHA was an important development because of the use of a shared medium, in which there was no direct control over who transmitted packets. Obviously, due to the number of collisions, a lot of time was wasted in coping with detecting these collisions. This problem was remedied by implementing time slots for each transmission. This later became known as slotted-ALOHA. Full details of ALOHA are given in Chapter 3.

By the middle of the 1980s, the introduction of LANs received a much needed impetus, the PC had appeared. What the PC did was to change the perspective of IT. Computer power was now available on a desktop and these independent desktop devices, although they solved the immediate business needs, worked alone. The sharing of information and resources was a prerequisite and hence the transmission of information evolved.

This need drove the development of the LAN — a term originally introduced in America by Xerox. Through the work of Xerox, Digital and Intel by 1981 LANs started getting more and more attention, especially when they announced their Ethernet LAN.

Ethernet has evolved considerably since then, and many commercial implementations of Ethernet are available today.

Other major developments that have influenced the evolution of the LAN are technological progress and the reduction in the price of implementing these tools.

Among the major LAN software implementations were Corvus's Omninet (which was used largely as a means of sharing a hard disk among several micros) and Novell's Netware. By 1983 IBM had saturated the market and dozens of IBM compatible networks evolved, including 3Com's EtherSeries, IBM's Network (1984) and IBM's Token Ring (1985). To date Novell are the market leaders for the number of their LANs implemented in the world.

The market growth in this arena has been phenomenal, but this has also meant that standards have been lagging behind for a while. The result was that during the late 1980s and early 1990s several different types of LANs were available that could not be linked together. This fortunately is changing, with the OSI reference model being the prime innovator.

The next development in the LAN scenario will lead LAN technology towards the concept of client-server computing. Client-server architecture is already being discussed in many circles as having arrived. Although the methodology may be here the applications are not and hence it is really a thing for the next decade.

The reasons why client-server technology has become so popular are relatively easy to comprehend. It is cheaper to employ a single powerful server (which serves a community of users with, for example, files, information, and processing power), than it is to similarly install the required power and devices on every user (or client). For further information on client-server computing read Chapter 6.

This and other technological advances will determine the future of LANS and therefore in order to continue into the next decade and further, networks will need to evolve and not be seen as an isolated tool. They will need to work with each other and with larger systems, those large systems they have at various times seemed to threaten.

TERMS TO REVIEW

Sage the Owl Recommends

14 *What are Local Area Networks?*

- LAN
- WAN
- MAN
- ALOHA
- Point-to-Point
- Multi-Point
- Multiplexing
- Circuit-Switching
- Message-Switching
- Packet-Switching
- Topology.

2
Technologies Available

INTRODUCTION

In Chapter 1, the particular characteristics which distinguish a LAN from any other type of network have been discussed. It was concluded that if wide area or long-haul networks interconnect devices on separate sites, and system buses interconnect separate processors within a single piece of equipment or a room, then LANs cover the area in-between. They normally interconnect separate devices on a single site.

Although the geographic spread of a LAN is extending every day, it is still safe to define a restricted area as the basic feature which can be assumed for all LANs. Practically every other LAN characteristic can be viewed as a consequence of this feature and, of course, the cheapness and compactness now possible for the electronic components which are needed to support the network.

In this chapter the main requirements of a LAN will be identified. The way in which these can be satisfied, and the consequences for design are also discussed. Furthermore, it will discuss some of the latest developments in the geographic extension of the LAN and how inter-networking will satisfy this requirement.

MAIN REQUIREMENTS

In today's ever changing business environment it is not enough to be able to communicate effectively locally we must also communicate internationally. This publication will not consider the wider international communications issues that need to be addressed to be able to effectively carry out today's business transactions. Nevertheless, whatever communications technology is implemented and used locally will obviously influence the wider international arena. Towards the end of this chapter this topic is investigated in terms of inter-networking and how LANs influence wider communications issues.

Therefore lets start by assuming that the decision has been made to keep the network within the confines of a single office building, factory or site. This means that the designer and user are free to choose whatever technology suits their local needs best. The user interface to the network does not have to be the same as those dictated by the public telecommunications authorities, and so a simple interface which is tailored to the particular needs of the user can be devised. In practice, of course, things are not quite so straightforward, as we shall see when the other requirements are considered. An unrestricted information transmission system which can work at a sufficiently high speed to satisfy every user, and which has enough capacity to cope with all the traffic offered to it, has great appeal, but these things can only be obtained at some cost.

Let us first of all list the main local environment requirements.

Low Cost

By *low cost* it is meant that the cost of the mechanism for connecting together the devices is low compared with the cost of the devices themselves. Thus the solution for connecting together expensive mainframe computers could be very different from the solutions for microcomputers or terminals. Naturally the other requirements for data transmission between mainframes are also significantly different, so that characteristic alone could result in a totally different network.

High Transmission Speed

The aim of a high transmission speed is to enable information to be moved from one location to another with the minimum of delay, so that devices can respond as quickly, or so it seems to the user, as they would if they were connected directly to the processors. To computer designers and users, the rate at which information is transmitted by the normal telecommunications network is very slow when compared with the data bus and peripheral access speeds with which they are familiar. LANs offer the potential to exchange data between separate devices at a rate comparable with normal computer working speeds.

Network Capacity

Network capacity is a measure of the ability to handle the information which is presented to it by all the attached devices. It is closely related to transmission speed, since unless each conversation on the network is given a channel which is completely separate from every other one, the available capacity will have to be shared by a number of users. The longer a message takes to pass through the network, the longer others will have to wait. There are ways around the problem for circuits with slow transmission speeds (such as FDM) which are discussed later.

Low Error Rate

Error detection and correction are required in circumstances where errors cannot be tolerated. Traditional data transmission techniques normally exhibit relatively high error rates when transmitting data. Various ways of reducing the transmission errors, and of detecting them reliably when they do occur, have been devised, but generally errors are still more frequent in a network than those experienced in computers. However, LANs with their short distances, offer the potential for fewer transmission errors.

Reliability

The data transmission network must be very reliable; failure makes it impossible for the users to perform their normal distributed computing functions and resource sharing, thereby losing most of the benefits of placing computers in different locations. In most cases the physical medium for interconnecting devices (usually a cable) is inherently reliable but the devices connected to it to make the medium carry the information in the required form are far less so. The designer of a LAN chooses the method of coding the information for sending through the medium in such a way that the devices to drive it and the method of access can be simplified. This means that the overall reliability is improved.

Easy to Connect to

A major problem in interconnecting computers today is the variety of different connection procedures and transmission protocols. A LAN should help to provide some degree of compatibility between attached devices and should itself not present any new problems when devices are connected to it.

Mixed Traffic

The convergence of computing and communications and their use of office procedures has been a discussion topic for some time. Convergence brings with it the problem of handling information in many different forms; digital data, text, voice, video, facsimile and signalling.

Use with other Networks

It would be irresponsible for any designer of computer systems not to recognise that his equipment may be used with equipment from another source. Similarly, computer networks are likely to be interconnected, either through a private or public network. Although LANs are wholly contained within one site, they will not be totally isolated from users, terminals, computers and networks in other locations. LANs at two or more sites are likely to be linked in order that the devices on one site can send information to devices on another. These networks will have to be linked by means of private or public wide area networks using bridges, routes and gateways. Thus, LANs must provide facilities to use their networks where these are appropriate.

18 *Technologies Available*

Services

As well as providing the basic service of moving information cheaply and quickly from one location to another, a LAN will also provide access to services provided by systems using the network. It should also provide, what are best described as, network services designed to enhance the network for the users. The services that are provided as part of the network are the choice of the designer, but they would typically include fault monitoring, printing and central filestore.

CLASSIFICATION OF TECHNOLOGIES

LANs can be classified in many ways, with each classification related to the class of network and its use. Many publications classify LANs in terms of the transmission medium or connection technique used. However, these classifications do not comprehensively describe all the LAN environments.

LANs can be classified firstly in terms of the physical connection method used, hard-wired or switched-through software. Once this distinction is made we can further break down the definition in terms of the level of intelligence used, ie whether they interactively switch or store data, (*see* Figure 2.1).

LAN Classification by Software Connection

Therefore in the software connection environment we have the following:

Intelligent

These LANs have been set up to react dynamically with the data being transmitted. They provide services such as electronic mail, servers, gateways, etc. Intelligent systems can be subdivided into *distributed* or *central*. In a *distributed* intelligent system (*see* Figure 2.2), the intelligence is distributed across several devices. Each intelligent device can communicate with its intelligent partner while non-intelligent devices (for example dumb terminals and printers) cannot be directly connected. In a *central* intelligent system a computer or server is required to which all the devices are connected to — here the intelligence is only located at the hub, (*see* Figure 2.3).

Non-Intelligent

These LANs do not switch or interact with the data continuously. These types of LANs only act to set up the connection and are not involved in the data stream. Within this category there are three sub-categories (*see* Figure 2.1), namely *PBX* (a switching device

Classification of Technologies 19

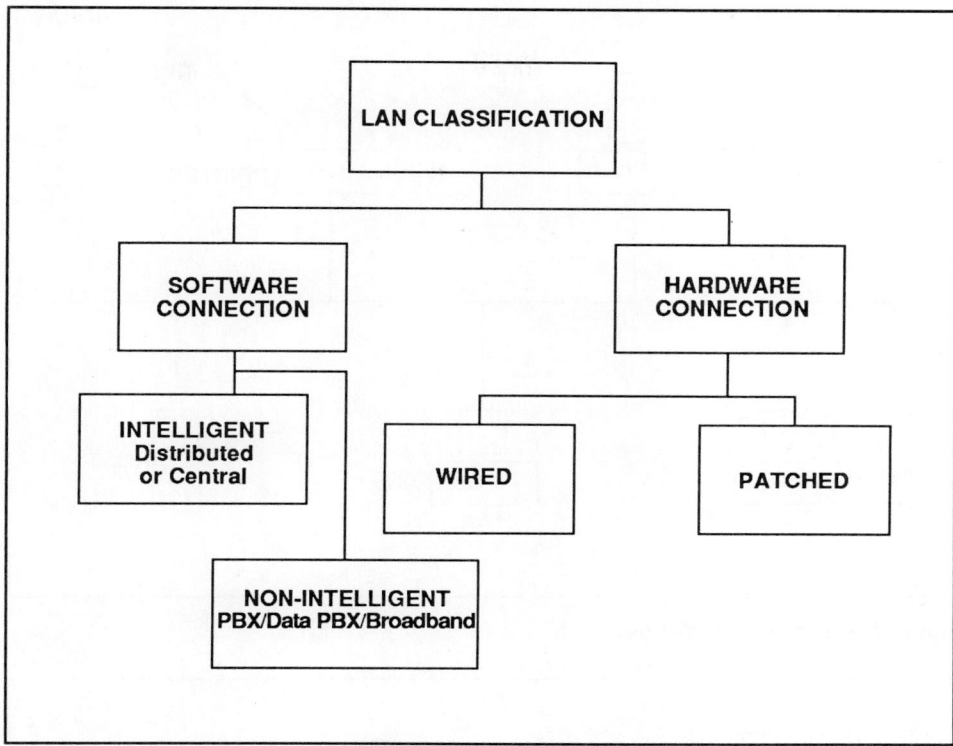

Figure 2.1 LAN classification

used for telephony), *Data PBX* (similar device, but handles computers, terminals and other data devices) and *Broadband* (this network uses a frequency division method to set up different channels, or bands, within a coaxial cable or other communications link). Broadband is further discussed later in this Chapter.

LAN Classification by Hardware Connection

Within the hardware connection environment (those networks that are made of straight wiring systems which connect the terminals or computers together) we have W*ired* and *Patched* systems.

Wired

In this situation the connections to the remote devices are via a system such as punch-down-terminations which require special tools and assistance to change. This system normally connects non-intelligent terminals to a central host (*see* Figure 2.4). Within this

20 *Technologies Available*

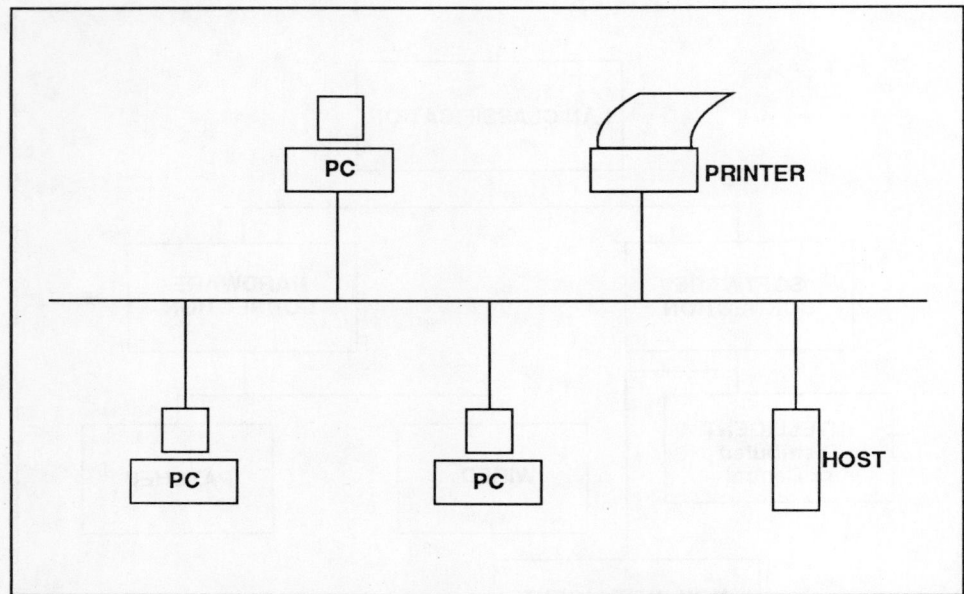

Figure 2.2 Distributed intelligent LAN

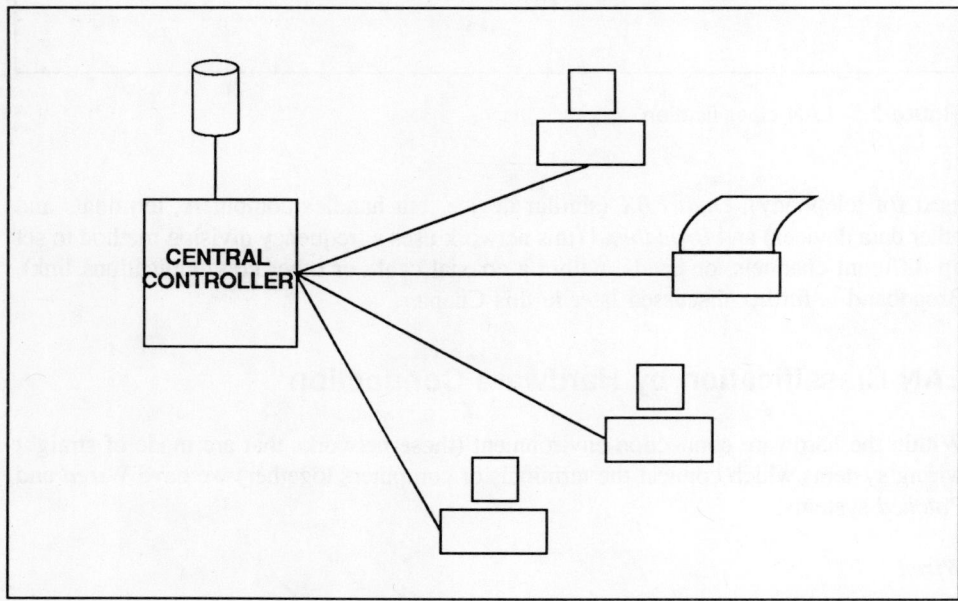

Figure 2.3 Centralised intelligent LAN

Classification of Technologies 21

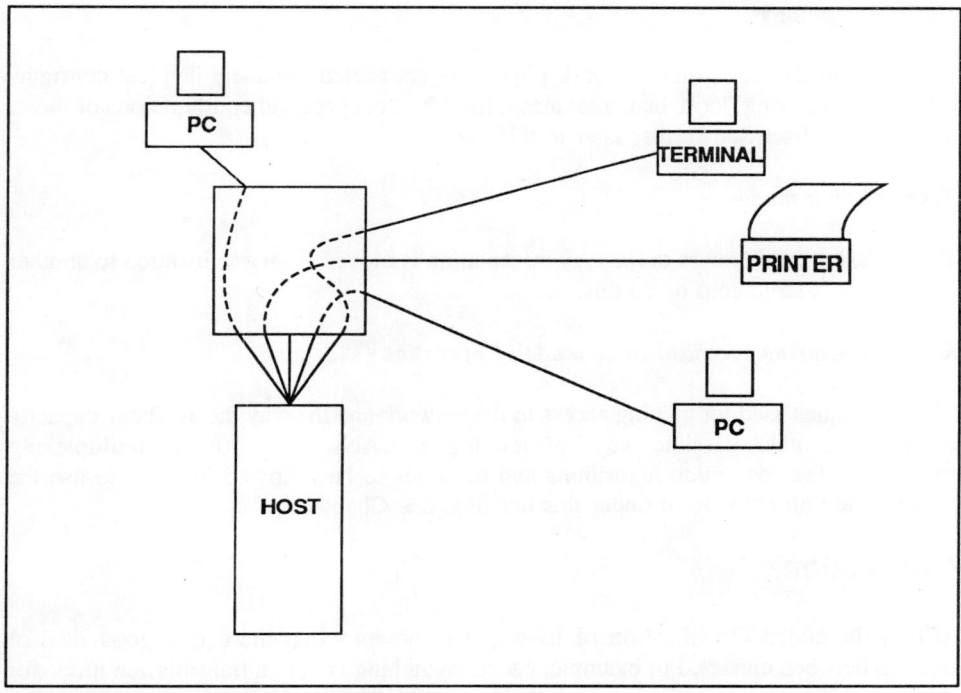

Figure 2.4 Hard connect wiring system

system you could also have a common wiring system for voice and data with cross connects establishing the connection at a common closet.

Patched

This system uses manual patch points to connect the devices and therefore can be modified by an operator without special tools. The system is normally centred around a central patch panel that does not require special tools for changing terminations.

Further Considerations

These classifications of LANs all have four common requirements that also influence the configuration and technology used within a LAN.

Physical transmission medium used

What kind of interconnection medium is used in the network? Possibilities include: coaxial cable, twisted-pair cable, flat ribbon cable, fibre optics, radio and infra-red transmission. These cables will be discussed further later in this chapter.

22 Technologies Available

Network topology

How are the devices in the network physically connected together? Typical configurations are: star, ring, loop, bus, tree, mesh, fully interconnect and combinations of these. This will be discussed further later in this chapter.

Transmission mode

Transmission mode refers to the way information is moved from one location to another and how it is structured to do this.

Resource-sharing mechanism or mode of operation

The techniques used for gaining access to the network and the way the available capacity is used are other possible ways of looking at LANs. The different multiplexing techniques, the contention algorithms and the rules to be followed in order to use the network, are all considered under this heading. *See* Chapter 3.

Conclusion

Within the stated classification of LANs, it is obvious that there is a good deal of overlap between classes. For example, packet-switching is both a transmission mode for the network and a network resource-sharing mechanism.

Some modes of operation are also applicable only to particular topologies or physical transmission media. For example, ring topologies require specialised access techniques and modes of operation. Each way of classifying LANs, whether via a soft or hard approach, tends to be suitable for some ways of looking at the problem and equally unsuitable for others.

TRANSMISSION MEDIA

In its simplest form, a LAN consists of a physical transmission medium (typically an electrical cable) linking a set of user stations which themselves contain sufficient logic and electronic circuits to enable them to use the network. Figure 2.5 shows the typical configuration at a tap in the network, where the transmission medium is the physical path between transmitter and receiver.

In this section the physical transmission media, its distribution and planning are examined. In many LANs the medium can be one of several options, or even combinations of media, but most experimental systems and current products are designed around one particular medium.

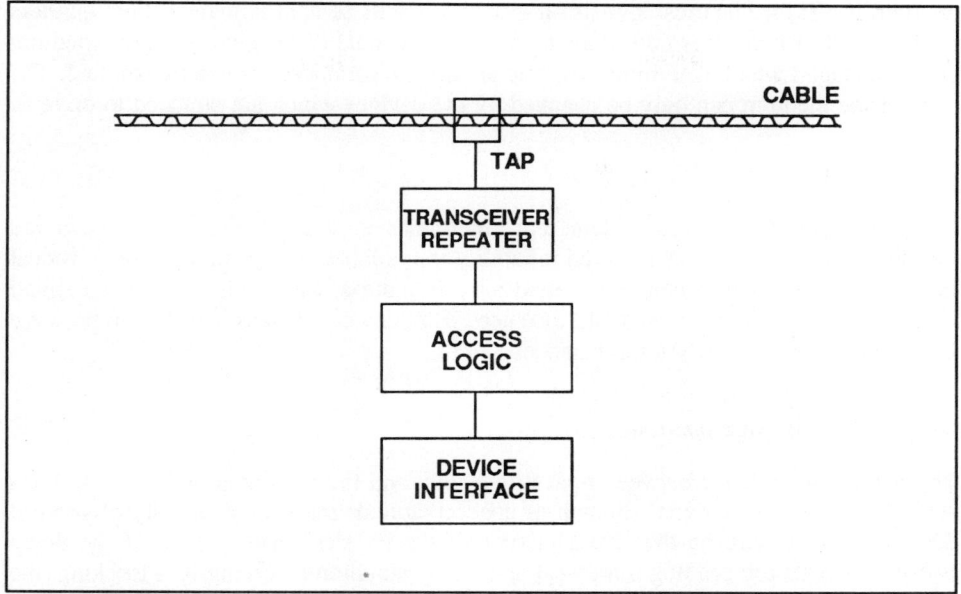

Figure 2.5 Tapping into a LAN

There are essentially two schools of thought regarding the choice of medium. One says let us choose the cheapest possible, consistent with the speed and reliability requirements. The other says that since the medium is going to be shared by a large number of users, and the prime requirements are high speed and low error rate, then the best interconnection medium should be used regardless of the cost. Other requirements and practical considerations naturally influence the final choice regardless of cost criteria used.

Transmission Characteristics

In examining the characteristics of the transmission media and their suitability for LANs, the following features must be taken into consideration.

Bandwidth

Bandwidth is the width of the frequency band that can be handled efficiently by the system. Indirectly it is also a measure of the transmission speed which can be supported by that system; a high transmission speed demands a system with a high bandwidth. It is not just a function of the physical medium, but also of the whole system needed to send and receive the information. Once digital information is on the physical medium, the rate at which it can move from one location to another is a function only of the medium itself; for electrical signals on a wire this will be approximately three quarters of the speed of light. It is only the rate at which the state of the signals on the medium can be changed which determines the rate at which information can be transmitted. The state of the medium can only be changed by the devices which are attached to drive it.

Connectivity

It is the connectivity of a system that determines how the nodes of a system are interlinked and whether the required reliability is available. For example, some physical transmission media are suitable for broadcast information, whilst others are better suited for point-to-point links. Some media also need extra devices such as repeaters to preserve the signals over relatively long distances.

Geographic coverage possible

The maximum distance between nodes on a link, and the total area which a LAN can cover, without loss of signal strength or unacceptable degradation of quality of service, does not just depend on the characteristics of the physical media alone. If the delay between one station sending a message and the destination receiving it is too long, the algorithm which is used to gain access to the network can be affected. If it takes too long for a message to reach all the devices on the network in a broadcast system for example, then two or more users may well try to transmit at the same time. The overall result could be a reduction in throughput on the network due to interference between devices.

Site topology

Some physical media used for LANs are better suited to particular site topologies than others. The location of the devices to be connected to the network will dictate the path the interconnection medium must follow and this may be difficult to accommodate with certain media. Allied to this are the requirements imposed by the various building and safety regulations, some of which may impose severe constraints on the choice of the medium and the route it can take.

Noise immunity

Ideally the physical medium chosen to transmit information should be free from interference from every outside source, but in practice this is not possible. This interference is normally undesirable or unwanted and is referred to as noise. Noise can be divided into four categories:

— *Thermal noise* which is due to thermal agitation of electrons in a conductor. It is present in all electronic devices and transmission media and is a function of temperature;

- *Intermodulation noise* which is due to signals of different frequencies sharing the same medium. The effect is to produce signals at a frequency which is the sum or difference of the two original frequencies;
- *Crosstalk* which occurs when two independent signal paths are combined together. For example, on a telephone line when you are able to hear another conversation as well as your own;
- *Impulse noise* which is non-continuous noise, consisting of irregular pulses or noise spikes of short duration and of relatively high amplitude. It is generated from a variety of causes, including external electromagnetic disturbances, such as lightning, and faults and flaws in the communications system.

Some media are relatively free from interference, whilst with others it is notoriously difficult to prevent extraneous signals and noise from corrupting the information being transmitted. As well as interference from outside signals, there is also the problem of noise generated by other devices such as electric motors. Noise is random information of varying amplitudes which is added to the signals being transmitted. Interference is other information from another source. Distortion can also be considered under this heading. This is where the signal is changed by the medium itself during transmission.

Security

Some kinds of physical transmission media radiate the signal they are carrying to their surroundings so that any unscrupulous individual can place a pick-up device close to the medium in order to eavesdrop on the messages which are being transmitted. Some media radiate much more than others, making the task of a potential eavesdropper easier. In some cases it may be possible for an eavesdropper to actually tap the medium directly rather than rely on the radiation. This can be very difficult to detect with some media without actually examining every part of the network, which can be almost impossible if the medium is ducted. In other cases the presence of an illegal tap can be readily detected due to changes in the transmission characteristics of the network.

This topic is discussed further in chapter 6.

Transmission technologies

Allied with the choice of medium and the topology of the network is the method by which information is moved from the source to the destination. The first choice is whether a digital or an analogue technique for the signal is used. Then various methods of modulating the signal to provide the information carrying capability can be employed, from an unmodulated system to many different analogue modulation techniques, each with their own advantages and disadvantages. As well as consideration of the modulation techniques, the way the information is structured for transmission can be affected by the properties of the physical media. Although packetising the information has become the accepted method for data transmission, the format of the packets, the addressing and the amount of error-checking information needed in the packet are affected by the quality of the service possible from the underlying physical medium.

Cost

Cost can be subdivided into the cost of the physical medium, its installation, maintenance, and the cost of the equipment needed to make it provide the kind of service the user wants.

Availability

Not least among the considerations of the physical transmission medium for LANs is its availability or otherwise. The very fact that certain types of cable were to hand during the initial design stage of some LANs has contributed to a major extent in their use for that system. In many cases other media would have produced superior results but were not so easily obtainable at the time. Generally the easier the medium is to obtain, the cheaper it will be to buy.

Restrictions imposed

The choice of a particular physical transmission medium is likely to restrict the number of applications within the network and the transmission technologies which can be used. For example, if fibre optic cables are used, it is considerably more difficult to design a broadcast network which can be tapped without disturbing the other users and the characteristics of the network as a whole. Fibre optic cables themselves may offer sufficient advantages to the user that he is willing to live with the restrictions, but this depends on many other factors which have to be taken into consideration when the whole network is being designed.

Cables

The main types of transmission media in use will be examined in the context of the above requirements, *see* Figure 2.6. There are many variations on these wires and it is not the intention of this publication to list them all.

Twisted-Pair Cable

This seems to be the most extensively used media for wiring within and outside buildings. LANs have traditionally used coaxial cable, so the idea of using this medium was initially viewed with some scepticism. However its success ultimately led to a new IEEE Standard (*see* Chapter 7). Recently twisted-pair transmission speed has been extended from its original 1 Mbps to approximately 10Mbps adhering to the IEEE 10BASET (10BASET stands for 10 Mbps, BASEband and Twisted-pair cabling) standard.

Twisted-pair wiring is the familiar standard telephone or telex terminal cable. It consists of individually colour-coded pairs of wires enclosed within a polyethylene, polyvinyl chloride (PVC), or a wood fibre, paper-like insulating layer. Each pair of wires is twisted together, at varying rates, in a helix in an attempt to provide fairly constant electrical characteristics.

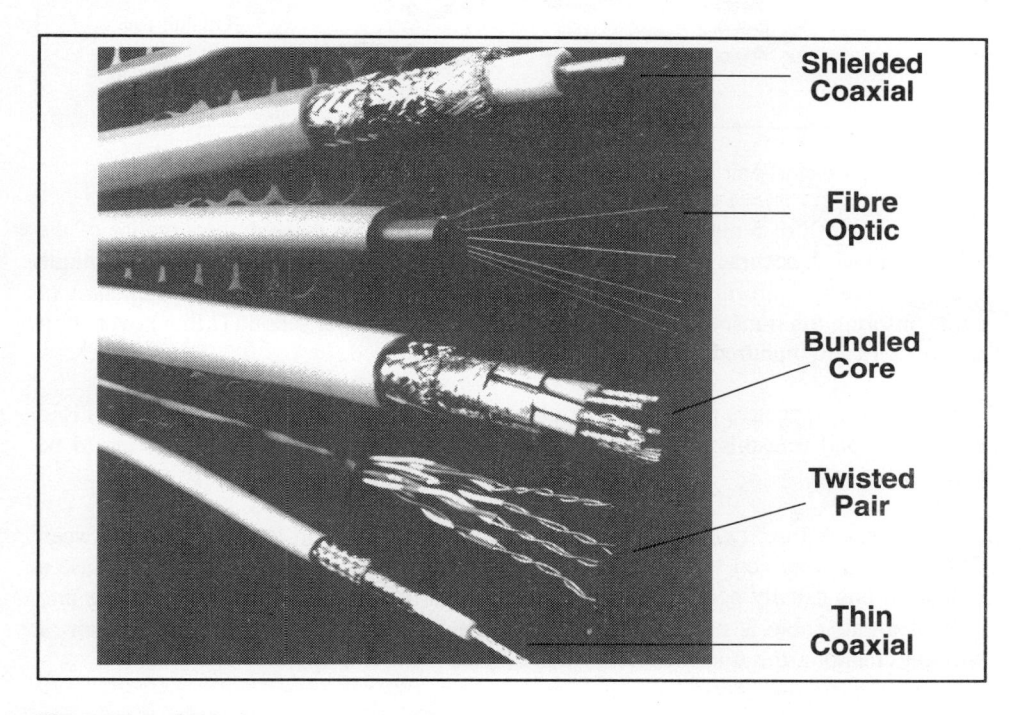

Figure 2.6 Cables

Usually several pairs are encased together, as a minimum two pairs, four wires, and this is what most telephone systems require. New developments in digital transmission, namely ISDN, have made four pairs (eight wires) more common. This construction attempts to minimise and randomise the coupling of noise and crosstalk. The general form of a twisted-pair cable is shown in Figure 2.7.

Twisted-pair cable is suited to both analogue and digital transmission (although *not* together on the same line) even though in the past its major use has been for transmission of analogue speech. For a number of reasons, (for example, when speech is transmitted, errors can normally be tolerated as crackle on the line by the human receiver, however data transmission errors are unacceptable) it is best suited for transmission of information over relatively short distances. The attenuation of a signal during transit can be fairly high and its waveform can be distorted. To minimise these

28 Technologies Available

problems, repeaters are commonly employed in the line to amplify the signal and regenerate the waveform.

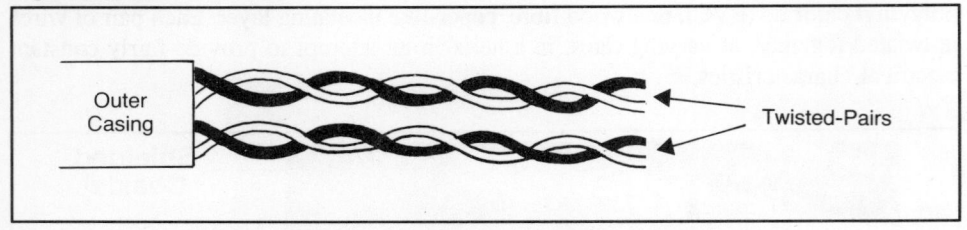

Figure 2.7 Twisted-pair cable

The bandwidth of a network based on twisted-pair cables depends on: quality of the conductors used, accuracy of the length of each component of the pair and the technique used to drive the information along the cable. With careful choice and installation of cable, information transmission rates of several million bits per second (Mbps) over short distances (a few hundred metres) can be reliably achieved.

By means of repeaters placed at shorter intervals in the cable and by using specialised electronics and transmission techniques, transfer rates as high as 100 Mbps could be reached.

By its very nature, twisted-pair cable is best suited for point-to-point links between devices or repeaters on the network. It is often used as a broadcast medium because a broadcast bus usually needs to be fairly long, distortion free and passive. Tapping into a twisted-pair cable is not easy without disturbing the other users on the medium or without changing the transmission characteristics significantly.

Twisted-pair cable of the kind normally and readily available is not shielded (normally known as Unshielded Twisted-pair (UTP)) and consequently it radiates to its surroundings when it is carrying information. This makes it very easy for an eavesdropper to place a pick-up coil alongside the cable to listen to the transmission without any fear of detection by devices on the cable, since the transmission characteristics remain effectively unchanged.

Furthermore, UTP has a greater propensity to interference caused by the close proximity of electric cables, motors, air-conditioning devices and fluorescent lights.

However UTP cables are easier to modify and troubleshoot than those based on coaxial or fibre. Shielded twisted-pair cabling is also easy to work with in terms of testing and modifying networks, but it is more expensive. Shielding can reduce, but does not eliminate the radiation and interference, and the individual wires in the cable can be balanced to help with this, but the main improvements obtained by these techniques are evident at frequencies below about 100 KHz. To be of most use, LANs should operate at much higher frequencies and hence higher data transmission rates.

As already discussed, twisted-pair cable typically has a high electrical capacitance which can severely distort the signal which it carries. The high capacitance can be partially offset by means of loading coils, but again the benefits of these are experienced mainly at lower frequencies than are considered useful for LANs.

Hence it may seem strange that something as unsuitable for high-speed data transmission as twisted-pair telephone cable should have been used as widely as it has. The reasons for its adoption are its availability, its very low cost and the fact that it is a well understood transmission medium which lends itself to a variety of different modes of use — a very valuable features for an experimental system. However, against this must be offset the large amount of care which is needed to adequately install it in order to achieve the desired transmission speeds.

Also, the fact that repeaters and other extra electronic devices are needed to ensure the cable performs in the right manner for high-speed digital data transmission over a sufficiently wide area adds significantly to the installation cost, thereby removing most of its advantages over some of its rivals.

Multi-Way Cable

Round multi-core or flat ribbon cable can be used successfully for LANs. Many of the characteristics of twisted-pair cable (eg high attenuation, susceptibility to electrical interference and ease of installation) are shared by multi-way cable.

Its main virtue is the fact that the control and data signals can be transmitted separately using different conductors, thus simplifying the interface problems. One conductor can be used as the busy indicator. When a device is actually transmitting on the network, this conductor can be switched on to indicate to the other users that the network is busy. One or more other conductors can be assigned to sending encoding methods which incorporate clocking signals.

Also, several conductors can be allocated the role of transmitting the data, so parallel rather than serial bit streams can be put onto the cable, the actual number of bits being determined by the number of conductors available.

The overall result of using the conductors in this manner is that the interface devices necessary to put information on to the medium, detect when someone else is transmitting, and read information off, can be simplified. High data transmission rates are possible if sufficient parallel conductors are used.

Against this must be weighed the fact that multi-way cable is much more expensive than either twisted-pair or ordinary coaxial cable. However, it is equally suitable for ring topologies and for bus systems which operate in a baseband mode. Data transmission rates in excess of 10 Mbps are achievable.

30 Technologies Available

Coaxial Cable

Coaxial cable consists of a single central copper conductor surrounded by a concentric ring of dielectric material which is surrounded by a metal screen which can be either solid or a mesh of wire. The whole assembly is protected from the outside environment by another layer which is usually an insulating material. Figure 2.8 shows the components of typical coaxial cables.

Coaxial cable is available in a wide variety of qualities ranging from the cheap and relatively low quality cable aimed at the domestic television and hi-fi aerial markets to that of very high quality which has low loss transmission characteristics, high immunity from interference and resilience to accidental damage. The latter can be very expensive and, because it can be very thick and stiff, it can be difficult to install, even to the extent of requiring special equipment to bend it round corners.

The electrical characteristics of coaxial cable make it eminently suitable for transmitting high-frequency signals whilst at the same time reducing the radiation from the cable and remaining almost immune from interference. Very little crosstalk is experienced between coaxial cables running alongside each other. Due to its inherently good features, very high data transmission rates using both digital and analogue techniques are possible.

In the case of LANs, the usual coaxial cable used is of the middle-of-the-road quality used by suppliers of cable television.

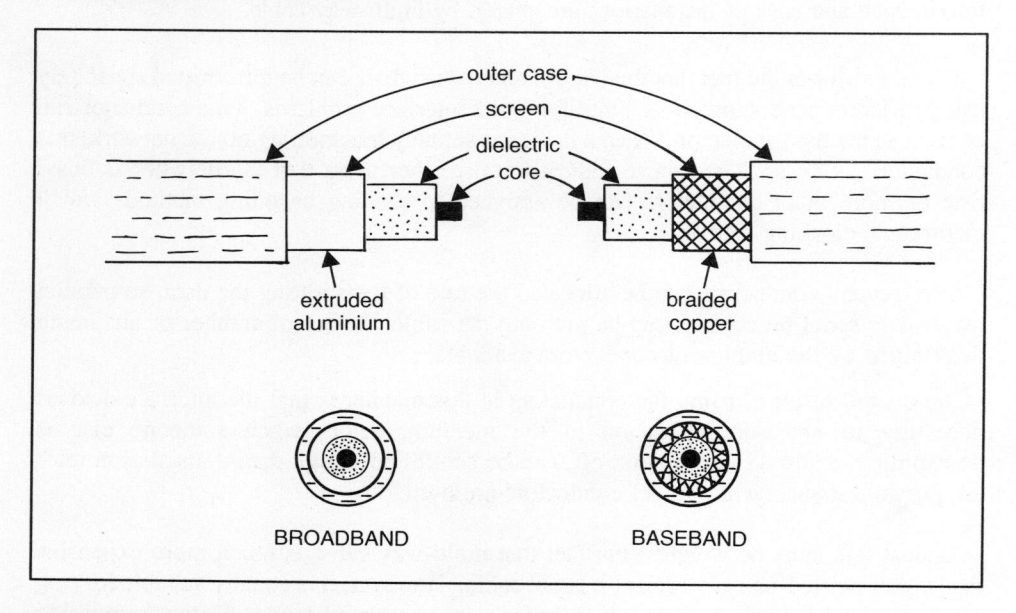

Figure 2.8 Coaxial cable types

Community Antenna Television (CATV), designed to provide services to remote areas, carrying numerous TV channels at ranges up to a few tens of miles, uses coaxial cable. This usage has meant that the cable is widely available and the technique for installing it is well understood. Added to this, equipment for tapping the cable, and amplifying the signal if analogue transmission is being used, is readily available off the shelf. The requirements of the domestic cable television industry dictate that the equipment used must have very high reliability since much of it will be outside and in relatively inaccessible positions. The mean time between failures of the line amplifiers is several years.

Coaxial cable can also be found in voice transmission (here using Frequency Division Multiplexing (FDM), the coaxial cable can carry over 10,000 simultaneous voice channels) and data transmission (as a high speed I/O connection to a video terminal).

Two modes of data transmission are possible using coaxial cable: baseband and broadband. In baseband signalling, the information is put on to the cable in essentially an unmodulated form. Each bit of data is represented by a discrete level of signal on the cable. Broadband, on the other hand, uses modulation techniques to transmit analogue signals. The differences between baseband and broadband transmission are discussed in much more detail later, together with the different techniques which are used to access and control the use of the medium.

The types of coaxial cable used for baseband and broadband differ slightly in their design. Generally for baseband it has a wire mesh screen made of copper and has a characteristics impedance of 50 ohms. The cable used for broadband is usually of heavier construction, having a screen made of extruded aluminium and with a characteristic impedance of 75 ohms.

The bandwidth of coaxial cable depends on the mode of transmission being employed, ie whether baseband or modulated signalling is being used. With baseband, the capabilities of the electronics which drive the medium largely determine the speed of transmission, but 10 Mbps is fairly easy to achieve; much higher rates are possible at increased cost.

The bandwidth of broadband systems is typically around 300 MHz, giving a possible digital data transmission rate of around 150 Mbps full-duplex. In practice, however, the available frequency bandwidth of a broadband system is divided into a number of discrete channels, the width of each being determined by the way they are used.

Baseband systems use an essentially passive physical medium and consequently they can be tapped without significantly disturbing the medium's characteristics. This is an advantage when new devices are being added but it is a positive security risk. Incidently, the fact that baseband signalling does not use modulation means that the cable radiates more than it would do if it were modulated. Thus it is easier to eavesdrop on a baseband network than on a broadband system.

Coaxial cable is ideally suited to a broadcast network system with each user attaching to the network wherever required. The geographic coverage possible depends on a large number of factors.

In principle, coaxial cable can cover long distances, provided that amplifiers and repeaters are inserted into the lines at appropriate intervals, but certain transmission techniques and access methods require that the transmission delay, distortion and attenuation be restricted to an acceptable level, which itself severely restricts the acceptable cable length. When we come to examine the methods employed for sharing a network, we will see that maximum end-to-end transmission delay greatly influences the length of cable used and the size of the packets of data which can be transmitted. Each must be traded off against the others.

Using typical CATV coaxial cable, the actual cost is a little higher than twisted-pair, but the cost of connecting to it and the lower cost of shielding it for security reasons may make the two comparable. Against this should be weighed the extra installation costs caused by the limited flexibility of coaxial cable of adequate quality.

Fibre Optics

Fibre optic cable differs from the types of cable previously discussed in that it transmits light rather than electrical signals. The cable consists of a filament for transmitting the light which is usually made from silica but can be plastic for low quality installations. The light conducting material is surrounded by another substance with a lower refractive index which minimises the loss through the cable and guides the rays of light by means of internal reflections.

The principle of the transmission of light through a tube of glass containing water was demonstrated as long ago as 1870, but it was not until the 1950s when glass rods were coated with a suitable refractive material that the idea became a commercial product. The first optic fibres were used for transmitting images and were often used by surgeons for examining internal parts of the body without surgery. It was not until lasers and Light Emitting Diodes (LEDs) were applied to the task of transmitting light along optic fibres that they were used for digital data transmission. This, and the discovery of low loss fibres, led in the 1970s to the development of optic fibres as a possible alternative to copper cables for the transmission of information. The basic raw material of optic fibres is silica which is potentially cheaper than copper and, provided it is of a high enough quality, should be able to offer a much higher bandwidth, and hence a higher transmission rate.

Various types of optic fibre are available which, coupled with different types of light source, permit a wide range of transmission rates at a wide range of costs. Figure 2.9 shows some single fibre types. These types vary as to the nature of the input light source, the size of the core fibre, and the complexity of the index of refraction boundary supplied by the cladding and the typical waveform it ultimately represents.

- *Multimode step index* which is a fairly dispersive type of fibre and is generally used in applications where it is important that the fibres can be joined together easily. It has the thickest core and cladding boundary. In terms of light it tends to deteriorate rapidly since the path lengths will vary depending on the angles of the light rays. These problems increase as the transmission speed increases and hence this medium can effectively transmit at a maximum of 20 Mbps for about a mile;

- *Multimode grade index* is the most widely used fibre. This fibre has a refractive index that varies with the radius giving different velocities of light depending on where the light starts, ie slower at the centre and faster at the ends. It is fairly easy to join together and has a larger core than single-mode fibre. While this fibre is not as fast as single-mode, it is nevertheless 50 times faster than the multimode step index.

- *Single-mode* is the simplest and also the most expensive fibre. Its expense is due to the critical tolerances in its manufacture and also because of its associated use in laser devices. Single-mode fibre has a central filament which is very fine. As a consequence, it is difficult to join two ends together. The fibre does have advantages for data transmission over other types because it can support much higher transmission rates.

It can be seen from the Figure 2.9 that fibre optic filaments are very small compared with traditional copper wires. Thus, more optic filaments than copper cables can be put in ducts.

Using the best quality fibres, a very small amount of light is lost in the cable. Experimental lengths of fibre with a loss of only 0.5 dB/km have been made, but using fibres of a much lower quality, transmission rates of around 50 Mbps over several kilometres can be obtained.

One great advantage of optic fibres over traditional electrical conductors is their immunity to electrical interference which makes them especially suitable for electrically hostile environments. Also the information which they carry cannot be detected merely by placing a pick-up alongside, so making them more secure from eavesdroppers.

A single optic fibre is essentially a one-way transmission medium, with a light source at one end and a detector at the other (*see* Figure 2.10). Two-way transmission is possible by means of a pair of cables, one carrying information in one direction and one in the other direction.

Tapping into a fibre is not easy to do since generally the light path must be interrupted and the information regenerated and retransmitted in the original direction. There are techniques for reading the information from a fibre optic cable without breaking it but these require special cables and even then they are not wholly satisfactory. Optical

34 *Technologies Available*

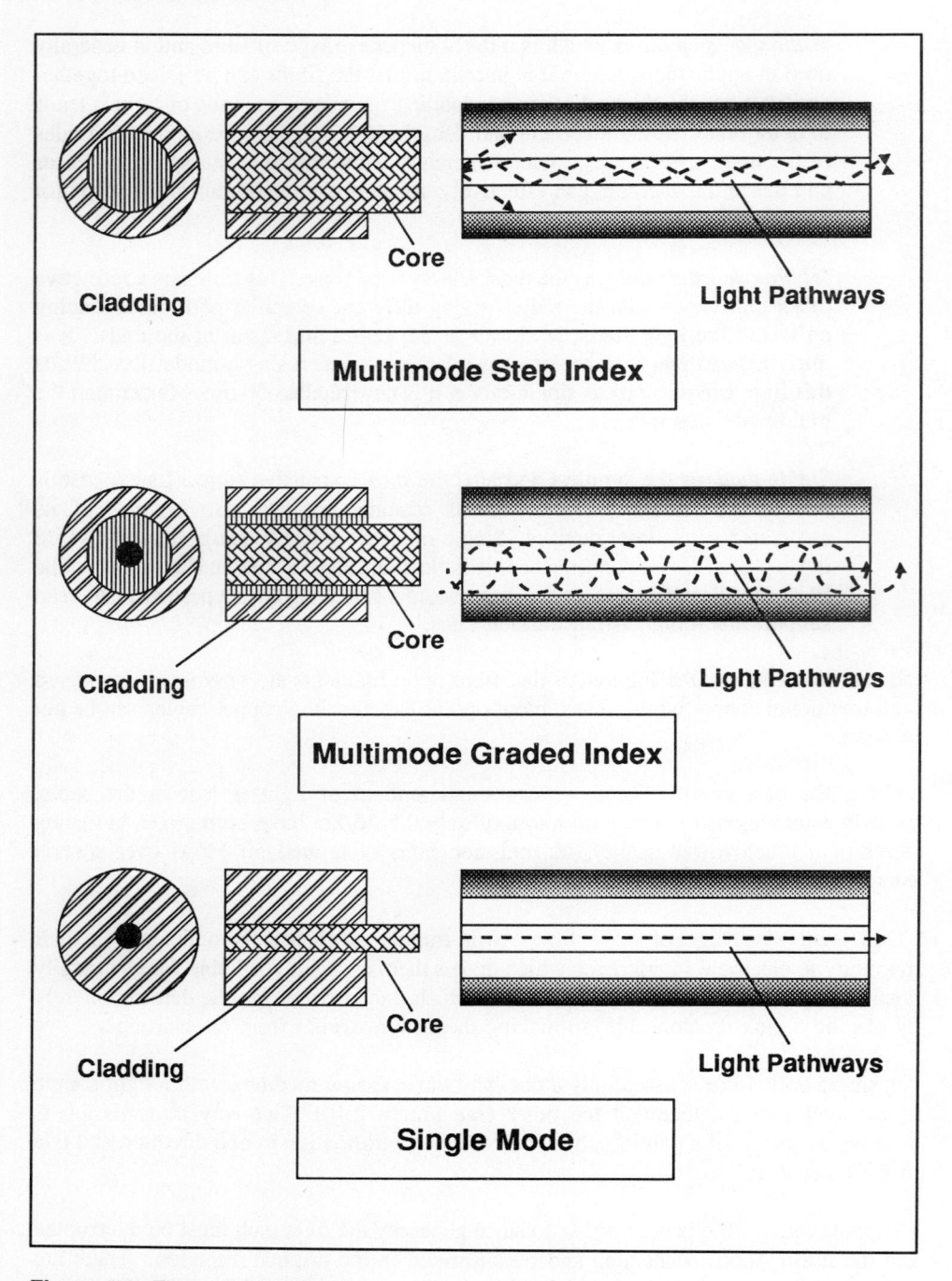

Figure 2.9 Fibre optic cables

fibres are ideally suited to ring and loop topologies, but the difficulty in tapping makes them less suitable for broadcast bus systems.

Each electrical connection to an optical fibre requires a special device to convert electrical signals to corresponding light pulses. The reverse system is required at each point where the cable is tapped. When repeaters are required, these must be optical-to-optical amplifiers.

Interconnection between different cable types

Any wiring of a building is sooner or later likely to encounter the problem of having to link two distinct types of cables together, as it is unlikely that a building will only contain one type of wiring. Therefore techniques and equipment are needed in order to achieve this task. There are two devices available which allow connection of two different cables.

The first is a BALUN, a small device which connects an electrically BALanced medium (ie twisted-pair cable) to an UNbalanced medium (ie coaxial cable). It is essentially a small transformer which does not change the speed of transmission, it only repeats the correct signalling technique on either side. Since BALUNS are basically one-to-one devices, care should be taken when using them as there are many different types available and their use is dependent on the signalling used. The most common use is to multiplex several twisted-pair wires into a single coaxial cable.

The second is an ADAPTER. These devices allow the connection of different cable types. For example a V.24 D connector and an eight wire cable (a four wire twisted-pair cable). Note, the interconnection of optical fibres and other cable types has not yet become popular, as the connection can be rather difficult and expensive. The reason for this expense and difficulty is the necessity to convert the optical signal into an electromagnetic signal.

Structured Cabling Techniques and Cable Distribution

Cabling has always been a fundamental part of a building's communications network. However most people view cabling as the support or servant territory of the IT function and hence it is viewed as rather drab and uninnovative.

This normally means that it is not taken seriously and as a consequence has been provided in an ad-hoc, unstructured manner. Frequently cables lie redundant, merely because no one has taken time to find out what the cable is there for and what it is supposed to be attached to. Furthermore in many organisations when a new computing facility is required what normally tends to happen is that more cable is laid, which can cause unnecessary cost and disruption.

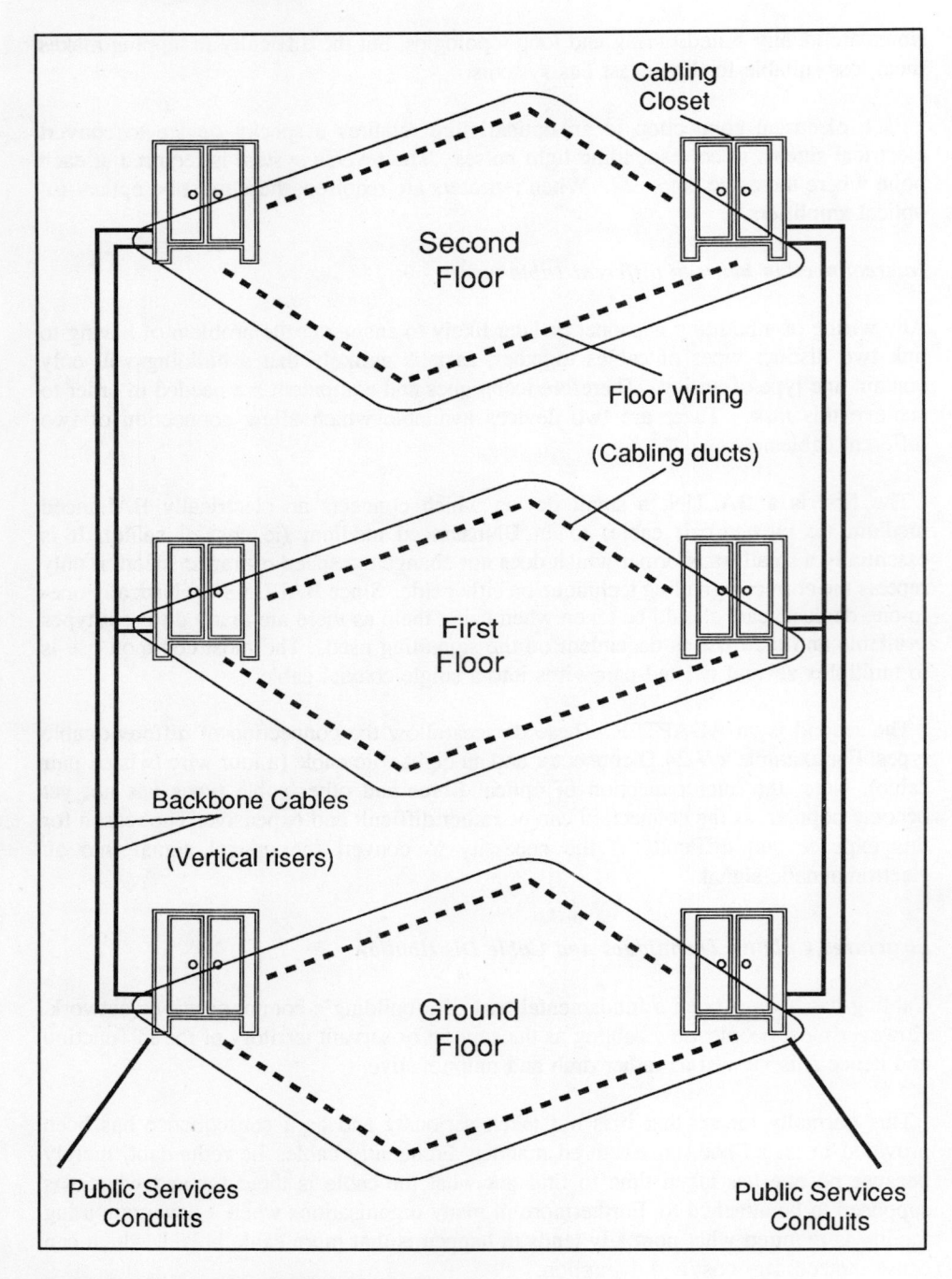

Figure 2.10 Structured wiring topology

Investigations into the use of cabling by companies has identified one major need, that it is normal for a company's telephone and data terminal to be moved on average every year. This means that if a structured cabling approach is not used in the first place then the cost of these moves and changes can be phenomenal. It has been proven that a structured cabling approach will reduce these costs.

With a continually evolving cabling technology, the need for a versatile and manageable cabling system is very important. Structured cabling methodology deals with every aspect of management and maintenance of existing cables as well as the future use of any advances in technology. It consists of the components and cables that are used to interconnect telephones, computers and office equipment within a building, which means that it supports a multi-product, multi-vendor environment. The methodology comprises of three main cable distribution elements, (*see* Figure 2.10).

The Vertical Component

The vertical component is designed to act as the high capacity backbone (or riser cabling element) of the system. It carries the high concentration of information between the main computer or frame rooms and the cabling closets between different floors of the building.

The Horizontal Component

The horizontal component is part of the cabling system providing flexible distribution between individual workstations and the floor distribution points, or cabling closets and the backbone or vertical elements.

Cabling Closets

This is the interface between the vertical and horizontal components. This element is normally situated adjacent to the building risers on each floor. Within these closets are various patching panels and termination facilities where the horizontal and vertical cabling sub-systems terminate. For example, a voice wiring system would normally have a distribution frame for the vertical cabling and another for the horizontal. These would be cross-connected as required. In data communications these closets would contain the BALUNS and adaptors for linking different cabling transmissions.

Cabling Structures

This cabling structure requires various physical elements to make it work. These elements will route the cables around a building and may well affect the structure of the building when being built or refurbished. When routeing there are three main issues to be considered. First, service access into the building. If all the services come into the building from one central point, then you are more vulnerable to failure as the risks associated with this configuration are centred around the one entry point. If it fails everything is affected.

Secondly, where and how many vertical elements exist. Again, if a building only contains one riser or two side by side (in a central position), then the level of protection against a disaster is obviously reduced. Finally, horizontal positioning of your cabling is the most difficult decision you are likely to ever make in the cabling arena. Here you will need to include, not only today's requirements but also predict as accurately as possible tomorrow's office floor plans.

With all this in mind lets now discuss some of the cabling elements within a building.

Cable Trays

These cable mounts are normally used in environments where cable configurations are continually being changed to accommodate a new environment. In this environment (which could be a laboratory or university) the main aim is to make the network function and therefore aesthetics are not a factor. Another area of use for these trays is as a tool for managing cables. Here trays can be used within risers so that cables can be tied up in an orderly manner or within raised floors or suspended ceilings in order to keep them in known locations.

The main advantage with cable trays is that they are easy to access because there is no lid to remove. Note that care should be taken when implementing them as future requirements must be taken into consideration. That is to say that if the trays do not have the capacity to cope with increasing cable requirement, then obviously you will need to reinstall larger trays. Therefore the trays used should not be more than 50 percent utilised in the first instance.

Raised Floors

Raised floors consist of some type of removable panels set on a metal grid-work above the actual building floor. This is a common construction in computer rooms as they offer the ultimate in flexibility in terms of cabling. However they can be rather expensive with the cost ranging from £50 to £150 per square metre, depending on the floor load. Furthermore these costs must include not only the flooring itself, but also the construction of ramps and the placements of electrical conduits.

Hung Ceiling

In this environment cables are routed through the space between the visible ceiling and the actual ceiling. The cables are then brought down on the walls or via specially built poles. The main advantage with this type of wiring is to reduce the amount of cabling used, as cables that are routed in this manner can follow the shortest route between two points. While this system of wiring can be the cheapest, it may mean that the wiring needed could be more expensive as they need to be fire-retardant.

Conduits

This system is either embedded in concrete or attached to building walls - it is a form of trunking. Trunking is a method of distributing cables within a modular system designed to fit with the floor or wall surface. These systems offer the maximum in physical protection for communications cables (as they enclose the cables to prevent damage), but can be expensive to install.

Cabling Closets

As you can see in Figure 2.10 the cabling closets form a major strategic part in the whole structure of a wiring configuration. These closets form an intermediate stage between risers and horizontal cabling. These cabling closets can act in various ways. First, they can act as termination points of each horizontal or vertical cable. Secondly, they cross connect different cables, for example, the horizontal to the vertical cable. Finally, these closets will probably be running 24 hours a day, 7 days a week. Therefore provisions must be made to ventilate them in order to avoid a fire or breakdown. This also means that access for maintenance purposes must be available.

Recording the Cabling Structure

Structured cabling and these cabling components will help Communications Managers keep accurate records concerning their installations' wires and cables. Obviously, they will still need to keep up-to-date records of their installation and the labelling of their communications components is a must. Furthermore, a structured cabling approach will help the Communications Manager plan for future expandibility requirements.

Other Transmission Techniques

The main discussion point in this section is centred around the possibility of having a Cordless Local Area Network (CLAN). Here transmission techniques are discussed in this context, for further information on CLANs themselves please see Chapter 10.

Before I discuss the three main LAN cordless transmission techniques, it is interesting to see where in the electromagnetic spectrum these transmission techniques are situated. Figure 2.11 illustrates this. As can be seen, the further we move to the right of the spectrum from radio to microwave and infra-red, the frequency increases from about 1 Megahertz (MHz) to many Gigahertz (GHz).

40 *Technologies Available*

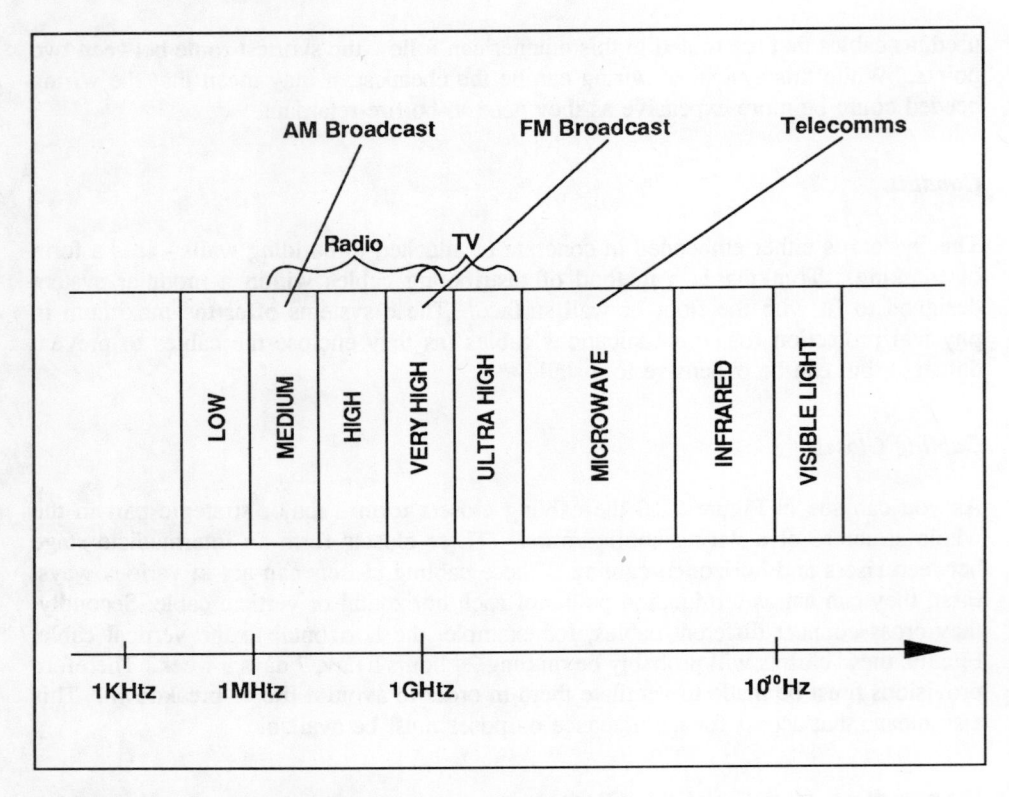

Figure 2.11 Electromagnetic spectrum

Radio Transmission

If the intention was to find the transmission medium which is widely available to everybody, then radio transmission would be the obvious choice. The principal difference between radio and microwave is that radio is omnidirectional and microwave is focused. The transmission medium used by radio is the 'luminiferous ether' which was thought of as the medium needed to carry all electromagnetic radiation through space. This is the origin of the name Ethernet (although Ethernet chose to use coaxial cables!). One of the earliest systems which could be thought of as a LAN, even though it covered a greater area than that commonly accepted for a LAN now, was the ALOHA network in Hawaii. This network used packet-radio transmission as the means of connecting a number of outlying ground based stations with a central computing system. The ALOHA network demonstrates many of the techniques now used by other broadcast networks and its main features are discussed in Chapter 3.

There are a number of problems associated with radio transmission which make it unsuitable for most LAN applications. One is that radio transmission is not restricted to the confines of the one office block or industrial site and so it is easy for transmission to be interfered with by other people outside using the same frequency channels. It is also easy for an eavesdropper to listen undetected to any transmissions made using the radio waves, so any security must be provided by an extra level within the systems which are using the ether for information transmission.

The communications bandwidth available to a user of a radio channel is a function of the frequency band and modulation technique being used. In order that the available frequency bands can be made available to as many different groups of users as possible, the individual channels are restricted in width so the actual transmission rates are also severely restricted in practice.

The range of the transmission possible is also a function of the frequency band used. Generally the higher the frequency band used, the wider the bandwidth possible, but the shorter the range. Greater range can be achieved using more powerful equipment but then the likelihood of interference to other users is greater.

Radio communications are very susceptible to noise and electrical interference, so a mechanism for detecting and correcting errors which are caused by extraneous factors needs to be included in any design.

Microwave transmission

Microwave communications (a form of radio transmission that emits Extremely High Frequency (EHF) waves) is defined as point-to-point (line-of-sight) radio transmission and hence only applicable over relatively short distances. Digital microwave communications is defined as the same type of communications but over a higher bandwidth.

The first real application microwave technology was radar, in the 1920s. Since then many developments have taken place, culminating in the use of microwave as a mode of transmitting digital data. Within the LAN environment this mode of transmission is normally used as a way of extending the network. A typical private microwave LAN link contains a parabolic antenna, a radio frequency transmitter/receiver, a microwave LAN interface device and a power supply. Microwave transmission can be about 1.5 times faster than transmission over cables.

Infra-red Transmission

Of the other possible transmission media, only infra-red and light beams have received any real consideration. Both have the problem that they can be obstructed by any solid object or even certain weather conditions and this severely restricts their use.

Infra-red transmission has been thought of as a substitute for microwave or as a basis for LANs. In this context a single room, possibly an open plan office is what is

42 Technologies Available

foreseen. An infra-red transmitter/receiver would be placed on the ceiling and all the devices in that part of the network would be within sight of it. The technique is employed by domestic remote controlled televisions. In the office environment, the transmitter/receiver would be connected by ordinary cable to the rest of the network. Apart from the obstruction problem already mentioned, the transmitter/receiver is the weak point in the network since all the communications in that area must go through it.

Infra-red has the advantage that it is unobtrusive, easy to install and has sufficient bandwidth for its range of application. It is however very easy to eavesdrop on other conversations and to interfere with transmissions in the same area and within sight of the transmitter/receiver. Within the range of application, these factors do not pose a serious threat. For quick installation of devices in offices where they may be moved around frequently, infra-red is a serious contender.

Infra-red can also be used to provide communications between buildings. For this class of application, relatively high data transmission rates are usually required so lasers are employed for the transmitters. Laser technology for data transmission is also used in fibre optics, so the technique is familiar. It is especially suitable for providing cheap, high bandwidth links between buildings, provided these are within sight of each other. Using the technique, several million bits per second (bps) can be transmitted reliably.

Case Study — The IBM Structured Cabling System

The IBM Structured Cabling System interconnects IT devices in a local area via a homogeneous, structured wiring approach. The basic components of this system are the cable, connectors and a distribution panel. This system has been chosen as a case study in order to give the reader an insight into a well known and widely distributed cabling system. Although to date, this is not the market leader in LAN cabling structures, it is the cabling structure recommended for connecting the biggest PC seller - the IBM PC DOS-device, whether it be an IBM device or a clone. IBM introduced this cabling system in 1984 before releasing its Token ring LAN, offering it in direct competition with existing coaxial and twisted-pair cabling systems. IBM market this product as a flexible and integrated solution covering voice, data and video. However, to date, the offering is limited to data communications components for Token ring and other IBM terminal types. The main advantage of IBM's approach is that it offers a single structured cabling systems for connecting IBM devices. The IBM cabling system components are:

Cable

The cables are used to connect workstations with distribution panels within wiring closets and also connect the wiring closets themselves. Users have a choice of ten cable types, each type will facilitate a particular requirement. *See* Table 1.

Type	Description
1	Two twisted-pairs of No. 22 AWG solid conductors enclosed in a braided cable shield covered by a sheath. Used for data communications. Maximum distance 330ft.
1 plenum	Same as Type 1 but with TEFLON or similar. Used for data communications. Maximum distance 330ft.
1 outdoor	Two twisted-pairs of No. 22 AWG solid conductors enclosed in a corrugated metallic cable shield with a sheath. Used for data communications. Maximum distance 330ft.
2	Two twisted-pairs of No. 22 AWG solid conductors for data communications, enclosed in a braided metal cable shield. Four additional pairs of No. 22 AWG solid conductors for telephones are also included inside the cable jacket. Maximum distance 330ft.
2 plenum	As Type 2 but with TEFLON or similar.
3	Four pairs of unshielded, twisted-pairs of No. 24 AWG telephone cables. Maximum distance 330ft.
5	Two 100/140 micron fibre optic cables. Maximum distance 660ft.
6	Two twisted-pairs of No. 26 AWG stranded conductors for data communications.
8	Two individually shielded, parallel twisted-pairs of No, 26 AWG solid conductors. Maximum distance 165ft.
9	Two twisted-pairs of No. 26 AWG solid or stranded conductors. Maximum distance 220ft.

Table 1 — Cable types

Connectors

The IBM cabling system contains connectors for terminating both data and telephone cable conductors. There are three connector types. *Data connector*; this terminates two twisted-pairs of copper data conductors. *Three-pair Telephone Jack connector*; this is a

44 *Technologies Available*

six-pin modular stack used to terminate three twisted-pairs of telephone conductors in Type 2 cable. *Four-pair Telephone Jack connector*; this is a eight-pin modular stack used for terminating the four twisted-pairs of telephone wires in Type 2 cables.

Distribution Panels

This serves as an accessible way of mounting cable connectors. Up to 64 data cables connectors are installed on a distribution panel. It can also serve as a patch panel in wiring closets.

There are many more elements to the IBM Cabling System which have not been described here, for example cable accessories, surface mounts (this provides the attachment of data and telephone jack connectors), faceplates (cable terminating devices), line surge suppressor and interfaces to other types of cables, for example, coaxial.

This discussion is only intended to give the reader a brief idea of the three basic components of a structured cabling system. For further information the reader is recommended to contact his local IBM office or dealer for help and advice.

TOPOLOGIES

The topology of a network is the pattern of the nodes and their interconnection. This topology together with the transmission medium used determines the type of data that may be transmitted, the speed and efficiency of communications within the network. In the past topology has been used solely as a means of categorising local networks. This was useful only when there were a few different local networks and their topology did in fact indicate the way the network operated as well as the interconnection of the nodes. Since LANs have proliferated, the same topology can be operated in many different ways; a classification based on some other criterion, such as the access mechanism or the network control technique, is more useful. In spite of this, a discussion of network topologies will still aid the later descriptions of the techniques and also since some techniques apply best to particular topologies.

Star

The most common topology for installations designed around a central mainframe computer system is the star network (*see* Figure 2.12). Today this central processing device can be anything from a large PC to a mainframe depending on the power required. Therefore the centre of the star can perform processing and/or switching of messages from one incoming line to another. More complex networks can be constructed by interconnecting the stars. One feature of this kind of topology is that each outlying device (which only needs minimal intelligence) is connected to the central system by means of a point-to-point link which is for its exclusive use or which is shared by only a small number of others on a polled basis, (*see* Figure 2.12). The central processing hub (or server) normally uses circuit-switching to establish a dedicated path from a workstation to itself or to another workstation. The shared resource in a star network is the central system and not the transmission medium as in the case of a true LAN.

In principle, the addition of new devices is easy in a star network because each one just needs to be tapped into an existing multi-dropped line, or a new line is put in-between it and the central system. In practice, it is not quite so straightforward. The installation of each new cable necessitates the whole route between the two sites being accessed in order to put the wire into ducts. The communications handling device at the central site also needs to have a suitable port available and the necessary communications software to handle the particular device which is being put on.

Thus in a star LAN which is serving 20 separate terminals, for example, a communications controller with 20 ports is needed with 20 separate lines between it and the terminals.

A star network generally operates in a polled (note, polling is described further in Chapter 3) mode with each outlying device being asked in turn if it has any information to send. If it has, the communications controller gives its full attention to that device until either there is no more information to be sent or the controller decides to give another device a chance. If the central device acts only as a switch, two devices can be connected together for a time so that they can exchange messages. During this exchange, other pairs of devices can be in conversation without affecting any other dialogues.

The star is an important topology for LANs. The hub is used primarily as a switch for connecting together the peripheral terminals, workstations, computers, etc. This is the purpose of the normal private on-site telephone network where the peripheral devices are telephones. In this form star networks become LANs, with suitably enhanced exchanges at the centre. The PBX will be discussed further in Chapter 3.

High security, easy fault detection and isolation are some of the benefits of this topology. However there are some major disadvantages of local area star networks. The obvious one is failure of the server (or hub) — if it fails then the whole network fails. Other problems include: deterioration of performance and throughput as traffic increases, as requests for service may be blocked at the switch; limitations are imposed on distances between the server and the nodes; the capacity of the server dictates the number of nodes that the network can deal with; the transmission medium used determines the speed of the network.

Ring

A ring network (*see* Figure 2.13) consists of a set of repeaters, each one of which is

46 Technologies Available

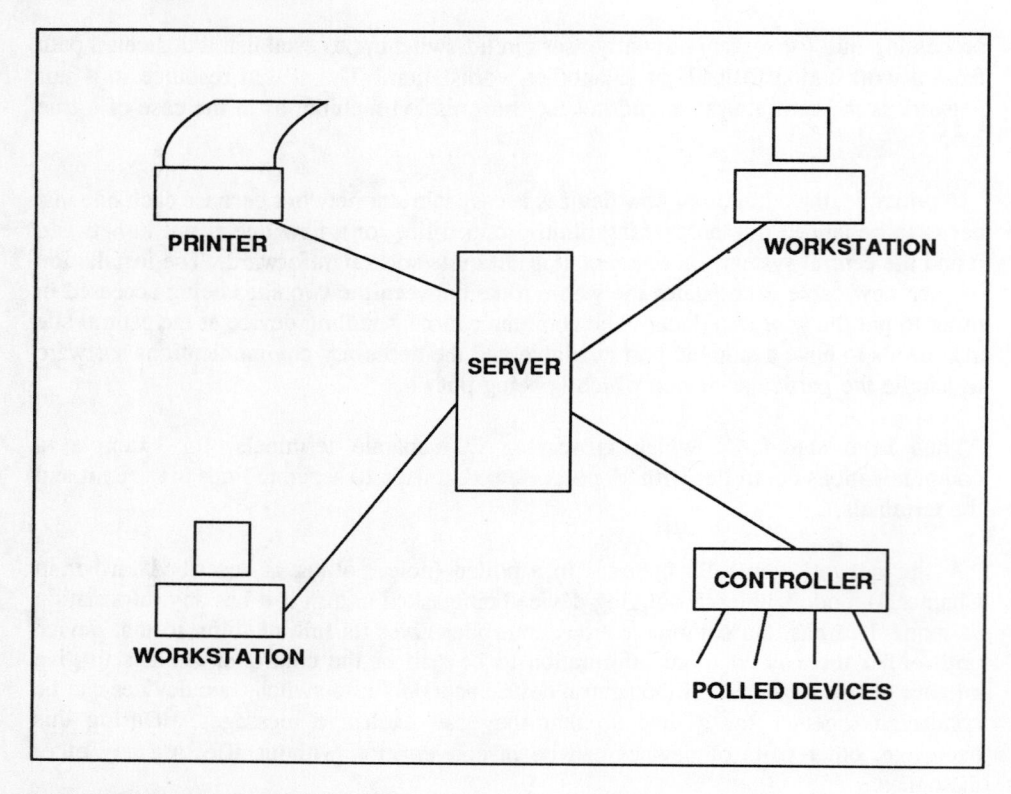

Figure 2.12 Star network system

connected to the repeater on either side of it in a unidirectional point-to-point transmission way to form a single closed ring or loop. The nodes are then connected to their own repeater. None of the nodes are responsible for controlling the network as a whole and each has equal status.

Unidirectional transmission means that information is received at one side of each node and is transmitted from the other and most existing ring networks are configured in this way. Bidirectional rings are possible but are necessarily much more complicated, in terms of the wiring which is required, the control mechanism which must be employed, and the higher level protocols needed to ensure that messages are received in order and erroneous ones are detected and retransmitted.

Ring networks were developed as computer networks as a result of looking for an efficient means of connecting together all the devices which need to be on the network. The aim was a network which would be both cheap and easy to control so that no one node could gain exclusive use of the network and every user would have a fair share of the available capacity. The challenge of the ring concept is in designing a system which would be fair and yet with a sufficiently simple method of control that a separate controller is not needed, and each node does not require to be excessively complicated. Probably the oldest ring type is the Token Ring topology, originally designed in 1969. This ring control technique is described in Chapter 3.

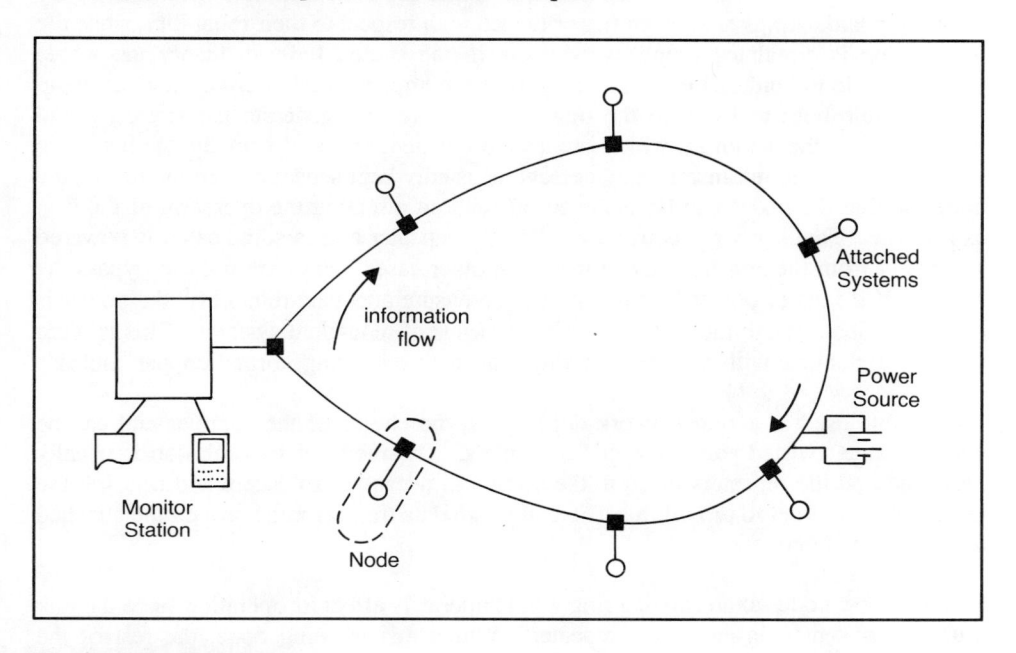

Figure 2.13 Ring network

Ring networks usually operate by means of a special message being passed from one node to the next. On receipt of this message that node is then able to transmit a packet of information. All the other nodes on the network will receive the information packet and will examine the address field to see if that packet is intended for them. If it is, they read it into a buffer and in some schemes they mark the original packet as having been received. Since everyone on the ring can actually receive each packet, it is easy to implement a broadcast message facility.

Many methods for transmitting information around a ring have been devised (discussed in detail in Chapter 3). They all operate by giving permission to transmit to a node which then is able to put a limited amount of information on the ring before handing over to another node.

Rings are capable of being run at a very high speed by means of suitable electronics at the points where the ring is tapped for the nodes. The actual observed point-to-point information transfer rate depends to a large extent on the methods used to control and access the ring.

Being usually unidirectional, rings are ideally suited to the use of optical fibres as the transmission medium. Most current ring-based products can either be obtained with fibre optics as an option or can easily be adapted. Some are even available with fibre optics as the standard. Rings are sometimes criticised with respect to their reliability, since the information is circulated round every node, if one station fails, in theory the whole network could fail unless bypass circuitry has been implemented. Furthermore, each tap must be able both to listen to the transmissions and to regenerate the messages and retransmit it to the next node which can lead to transient errors. Normally, the hardware which receives and retransmits the message is usually kept separate from the rest of the nodes so that the nodes can be switched off without affecting the operation of the ring as a whole. This hardware is usually called the repeater and in some cases is powered separately from the attached device itself. In other cases, relays are used to bypass the repeater if it fails or power to it is cut off. To ensure adequate reliability, the power is often supplied through the network itself by means of redundant systems. This is more difficult to achieve with a fibre optic ring than with one using normal copper cables.

The cable used in a ring network depends on the choice of the supplier and can be coaxial cable, twisted-pair cable or fibre optics. The mode of transmission is usually baseband and the repeaters perform the minimum necessary to accept and transmit the information in order to provide a sufficiently high data transfer rate between the attached device and the network.

Adding new nodes to an existing ring will temporarily affect its operation since the link must be broken to insert a new repeater. Whilst this is being done, the rest of the devices will be unable to use the ring. This can be avoided by duplicating the path.

Although it is not strictly necessary for the operation of the ring, it is commonplace to include a special device to monitor the traffic and remove packets of information which get corrupted and which would otherwise circulate without being removed or re-used. The monitor can also be used to pinpoint nodes or repeaters which are not functioning correctly. To do this, any node or repeater which detects a packet with an error in it sends a special message to the monitor which can be used to work out where the error occurred. Monitors can also be used to gather statistics about the use of the network to assist in planning future developments of the system.

Robustness, low error rate and costs are the prime incentives for using a ring topology. However, apart from the already discussed reliability problem, other issues include: distance limitation imposed both on total distance, and distance between nodes; capacity of server dictates number of nodes on the network; throughput decreases with each added node; performance is highly dependent on the number of nodes and server capacity.

Bus/Tree or Highway

A bus network consists of a main highway for transporting information between the devices which are connected to it. A bus is just a unique case of the tree, where there is only one trunk, with no branches. (*See* Figure 2.14 — a bus configuration could be any of the four options described on the diagram). It is a development of the data bus which is built into computer systems for interconnecting all the various components such as the processor, the memory and the peripheral controllers. The idea is that all the components in the system are connected to the same multi-point transmission medium and share in its use. In the case of a LAN, each node is given a unique address which the others use to append to the messages which they send to it. Since there is only one transmission path available in the whole network, there must be sone scheme for sharing its use as fairly as possible amongst all the devices connected to it.

Many schemes can be devised for sharing the bus, ranging from each node being given a time slot in which to send information, through a frequency division system, to a completely random method in which any device can send information at any time. In all cases the nodes must be sufficiently intelligent to handle the problems which occur when the channel is already in use or when data gets corrupted by colliding with somebody else's. Note, since all devices share a common communications medium, only one pair of devices can communicate simultaneously.

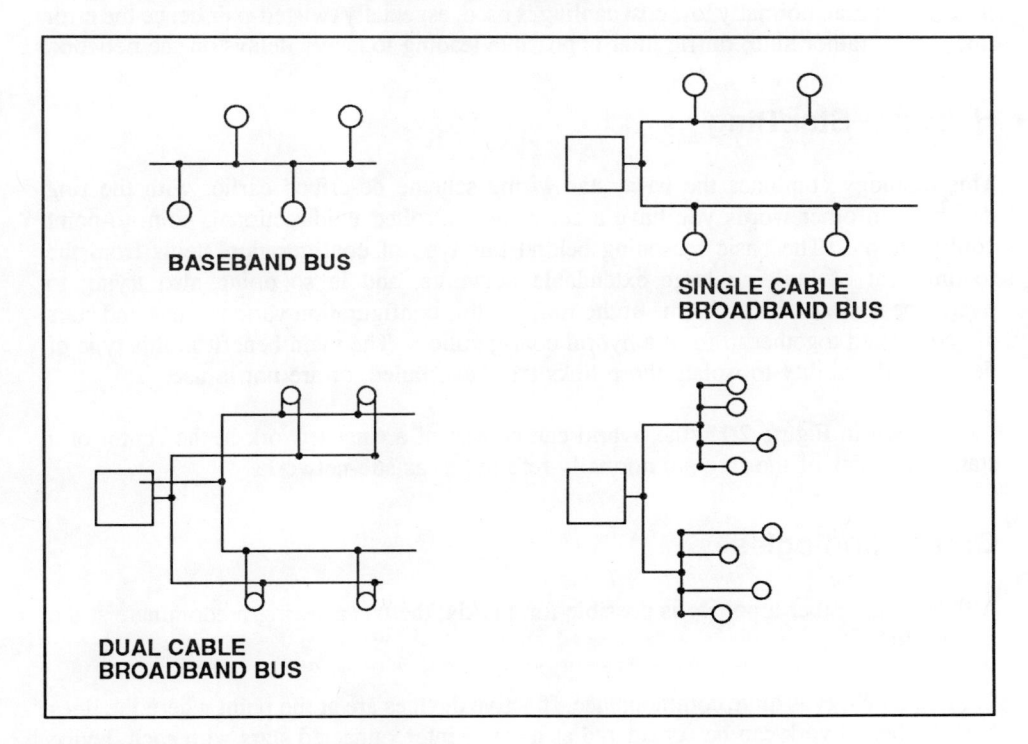

Figure 2.14 Bus network configuration

The data bus itself is completely passive, unlike those employed in ring networks. Each node must listen all the time to the network to detect information which is being sent to it. Also, the nodes must implement a set of high-level protocols to provide the functions of ensuring that the data received is the same as that which was sent, because the high possibility of collision with some techniques makes it very likely that information will be damaged in transit. The access method is the most important single factor in obtaining efficient use of the network.

The major techniques used in baseband, broadband, time division multiplexed and frequency division multiplexed bus systems are discussed in more detail in Chapter 3.

This low cost, limitless in terms of topology, flexible in terms of adding or deleting nodes, and reliable configuration is one of the basic LAN designs used today. The most well known uses of this topology are Appletalk and Ethernet. Through their market penetration it has become a well-understood design. However there are also some disadvantages with this topology, namely that throughput may decrease with each node added, especially in high volume, steady traffic environments; addition of a node directly affects the performance of the whole network; since this is a low-cost LAN implementation, normally low cost cabling is used, especially twisted-pair hence the error rate can be rather high; traffic jitter is possible leading to heavy delays on the network.

Hybrid — Star/Ring

This topology combines the basic star wiring scheme described earlier with the ring design — in other words you have a centrally controlled unidirectional, point-to-point configuration. The basic reasoning behind this type of configuration stems from the requirement of building large extendable networks, and in so doing also trying to overcome some of the problems of the ring. In this configuration various rings and stars are connected together to form a hybrid configuration. The main benefit in this type of design is the ability to isolate those links that have failed, or are not in use.

As shown in Figure 2.15, the hybrid can consist of a ring network at the centre of a star. The nodes of the ring are normally referred to as sub-networks.

Other Topologies

Although any other topology is possible for a LAN, the bus and ring predominate at the present time.

A tree topology is quite commonplace. If active devices are at the point where the lines branch, the network can be considered as a set of interconnected stars with each device connected by a dedicated line into the network. Bus networks can often be designed as tree shapes with the branches occurring at points in the cable.

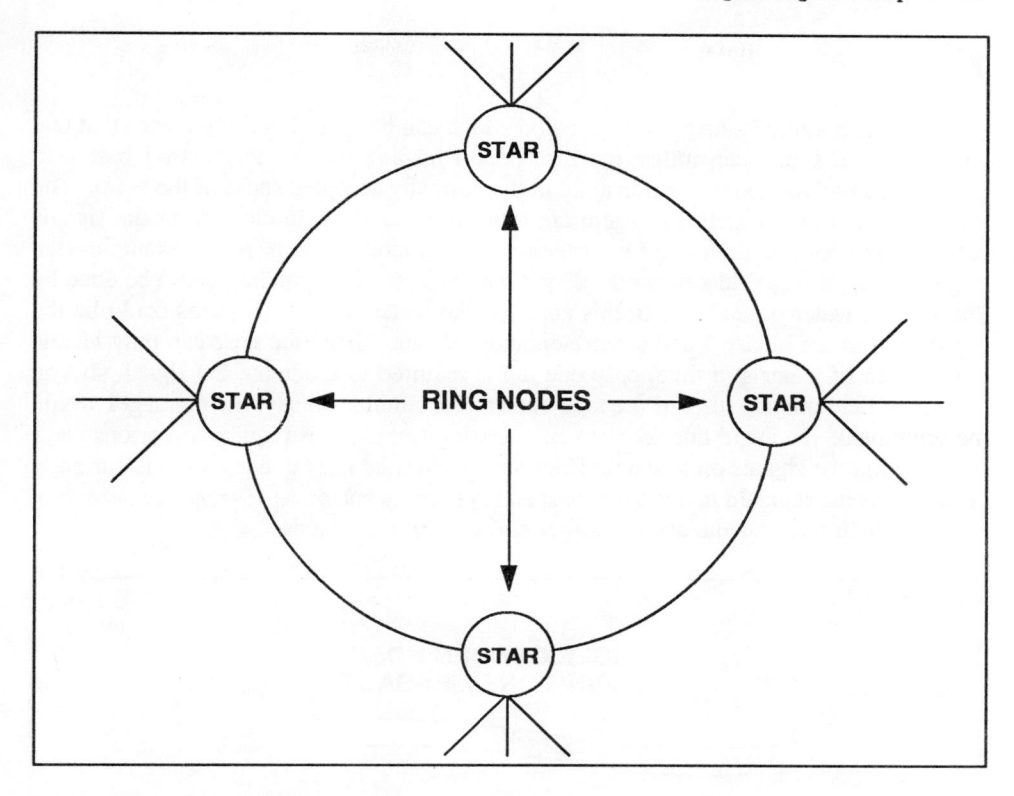

Figure 2.15 Hybrid network

Fully interconnected networks or meshes are sometimes required where it is important to have a lot of redundant connections, possibly to handle exceptional traffic loads or provide a high degree of security from line failure. Generally these cost significantly more to implement than would a typical LAN or even a typical star. One of the reasons given for implementing a local area network is to reduce costs by providing a shared data transmission network, and this is not generally consistent with the design aims of a mesh network.

SIGNALLING TECHNIQUES

To transmit information successfully from one location to another over a cable or other transmission medium requires the information to be coded in a manner which is suitable for the medium and information type involved. For LANs, two classes of signalling techniques are generally used: baseband or broadband.

Baseband

Baseband signalling is the simplest method which can be used (it simply means that one and only one signal can utilise the distribution media) and for this reason baseband signalling involves no modulation at all in the normally accepted sense of the word. The digital signals on a baseband system are transmitted as discrete changes in the signals which correspond to the digital information of the incoming data. As an example, (*see* Figure 2.16), if we build a network using a garden hose, the signalling could be done by turning the water on and off. In this analogy, the water on and off states could be the equivalent to the binary 1 and 0 representation of data. Since the hose can only handle one stream of water at a time, only one tap is required to modulate the signal. If you use more than one tap, then if the taps transmitted simultaneously, the messages would be scrambled. To avoid this problem an encoding technique is required. Various ways of encoding the signals on to the medium have been tried but the one which is currently accepted as the standard method for baseband systems is known as *Manchester encoding*. Others which are possible are the Miller and bipolar techniques.

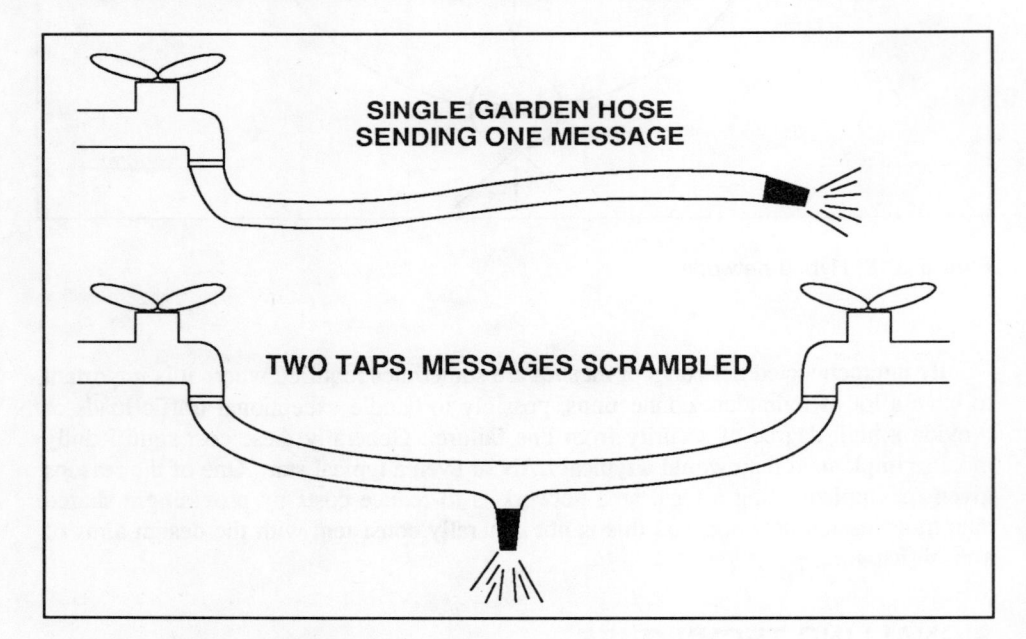

Figure 2.16 Baseband garden host analogy

Manchester encoding is one of the simplest to implement and has one feature which makes it very valuable for data communications systems; it has a built-in clocking scheme which enables every system on the network to remain in synchronisation. Manchester encoding works in the following way. The time interval is divided up into equal cells, each of which is used to represent a single bit. Each cell is itself divided in half. During the first half of the cell, the signal transmitted is the complement of the bit value being sent in that cell. In the second half of the cell, the uncomplemented value is sent. In this manner there is always a signal change during a cell, at the half-way point, which ensures that devices can be kept in synchronisation without the necessity for separate synchorisation signals. Figure 2.17 gives an example which is useful to illustrate the process.

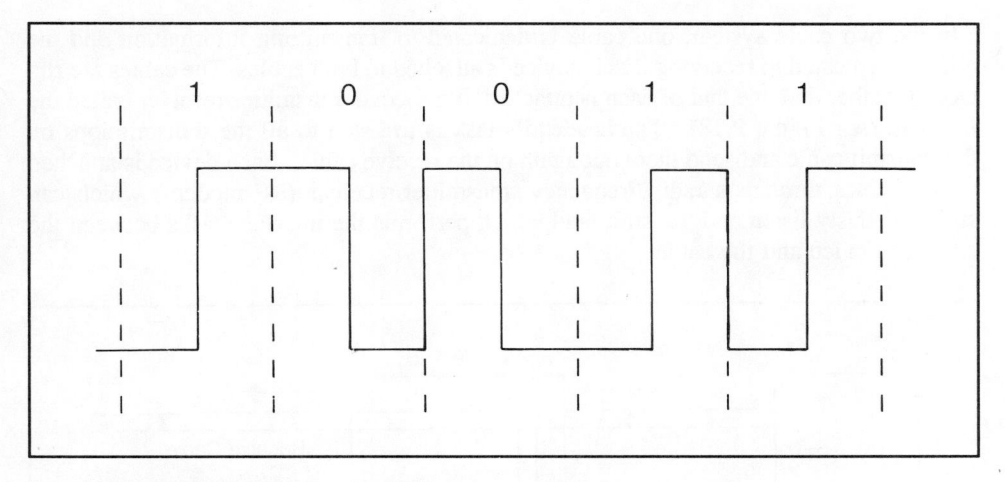

Figure 2.17 Manchester encoding

The most popular baseband network system is the Ethernet system. This transmission system makes use of a high speed trunk. The trunk is then time-shared competitively (*see* Chapter 3) to allow all of the users to send their data. The baseband system is a very cost-effective way to transmit data which can be handled in a burst mode but it should not be used for voice or video which may require a full data channel.

Broadband

One of the problems with baseband signalling is that the cables can attenuate the signal below a certain level, making it difficult to determine what is noise and what is data. Over the relatively short distances involved on most LANs which are in use today this is of little importance. For longer distances, in the past, the technique which was employed was to modulate the information on to an analogue carrier wave and to use complex modems to encode and decode the signal. Today digital WANs carry information totally in a digital format.

Another allied technique which has found favour with designers of LANs has been the broadband technique which has its origins in the CATV market. Essentially it is a

54 Technologies Available

method of frequency multiplexing many users on to a single cable so that in effect several channels are created. Typically a broadband system has a bandwidth of around 300 MHz so there is ample bandwidth available for data transmission services with plenty left over for other analogue based transmission systems.

The way a broadband system works is as follows. Two or one cables are used to link all the systems on the network.

In the two cable system, one cable is dedicated to transmitting information and the other is dedicated to receiving. Each device is attached to both cables. The cables are run close together and one end of each is attached to a special transmitter/receiver called the *headend (see* Figure 2.18). The headend's task is to listen to all the transmissions on the transmit cable and send them out again on the receive cable. Each device is attached to the cables through a radio frequency transmitter/receiver (RF modem) which can simultaneously listen and transmit, and which performs the interface tasks between the attached device and the cables.

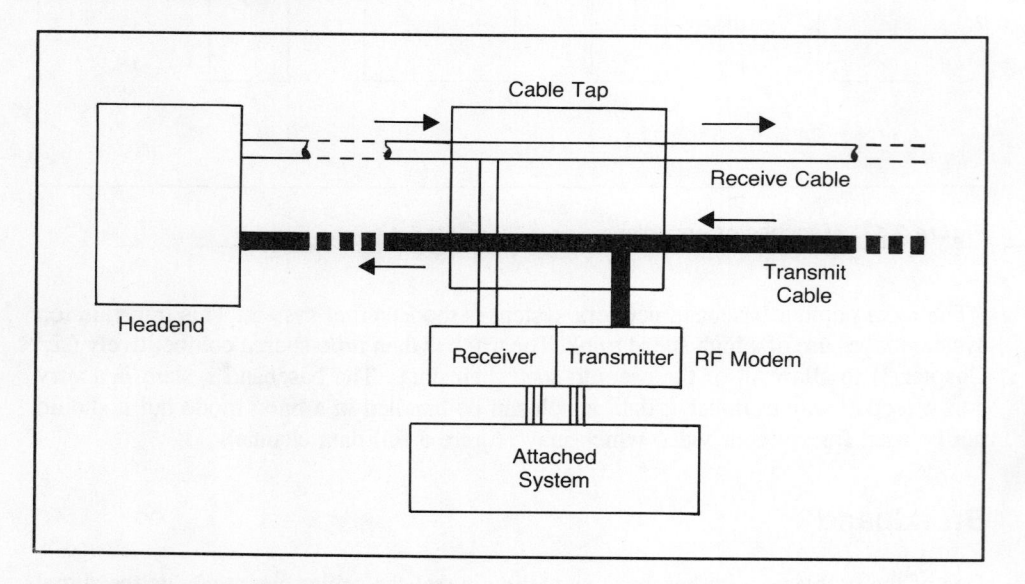

Figure 2.18 Two cable broadband bus

Normally the two cable system is adapted to use a single cable in the following manner. The available bandwidth of the cable is split into two separate bands, say, 150 MHz each. One band is allocated to information being transmitted and the other to the reverse.

Thus a system which is transmitting data uses one frequency band and this information is received on this frequency band by the headend device which retransmits it again on a different frequency, this time within the receiving band. All the systems on the network listen to the receiving frequency and they accept information which is destined for them by recognising their address on the packet of data. Figure 2.19 shows the main hardware components of a one cable broadband network.

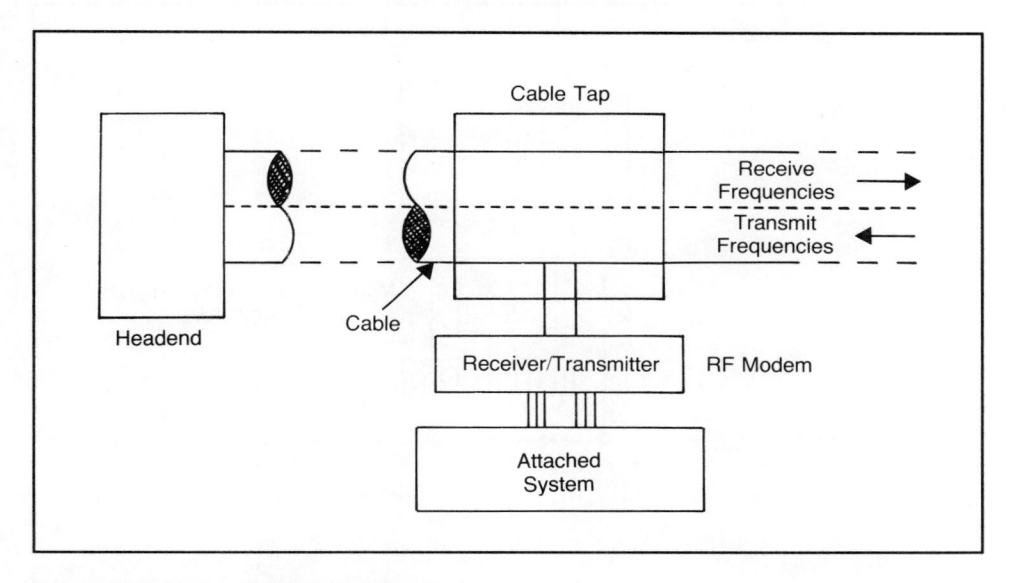

Figure 2.19 One cable broadband bus

Thus a broadband system can be full-duplex in operation, since separate frequencies are used for sending and receiving.

In practice, the transmitting and receiving bands are themselves split up into a number of different channels so that many different users and services can share the same physical medium without any fear of interference with each other. The technique originally adapted using the two cable broadband transmission was to allocate a separate channel to each pair of users.

Thus a total bandwidth of 300 MHz, say, is split into a large number of channels, each with a limited bandwidth specifically suited to the application being served. On a single channel, a number of separate terminals could be used in the normal way for a multidropped line. If the transmission requirements are such that the channel cannot be shared adequately by more than one conversation, one pair of devices would be the exclusive users of it. Using this technique, channels with transmission speeds as high as the users desired could be implemented.

The major problem with this approach is when a single device, such as a mainframe computer, needs to be in dialogue with a number of other devices, possibly at the same

56 *Technologies Available*

time. The way to do this would be to install a pair of modems for each of the channels which are being used as illustrated in Figure 2.20.

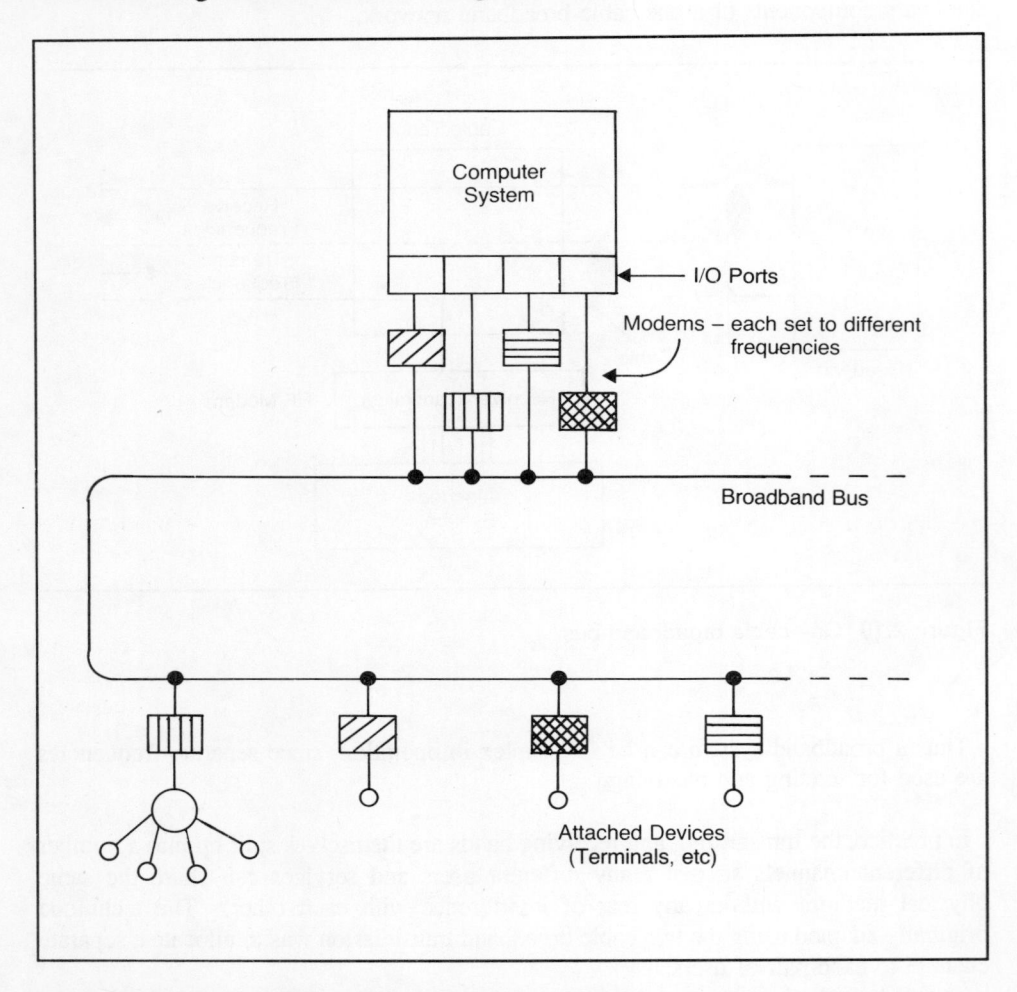

Figure 2.20 Connecting a computer system to a broadband bus using fixed frequency bands

The obvious disadvantage with this approach is that one pair of modems is needed for each channel and one hardware port on the mainframe computer is needed for each supported device. It prevents one device from talking to another without a lot of difficulty unless they both have modems of the same frequency. It is possible to attach multiplexers through the modems or PADs to the channel to minimise the number of modems and ports needed and to maximise the number of devices which can be supported, and this is the solution which is normally adopted.

Signalling Techniques 57

Better alternatives could be found. Advances, both in the hardware (eg the use of PADs) and the techniques used for accessing and using shared packet systems provide the key to the greatly increased potential of the broadband network as a viable system for a LAN.

One technique is to allocate one or more channels (in fact pairs of channels - one for sending and one for receiving) to the buses which can be shared using one of the techniques which have been developed for time-division multiplexing. With a channel bandwidth sufficient to permit a data transmission speed of a few million bits per second, it is possible for a large number of users to share a single channel without affecting the service which the user receives.

Another technique which can be used is to employ what are know as frequency agile modems. These are standard radio frequency (RF) modems except for the fact that they can switch from one frequency band to another. In this way, a single device need have only one modem for it to be able to communicate at different times with a number of other devices. For each conversation the devices involved must first agree on the pair of frequencies they will use and then switch both their modems to them. This assumes that the frequencies are not being used by anybody else. A network controlling device is usually employed to allocate the frequencies to the devices wishing to be in conversation. In practice, the device which is initiating the conversation asks the controller if the device it wishes to send to is in a position to receive information. The controller checks the availability of the other device and, if it is free, informs it that someone wishes to communicate with it and tells it which frequency to use. The controller also informs the initiator of the conversation which frequency to switch his modem to. That frequency band is then allocated solely to that conversation for its duration.

The modems which are needed to connect a piece of equipment are essentially VHF transmitters and receivers which use two separate frequencies to transmit and receive. Rather than transmitting using an aerial as would a normal transmitter, these modems use coaxial cable. With present day technology, RF modems which can support a data transmission rate of around 19 kbps are readily available using the modulation techniques normally associated with data transmission over standard telephone lines. RF modems which can operate at much higher rates of around 2 Mbps and which require a bandwidth of 6 MHz can also be obtained. It is these special modems and the fact that a special device is needed to translate all signals from the transmit frequency band to the receive band that puts up the cost of the broadband system.

The system is very well suited to carrying analogue signals such as telephone traffic and, more especially, television signals. Thus a broadband network can devote some of its channels to carrying computer-generated information, and other channels to analogue signals including real-time colour video. This is totally beyond the capabilities of most other LAN systems.

58 Technologies Available

Standard cable television line amplifiers can be used to give a long range to the network. A cable length of many kilometres is possible without noticeable degradation of the signal, but if a broadband bus is implemented on one of the channels which is operating in a contention mode, then the access algorithm and the length of the packet of information could severely limit the practical length of the cable.

The cable used for cable television and hence for broadband networks is similar, but not identical to, conventional coaxial cable. It exhibits a high immunity to interference so that it can be run in electrically hostile environments. Special tools are available to enable the cable to be tapped without cutting it, severely damaging it or interfering with the transmissions it is carrying at the time. Some doubt has been expressed about the reliability of these devices and some suppliers prefer to cut the cable and make a normal connection.

In summary, the main advantage with broadband is the capability of mixing totally different networks within *one* cable; hence allowing multiple distinct users and applications the ability to share the same transmission medium.

THE USE OF LAN SERVERS

All local area networks must utilise in some form the concept of a *server*. The server is a computer (normally another PC, although any intelligent device capable of providing a service can be used) that is used to provide the LAN peripherals with some kind of service, for example, disk storage, access to a printer or access to a public communications network. In the past LAN servers were normally a general purpose PC which was used both as a personal computer by a user and as a method of providing a LAN service. This obviously was slow as the PC had to resource to distinct functions at the same time. The tendency today is to configure a server as only providing one function, that of serving the LAN community. This specialised computer (which normally is still another PC - although only used for this purpose) provides a faster response for all the workstations.

These servers usually provide the following functions: division of resources among the workstations and other peripherals; sequential access control to specialised hardware; security management and data management.

There are various types of servers on the market today, these can be categorised as follows.

Terminal Servers

These servers are designed to connect dumb terminals, modems, PCs, minicomputers, printers or any other non-intelligent devices into a LAN. Terminal servers replace point-

The use of LAN Servers 59

to-point circuits with electronic virtual circuit connections between terminal devices and host systems over a network. These terminals are normally simple asynchronous RS-232 devices (although IBM synchronous terminals servers can also be found on the market today) used for elementary data entry and screen display. Directly these terminals cannot support LAN connections and therefore a small unit (that can handle all the LAN network protocol required) is used to allow multiple terminals to be connected to the LAN. This unit is seen by the LAN as a single device. Figure 2.21 shows this configuration, you will notice that this type of server can also provide a gateway facility which is described next.

Terminal servers are an essential part of an efficient LAN.

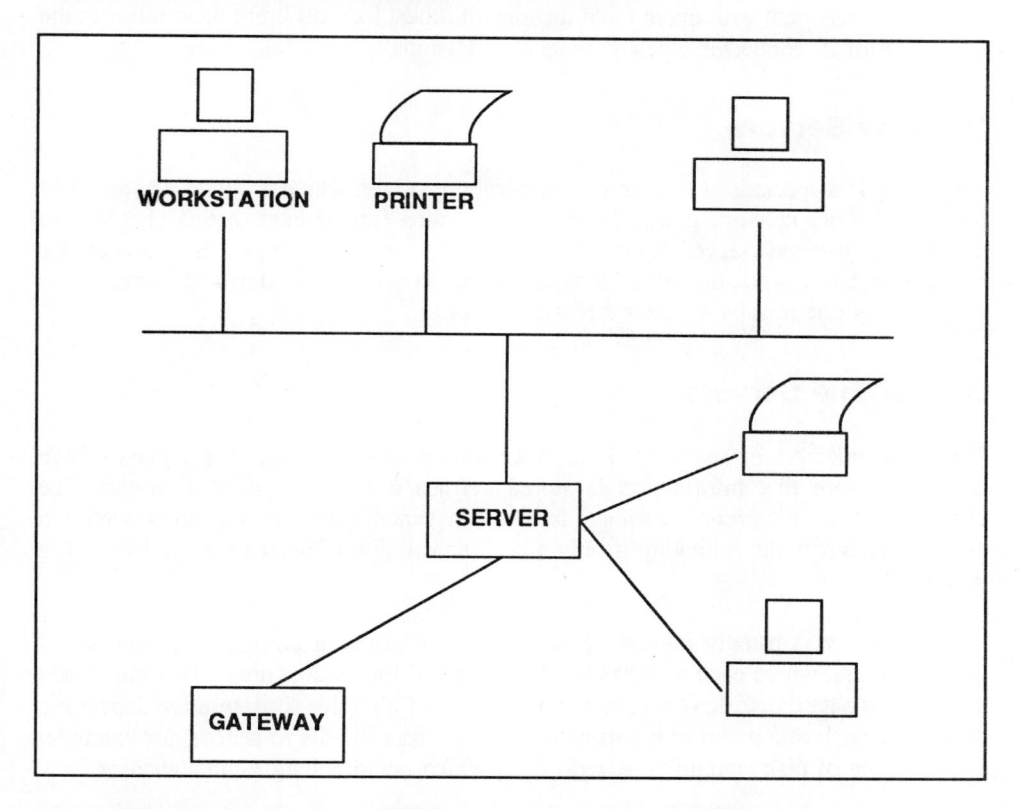

Figure 2.21 Server providing connection for non-intelligent devices

In general, most communications servers today have the following characteristics:

— they permit dumb terminals to be connected to multiple hosts;
— they provide a transparent data transport and control mechanism. Furthermore the server does not communicate characters to a host system as they are entered

60 *Technologies Available*

- by the user, instead it collects characters and periodically (or at screen fulls) transmits them to the host in one go;

- they support high-bandwidth LAN technology;

- they provide automatic configurations and directory facilities where the communications server can determine, without manual intervention, the names and addresses of hosts and terminals/workstations on the network;

- a server can manage, simultaneously, the operation of up to 8xRS-232 devices sharing a single network connection;

- servers deal with operational incompatibilities, like different baud rates, frame format, connector types and signal distortions.

Gateway Servers

A gateway is a specialised form of communications access which provides a connection between distinct network protocols (this is described further later in this chapter). In terms of a gateway server device, what it facilitates for example, is a device for connecting LAN workstations to a host. In this configuration the host computer is accessed via one link by all the other workstations.

Disk or File Servers

The main objective of any LAN is to share information, the way that it does this in terms of where that information is stored defines it as a file or disk server. The difference in these servers is a subject for some argument (and will depend on who you ask) and therefore the following is only a brief description of what I term a disk or file server.

A *disk server* is usually referred to as a disk that has been portioned for the use of different users, where each user has his own reserved file storage area. This eliminates the need for a hard disk drive on every workstation. Within this configuration depending on the access levels given to a particular user, the user is able to access, for example, a whole area of disk containing several files, which could belong to another user.

A *file server* is normally an intelligent disk server with the added responsibility of classifying every file according to who owns it and the security access classification the user wishes to give it. In this configuration a user is only able to see one file at a time depending again on the access levels given to the files.

These types of servers have recently been developed further in terms of their performance. A new breed of computers — the super PC with multi-gigabyte storage, dual processing motherboards, Micro Channel (MCA) technology and the use of advance

RISC (Reduced Instruction Set Chips) technology — has revolutionised the use of them. Today a dedicated super-file server is becoming the norm within many large LANs.

Printer Servers

Printer servers are designed to equitably apportion time on the printer(s) to every user. This server is seen as the basic requirement of any LAN as it is seen by many as one of the main ways of saving money. In other words this type of server is used to share scarce or expensive resources, like a laser printer, and is normally used to justify the use of a LAN. In addition to letting a user share a printer, this server normally stores print jobs on a server disk drive and sequentially sends it to the printer as it becomes ready. This characteristic is called print spooling.

Printer servers are also used to direct print jobs to remote printers. In this way any special print job can be printed at any location where there is a printer that is connected to the network. The reason for this is that generally every printer on the network is assigned a unique address (which should be transparent to the user) and therefore this means that the data can be directed to it.

Other Servers

The server concept can be used for anything that can be shared, and hence there are many types of servers that a LAN could in theory be attached to. For example, a Fax server (normally a dedicated device) where all the workstations can prepare the fax document and send it to the fax server for transmission. Others include electronic mail server, database server or even OS-2 server.

INTER-NETWORKING

The limited range of the local area network has meant that there has always been a necessity to link together multiple LANs and LANs with other communications environments. Now with greater availability of high-speed communications lines and the phenomenal growth in the use of intelligent workstations and LAN technology, more and more organisations are looking towards interconnecting their LANs. If LANs are situated within the same building then this interconnection is normally achieved directly, however if they are located in different geographic locations, then inter-networking can only be achieved by using a public communications carrier or private WAN technology. The main requirements of any communications inter-networking environment are as follows:

— provide a link between networks;
— provide for the routeing and delivery of data between applications and systems;

62 Technologies Available

- provide a transparent communications environment by accommodating the following network differences if they exist:
  - addressing schemes;
  - maximum packet size;
  - network access mechanisms;
  - timeouts;
  - error recovery;
  - routeing techniques.

Inter-networking has now become a viable solution to linking dissimilar LANs, whether physically or logically different. In the last few years, the devices used to achieve this, have been repeaters, bridges, routers and gateways (which are explained later). These devices have been developed to use existing and future LAN technology and are achieving greater and greater levels of effectiveness and speed. New developments in digital communications within both LAN and WAN environments will undoubtly change inter-networking beyond recognition. In order to keep the discussion into this topic on a realistic level, I will only describe those components of inter-networking that have a proven track-record or that are the basic foundation blocks of the topic.

Bridges

These are normally simple devices that 'bridge' the gap between LANs (usually physically distinct), *see* Figure 2.21. However in recent years this technology has evolved and now supports functions that are normally associated with routers. Their main function is to link LANs that are identical across the *Data Link* and *Physical* Layers of the Open Systems Interconnection (OSI) Model (*see* Figure 2.25 — note, OSI and LANs are described further in Chapter 8), normally the Media Access Control (MAC) level. See Chapter 3 for further information on OSI and Chapter 7 for more information on MAC.

This means that a bridge will extend the Data Link address space across the inter-networking environment and could bridge two different networks as it simply passes data packets and ignores the higher level protocols. The way a bridge functions can be split into three distinct entities - learning, filtering and forwarding. In this way it will limit the traffic between network segments.

In terms of learning, when it receives a data packet, it determines its source address and compares it to the entries in its routeing table. If the source address is not already there, then it will add it. This means that new devices can be added to the network without having to reconfigure.

If the destination address is on the same network segment as the source, the bridge will automatically discard the packet, this is known as filtering.

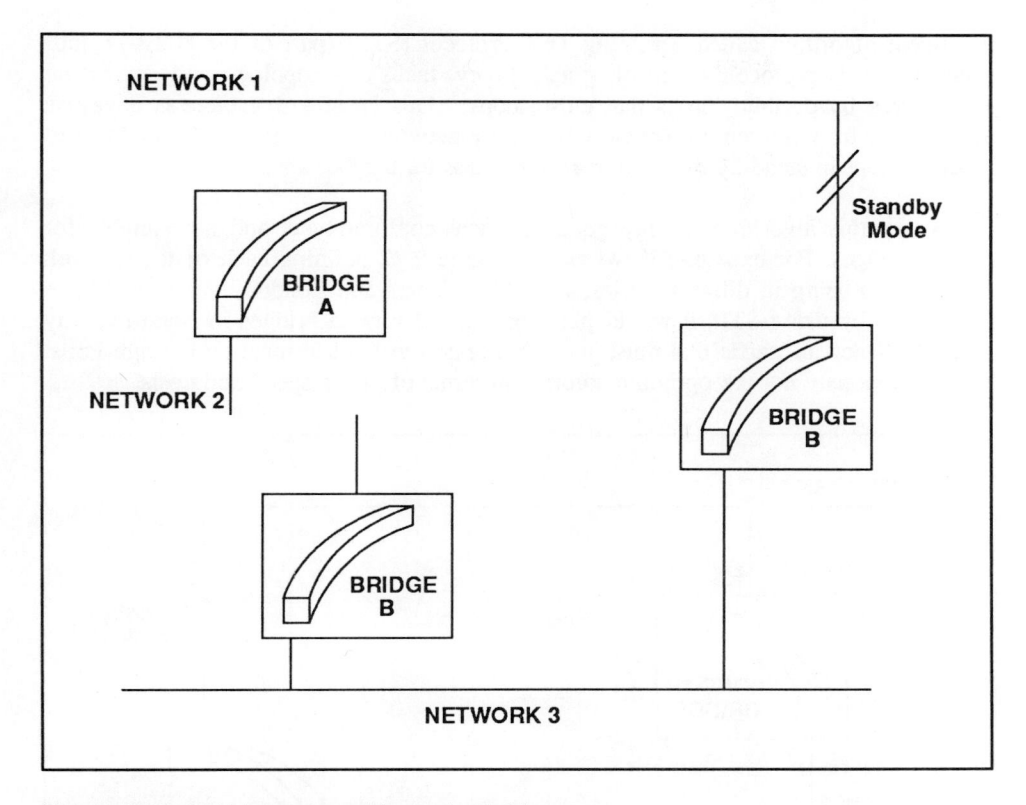

Figure 2.22 LAN inter-networking using bridges

Finally, if the destination is on the routeing table, the bridge determines the device associated to it and forwards the packet on to that device. If the destination address is not on the routeing table, then the bridge will forward the packet to all the devices except the one on which it was received.

These bridges assume that only one path (whether physical or logical) exists between any two devices on network segments connected by local bridges. Normally this will not always be the case, the possibility of creating multiple paths between devices is always a great problem. These multiple paths are also known as loops (*see* Figure 2.22).

This could lead to an unknown number of duplications of packets. This redundant traffic would obviously degrade the performance of the network as a whole and in complicated configurations can lead to a great deal of confusion at the end stations.

This problem has been under investigation for some time now, with the Institute of Electrical and Electronic Engineers (IEEE) producing a bridge-inter-networking

64   *Technologies Available*

intelligent algorithm called Spanning Tree Protocol (STP) (part of the 802.1-D draft standard). This protocol, based on graph theory, takes any topology and derives an acyclic tree by disabling links that close loops. This ensures that there is always a unique path from any device on the whole inter-network to any other. These disabled links are kept in stand-by mode until required due to, maybe, a station failure.

However this algorithm is only good for local configurations and not suitable for remote bridges. For example, if we extend Figure 2.22 defining each of the network segments as being in different cities, ie, Paris, Madrid and London, shown in Figure 2.23. Then by using STP, it would place one of the remote bridges in stand-by, (say Madrid), hence all traffic that must go from London to Madrid must go through Paris. This is obviously not the optimum solution in terms of either speed and costs.

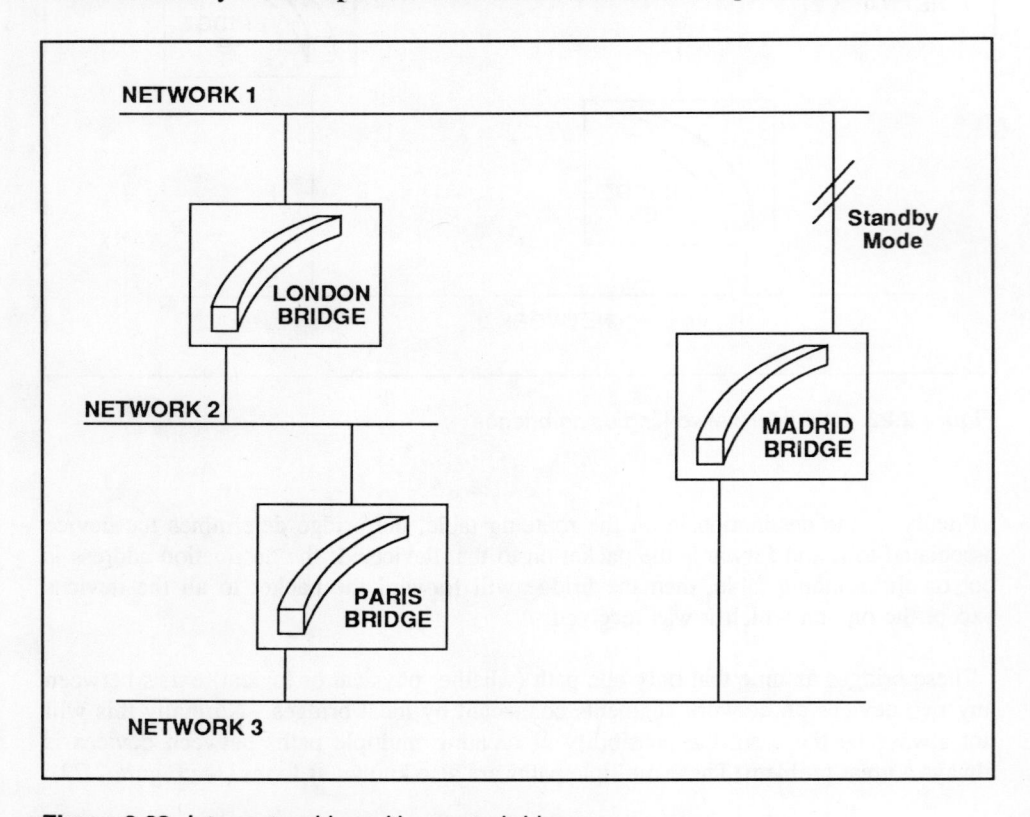

Figure 2.23 Inter-networking with remote bridges

Another bridging technique which also deals with the local environment, but this time not transparently, is called Source Routeing (part of the IEEE 802.5 standard). This technique is normally used in ring environments, where the source station needs to supply the routeing information in the frame. The bridge simply inspects the frame and follows the routeing instructions within it. One of the main elements within this technique is that it requires a unique bridge and ring numbering system.

IBM has extended this technique to remote bridges by treating pairs of interconnected bridges as one local bridge (*see* Figure 2.24). As can be seen the remote bridges A and B are logically configured as bridge 1 and so on. The only limitation to this configuration is that each remote bridge can only be connected to one other remote bridge.

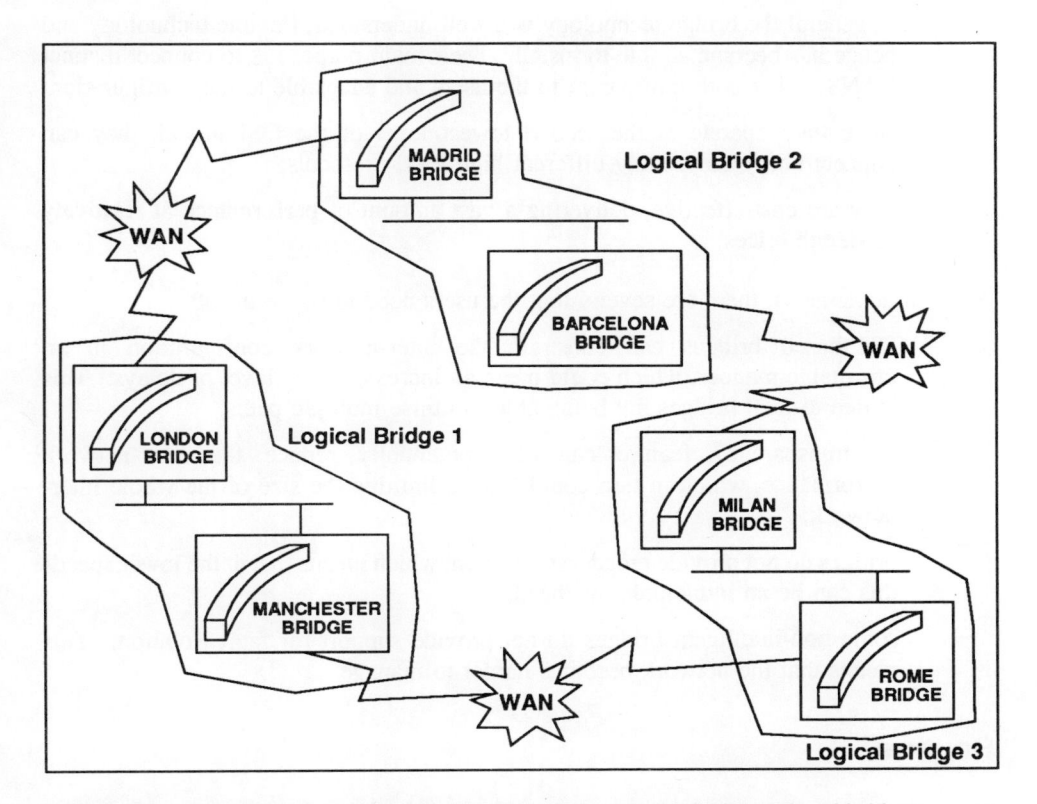

Figure 2.24 European remote bridge configuration – logically it is a local bridge

Bridges interconnect different LANs in various ways. There are many new developments to come in this arena, for example, work is being done on the production of source routeing transparent bridges. Therefore it is expected that the story of bridges will not end here. However whatever happens the users need to be aware of several issues when implementing a bridge solution to their inter-networking requirements. I have described them here in terms of advantages and disadvantages. The main advantages of using bridges are:

- in terms of control and management the network can be partitioned into self-contained segments. This means that fault detection is much easier. Furthermore, this isolation of segments can also increase overall network security since sensitive areas can be isolated;

- in general, performance on most LANs declines as the number of nodes increases. By using bridges, smaller LANs can be created and logically linked together to form a bigger LAN;

- in general the bridge technology is a well understood, flexible technology and hence has become simple to install. Their main purpose is to connect distinct LANS, being both transparent to the users and adaptable to the configuration;

- since they operate at the second lowest level of the OSI model, they can connect networks running different high-level protocols;

- they are cost-effective, delivering a vast amount of performance at relatively moderate prices.

As to disadvantages, there are several that the users need to be aware of:

- STP-based bridges can constrain the inter-network configuration in an unsuitable manner, which could mean an increase in the level of delays. This is due to STP bridges not being able to utilise multiple paths;

- its transparency feature can also potentially reduce the inter-network performance, which in turn could lead to limiting the size of the whole inter-network;

- bridges do not provide broadcast isolation, which means that at the lower speeds this can be an intolerable overhead;

- some non-intelligent bridges do not provide support for fault isolation. This means that the network becomes harder to manage.

Routers

These devices function in much the same way as bridges, except that they operate at a higher level of the OSI model, the Network Layer (*see* Figure 2.25). This means that they must possess a much higher level of software intelligence than bridges in order to be able to intelligently select the most efficient route for transmitting data and due to this can link together dissimilar networks, for example, CSMA/CD with ring protocols (for further information refer to Chapter 3). Routers can also link into WAN, running for example, TCP/IP via leased lines or X.25.

This makes them very suitable for inter-networking since they can support complex and large inter-networks with redundant paths. Furthermore with the use of a hierarchical addressing scheme routers can logically separate the inter-network into sub-networks.

This means that it becomes a much easier task to administer than a bridged inter-network.

The way a router works is totally dependent on the existence of a routeing table. It uses this routeing table to identify how to transmit its data, the address of an individual device and the paths available. From this and other inter-network information it calculates the most effective method and path to transmit the information. Routeing decisions are often based on an algorithm (eg open shortest path first (OSPF), a link-state algorithm that sends routeing updates only if changes have occurred or simply a least-cost algorithm) that can calculate the number of hops from one inter-network segment to the other and in conjunction with the link speed, cost and link congestion can then determine what is the shortest, fastest and cheapest route available.

The principal limitation of routers is that they cannot inter-network dissimilar Network layer protocols, for example TCP/IP with DEC Local Area Terminal (LAT) protocol. This limitation has prompted several suppliers to develop multi-protocol routers and *brouters*. The multi-protocol routers, as the name indicates, act as normal routers supporting more than one protocol. The *brouter* is basically an intelligent multi-protocol bridge that can also handle simultaneously different protocols. But unlike the multi-protocol router, if it encounters a protocol that has not been defined within its logic it will act as a bridge.

As always there are advantages and disadvantages with using these types of devices. If we first look at the advantages:

— routers link like protocols, communicating with other networks directly as they receive the address of every node (whether workstation, other router or bridge), with this and network configuration information it makes intelligent routeing decisions. This means that in theory, routeing should be the most cost effective inter-networking solution;

— all routers are configurable, this means that the network manager can alter the way an inter-network operates depending on his knowledge of where the load will be. For example, if the network manager knows that on Mondays, between 10am to 10.30am the internetwork load is going to increase by 200 percent then he can configure the network accordingly. Furthermore, since they are better at optimising usage and dealing with failures, errors or congestion than bridges, then it could be the prime network management tool of any network manager;

- in terms of providing an effectively secure and available inter-network, they can logically isolate segments. This means that if an incident occurs within one sub-network, this can be detached from the inter-network leaving the rest of the network to function as if nothing had happened;

— routers are not affected by the time delay that occurs within bridges. Furthermore, unlike some bridges they permit active loops, which allows the load-splitting of certain applications;

68 Technologies Available

- many of the LAN protocols include Network Layer features, this means that from the start they were designed to be routed.

In terms of disadvantages:

- routers are more complex and hence are more difficult to configure and install;
- routers are protocol-dependent devices, this means that all the protocols required within the inter-network must be accommodated on every router, otherwise the inter-network will fail;
- although many of the LAN protocols are accommodated in routers, there are still two major exceptions, IBM's DLC (Data Link Control) and DEC's LAT.

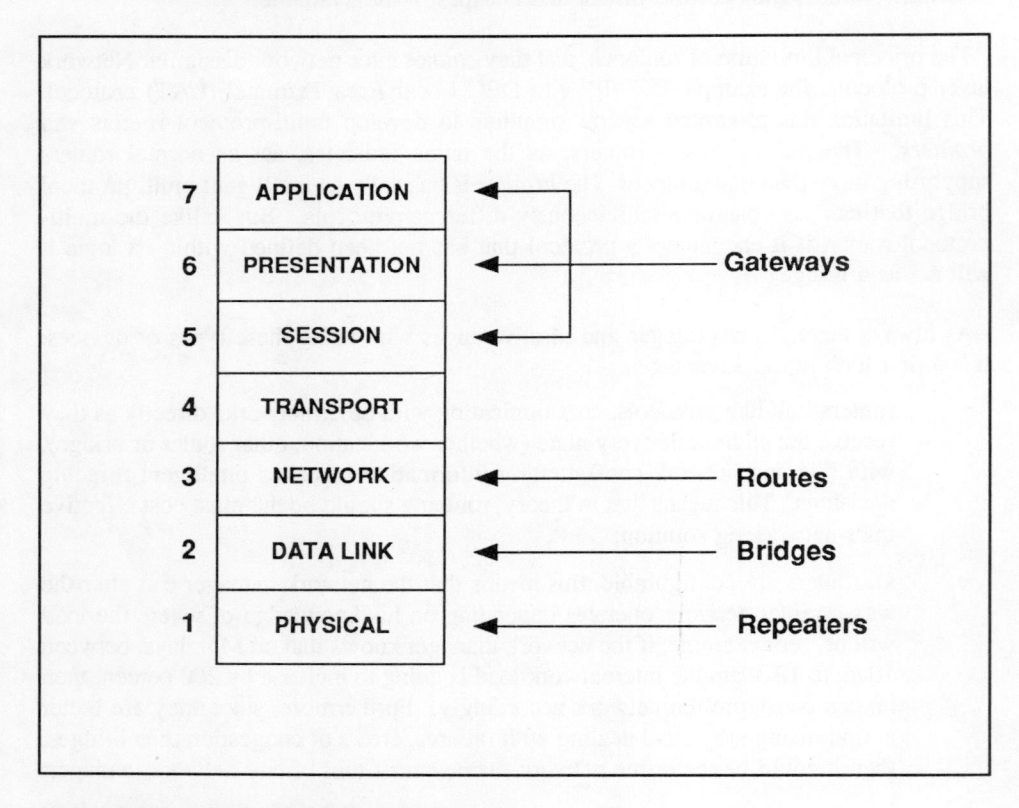

```
7  APPLICATION   ◄─┐
6  PRESENTATION  ◄─┤────── Gateways
5  SESSION       ◄─┘
4  TRANSPORT
3  NETWORK       ◄──────── Routes
2  DATA LINK     ◄──────── Bridges
1  PHYSICAL      ◄──────── Repeaters
```

Figure 2.25 OSI view of inter-networking

Gateways

A Gateway is a specialised device that links two different communications environments, normally running their own proprietary protocols. Figure 2.25 describes where within the

OSI Model these devices are normally defined. Its main objective is to convert incompatible protocols, networks and applications, in order to create a transparent inter-network. An example of a gateway could be the link between a LAN and an IBM SNA network into an IBM mainframe environment. Here the connection would be made through a gateway PC running 3270 simulation software.

Repeaters

Repeaters work at the lowest level of the OSI network configuration (*see* Figure 2.25). Their main function is to extend the maximum usable length of the cable used within a network. Although in theory this device is not strictly an inter-networking device, it is placed within this section for completeness as it is normally used with all the inter-networking devices discussed so far. Furthermore, the fact that they extend the network geographically, could indirectly imply that this is an inter-networking device.

TERMS TO REVIEW

Sage the Owl Recommends

Due to the size and content of this chapter, I have split this part of the chapter into different chapter sections.

Main Requirements

— Cost
— Transmission Speed
— Network Capacity
— Error Rate
— Reliability.

70 *Technologies Available*

Classification of Technologies

— Intelligent LANs
— Non-intelligent LANs
— Wired
— Patched.

Transmission Media

— Tap
— Bandwidth
— Connectivity/Availability
— Security
— Topology
— Noise
— Twisted-Pair Cable
— Multi-way Cable
— Coaxial Cable
— Fibre Optic Cable
— Balun
— Structured Cabling
— Radio Transmission
— Microwave Transmission
— Infra-red Transmission.

Topologies

— Star
— Ring
— Bus
— Hybrid.

Signalling Techniques

— Baseband

- Manchester Encoding
- Broadband.

The use of LAN Servers
- Terminal Servers
- Gateway Servers
- Disk and File Servers
- Printer Servers.

Inter-networking
- Bridges
- Routers
- Brouters
- Gateways
- Repeaters
- OSI.

3
Network Sharing Techniques

INTRODUCTION

In the previous chapter the basic components of local area networks were described. However, more than just a few lengths of wire, intelligent devices (servers, bridges, etc) and some modems are required to make a network operate. Methods of using the network must be devised to make it suitable for carrying data.

As we have seen, networks with the same topology can be used in several different ways and can use different media to effect interconnection. Thus, neither the topology nor the medium are wholly suitable as a method of classifying LANs. It is much better to approach the problem through the way the network operates and the access and control procedures which have to be followed to make it operate as desired, although even here the same method may be applicable to several different topologies and applications. However, a classification based on the access and control methods is the one which is most relevant to the products and research systems in existence today. It also serves to illustrate a number of important features of LAN technology.

Some of the techniques described here are of general applicability and others are relevant only to a particular type of configuration. The type of network which is the most relevant to the method being described is identified.

MULTIPLEXING TECHNIQUES

The idea behind multiplexing is to enable more than one user of a single circuit or network to access it with other users. Many techniques have been tried for multiplexing but only those which are particularly useful for local area networks will be considered here.

Multiplexers share a high speed I/O line amongst a number of lower speed devices. An example of multiplexing is the multi-drop line. In this situation a number of intelligent devices and one host intelligent device share the same line.

Time-Division Multiplexing

Time-Division Multiplexing (TDM) also known as synchronous TDM, is possible when the available bandwidth exceeds the data rate of digital signals to be transmitted. Therefore multiple digital signals are carried on a single medium by interleaving portions of each signal in rotation, giving a slice of time to each signal. For example, consider the situation which is illustrated in Figure 3.1. A number of relatively slow devices each want to use a circuit to another device. Usually the other device is at a distance away from the cluster of low speed devices and it makes economic sense to share a long line amongst as many users as possible. The example is typical of a group of terminals which are located in one site, all using a computer in another location and requiring the provision of one or more leased lines between the two locations.

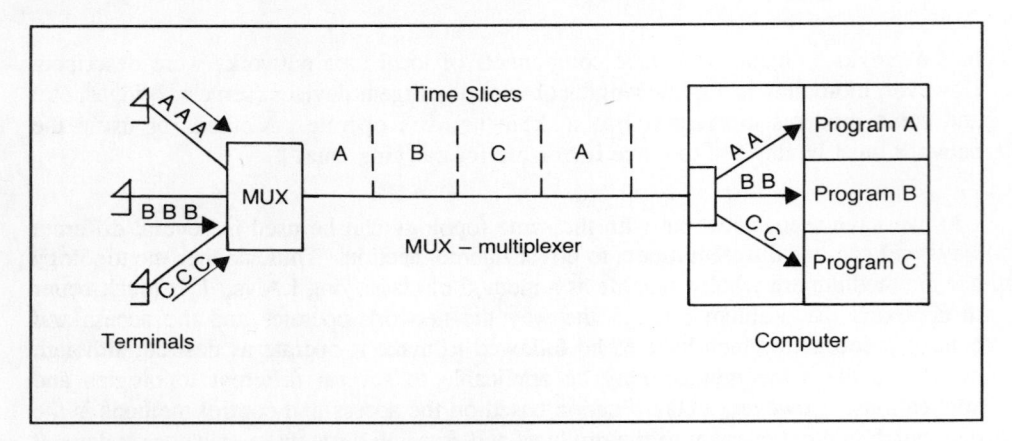

Figure 3.1 Line sharing by low speed devices

The cost of providing each low speed device with a separate leased line would be phenomenal, so multiplexing is used to share the relatively expensive high speed resource. This is parallel to the situation of a local area network where economical interconnection can be achieved by means of sharing the data transmission network amongst all the devices connected to the system.

The multiplexer in the diagram allocates each of the attached devices a time slot for them to have exclusive use of the shared high speed circuit. Information flows between the end devices and the multiplexer at a steady rate determined by the end devices themselves and not by the multiplexer. The time slots allocated to each device are kept fairly small in order that each device can have frequent use of the shared circuit, at the multiplexer itself.

The data which passes along the shared circuit is more or less a continuous stream of binary digits or characters. To unscramble this at the other end requires the presence of a reverse multiplexer which is synchronised with the multiplexer and which can then divide up the incoming data stream into individual data streams corresponding to the ones produced by the devices at the other end.

TDM is an important technique for a number of local area network technologies, especially those based on ring topology. In rings, each station is normally given the opportunity to use the ring for a fixed period of time. Normally no actual physically separate multiplexer is used, since the mechanisms for accessing the ring, which are built into the repeaters, are inherently time-division multiplexing techniques.

An extension to TDM is what is termed as the Time-Division Multiple Access (TDMA) protocol. Multiple Access techniques are discussed later. However TDMA works by assigning a time slot to every node in which each node can transmit. The time slots are synchronised by the control node that transmits a short timing message, following which each node counts time intervals until its interval arrives. The node may now transmit its message otherwise this time slot will go unused.

Statistical Time-Division Multiplexing

Using normal time-division multiplexing techniques, channel capacity is wasted unless every device is transmitting data all the time, and this is unlikely to be the case in a practical situation. If time slots could be allocated only when they are actually required by the devices connected to the multiplexer, then a much better utilisation of the capacity of the shared channel could be achieved. This is the idea behind statistical time division multiplexing (STDM) - also known as asynchronous TDM. The devices which are connected to the STDM multiplexer actually contend for use of the shared circuit. The multiplexer is a complicated device which has enough intelligence to allocate the channel efficiently to the devices connected to it.

Statistically it is unlikely that all the devices served by the multiplexer will be active at the same instant in time, so an STDM system can be made to serve a larger number of devices than can a multiplexer using ordinary TDM nethods.

Local area networks which rely on contention to allocate the network such as those employing the carrier sensing techniques described later, are essentially STDM methods, since the time slots on the network are allocated on demand from the devices connected to the network.

Like local area networks which use standard time-division multiplexing techniques, the intelligence needed to perform the multiplexing is distributed around to every device on the network and is inherent in the access mechanism involved.

Frequency-Division Multiplexing

Every transmission channel has a certain frequency bandwidth (ie the difference between the highest and the lowest frequency which can be transmitted successfully).

76 Network Sharing Techniques

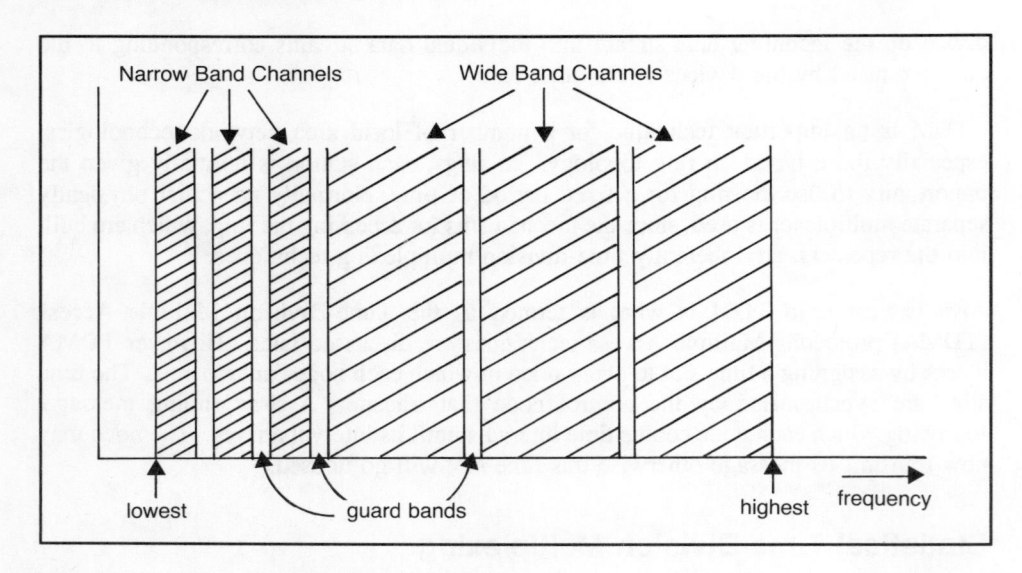

Figure 3.2 Frequency-division multiplexing

If the bandwidth is sufficiently wide, it can be split into a number of bands which can each carry a frequency band equal to or smaller than their width. Each of the individual channels may still have sufficient bandwidth to be able to transport information at an adequate speed for many purposes.

The way the bandwidth is split up is shown in Figure 3.2 which is a graph of frequency plotted against signal. As can be seen, the individual channels need to be separated from their neighbours by a narrower band in order that the data being carried by one channel does not interfere with that being carried by the adjacent channels. These bands which separate the information-carrying bands are called *Guard Bands*. Using the technique of frequency-division multiplexing, a number of information channels with low bandwidth requirements can share the wide bandwidth provided by some transmission media.

Polling

Polling is not normally considered to be a multiplexing technique although it is a well understood method of sharing one communication circuit amongst several devices which do not need to transmit continuously. Consider the simple situation illustrated in Figure 3.3.

The devices labelled A,B,C,... are connected by the same circuit to the controlling device, which may be a computer or just a terminal controller. If all the devices tried to transmit at the same instant and there was no method of deciding which was to have

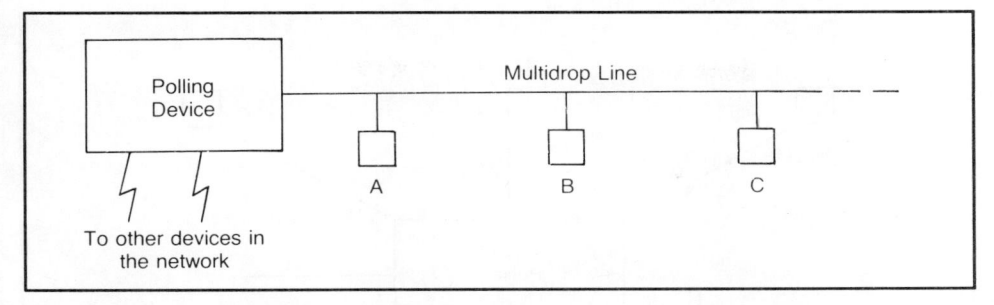

```
                                    Multidrop Line
  ┌─────────┐─────────┬──────────────┬──────────────┬──── ── ──
  │ Polling │         │              │              │
  │ Device  │        ┌─┐            ┌─┐            ┌─┐
  └─────────┘         └─┘            └─┘            └─┘
      ↙ ↙              A              B              C
  To other devices in
  the network
```

Figure 3.3 A polled system on one line

priority, the signals which would appear on the circuit would be incomprehensible. The normal solution to the problem is for the controlling device to ask each of the devices on the circuit whether they have any data to send and, if they have, to let them have exclusive use of the circuit to transmit their message. Various systems of priority can be used to allow those devices which need to transmit information more often than the others to be given the opportunity to use the circuit more often. Each device knows which requests are directed to it by means of a unique address which is placed at the head of each message.

Incoming data is handled in a similar way, the controller adding the address of the destination device to the message before it transmits the message on the circuit. The target recognises its own address and reads in the message.

Polling is also frequently used in centrally controlled systems of the type illustrated in Figure 3.4. The device at the centre of the star could be a computer system or a controller serving a computer system which is incapable of handling more than one message to or from any device at a time. In this situation, the end devices are each allowed to have exclusive use of the controller or computer rather than the communications medium as in the previous example.

Polling is a technique which is more often associated with a computer system or a concentrator which is serving a number of low-usage terminals.

Within the LAN environment this protocol will cause some problems. Firstly, as already stated, it requires a central controller, therefore if this central controller fails then the whole network fails. Secondly, as the size of the network increases, the speed of node-to-node communications will diminish dramatically since everything has to first go through the central controlling node.

BROADCAST BUS SHARING TECHNIQUES

A broadcast bus can conveniently be thought of as a single data transmission channel to which all the systems on the network are listening all the time. A message from any one

78 Network Sharing Techniques

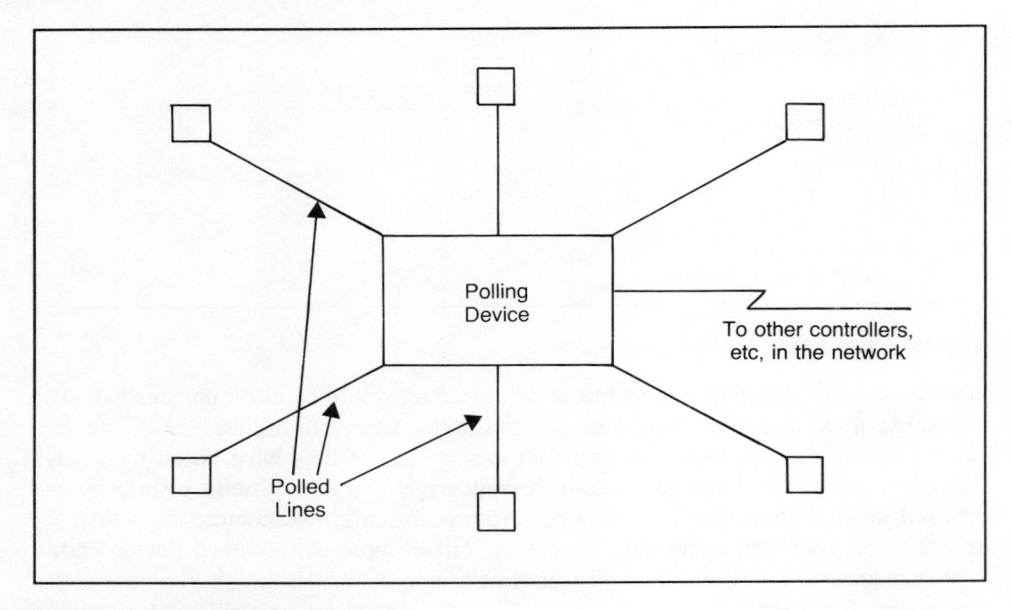

Figure 3.4 Star polling system

user of the bus to any other is 'broadcast' in the same way as a radio message is broadcast on the airwaves for anybody with the right sort of receiver to be able to listen to. In the context of local area networks, the airwaves are normally replaced by a physical cable (note this is now slowly becoming redundant with the advent of cableless LANs — *See* Chapter 10 for further information) of some sort, generally an electrical cable or a fibre optic link.

The other main feature of a bus is that it is shared by every user on the system. In order to share the use of a broadcast bus in a LAN, it is necessary to devise a method by which each user is given a fair chance to transmit information. More than one user is unable to send information at any one time, since to do so on a broadcast medium would mean that the messages would become intermingled and the result would be indecipherable. One possibility is to allocate time slots to each of the users during which they have exclusive use of the network.

Another alternative is for each user just to transmit his messages as and when they are ready and if someone else is using the medium at that time to retransmit the messages which collide. The latter method has been tried but it was found that, in its basic form, it made poor use of the available transmission capacity, especially when there was a large amount of traffic on the network and the likelihood of a collision was very high.

The solution usually adopted for current systems is that in which each user contends with the others in order to obtain exclusive use of the medium. If someone else is using the network, they do not attempt to transmit. In the relatively rare instance of two users trying to transmit at the same instant, both users involved should cease transmission and make another attempt at a later time.

Whichever solution is chosen, since all the systems using the network must listen to every transmission, a comprehensive addressing scheme is required. Also, in order to ensure that the network is fair to everyone, a set of rules must be devised which all the users must observe. It is quite possible that one unscrupulous user who knows that everyone else is abiding by the rules could gain an unfair proportion of the available capacity by deliberately not following them.

It may appear at first sight that allowing each user to contend for exclusive use of the network is liable to cause problems, since collisions can be expected to occur frequently, which would result in two or more messages being corrupted. However, by careful design of the access algorithms, combined with rapid transmission and access logic speeds, we can achieve a high degree of efficiency.

Efficiency can be measured as a percentage of the transmission capacity of the network which is actually used, ie if the network has a raw transmission rate of 10 Mbps, and this is capable of transporting 9 Mbps of information without errors, then it can be said to be 90 percent efficient. But, in a ridiculous situation, this may be the same data stream over and over again, or control information being transmitted continuously, whilst end-user devices are trying to place their data on the network but are unable to gain access. Possibly the best measure of efficiency is the ratio of information transported successfully by the network to that offered to it for transmission.

We must, therefore, be careful in deciding exactly how the efficiency of the network is quoted, as the method used to calculate it can produce very different results. In the case of most broadcast bus systems which rely on contention to allocate the network to the users, the quoted efficiency can only be the statistical average and could be much better or worse under certain circumstances. It is not impossible that every user on the network will attempt to transmit at the same instant, so causing the loss of every message, but it is statistically unlikely.

In common with other data communications techniques in use today, LANs based on broadcast buses typically use packets to send their information. A message is split up into a number of separate blocks and each is transmitted separately with a certain amount of extra information placed in headers and trailers. This is similar in concept to the frame which is now the standard mechanism used for data transmission. The format of a typical packet or frame is shown in Figure 3.5.

The header of a normal packet includes the address of the node which is sending the data and the node to which it is being sent, information about the packet itself (for example, whether it contains data or is a control packet), the length of the data field, etc. The trailer usually contains a special field (field check sequence) which is examined by the destination node to see if the packet has been damaged in transit, another field which

80 Network Sharing Techniques

indicates the end of the packet. The advantages of packet formatting are associated with the detection and correction of erroneous information, and with the fact that any arrangement of data can be sent without fear that it would be interpreted as a control field.

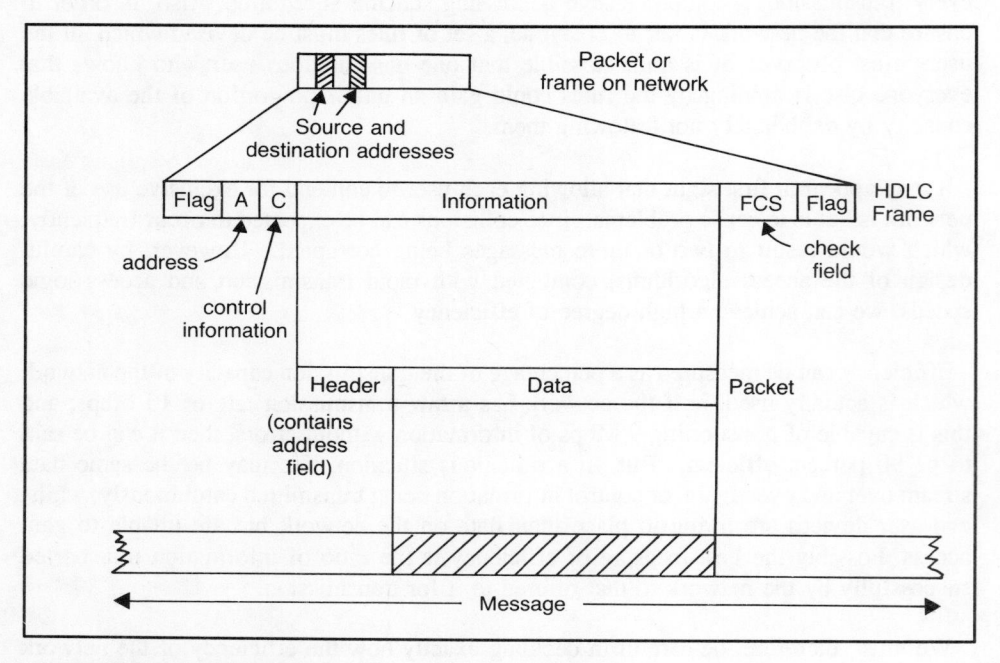

Figure 3.5 Packet format

Whenever a packet is received by the destination node, the error detection fields are examined and the information contained in it is compared with that calculated by the destination node itself using the known algorithm. If the two differ, the destination node can transmit a special packet back to the source node telling it that a certain packet has been incorrectly received and requesting retransmission of it.

The source node need only retransmit the erroneous packet and not the whole message.

The length of the packet can be chosen to suit the characteristics of the transmission medium, the devices using the network or the network itself. Generally the choice is a compromise between the length which is most likely to be transported without error, the time which is needed to place the packet on the network, and the amount of usable information contained in it in proportion to the rather large overheads imposed by the header and trailer information fields. Packets generally used for broadcast bus systems are variable in length with a maximum of around 8000 to 10,000 bits.

The other major advantage of the packet format for data transmission is the freedom it gives the user in the choice of characters. Older data transmission techniques used to control the device at the other end of the link. Thus, if the character stream which was being sent included some of these control characters, special precautions had to be taken otherwise the device at the other end would check for the known control characters, and when they occurred would replace them with another character sequence which would be recognised at the other end where the device would replace it with the one which was originally intended. Packetising the data effectively overcomes this problem since the data is enclosed inside a set of header and trailer fields which have a fixed format and serve to delimit the data field as well as define its length.

In a broadcast bus system, every user terminal is attached to the same circuit, so each must have its own unique address on the network. Packets include in their header field the addresses of both the sender and the destination. Thus, when a packet is transmitted on to the network, each node connected to it examines the destination address field to see if the packet is intended for itself. If it is, then it reads the packet into its internal storage where it takes the action it feels is appropriate. If the destination address is that of another node, it ignores it. This is another reason why the packet format for data transmission on a broadcast system is so useful since it is impossible to tell the source of a message merely by looking to see which wire the data came along.

The technique most commonly encountered for broadcast bus local area networks will be examined below and their major features explained. It is inappropriate at this stage to discuss exactly how each of the techniques is implemented in practice since one single technique can use an infinite number of packet formats and access algorithms. Such considerations are best left to the full descriptions of the products themselves which can be obtained from the suppliers.

ALOHA

The ALOHA techniques for using a broadcast medium are those which were used in what was probably the first of the broadcast packet networks to be implemented. It is now mainly of historical interest only in the context of local area networks, since the technique is not efficient enough to be used for them although it does have the virtue of simplicity. However, it has proved such a great influence on the subsequent design of local area networks that it should be discussed as it does throw some light on the way the techniques have evolved.

The University of Hawaii Computer Centre is based at Honolulu, although it serves a large number of terminals scattered around many of the islands in the Hawaiian archipelago. To provide an easy method of access from these widespread terminals to the central computer centre, a radio broadcast medium was used. Naturally the medium was accessible to everybody with the right equipment and used the so-called 'luminiferous ether' through which all electromagnetic radiation was once thought to pass. Therefore, packet broadcasting was the first choice from the point of view of reliability (ie the likelihood of damaged packets through noise was very high), and the need to employ an addressing mechanism. The ALOHA methods come in two main

82 Network Sharing Techniques

types (pure-ALOHA and slotted-ALOHA), although other methods have been experimented with.

Pure-ALOHA was the first attempt to set up a usable packet broadcast system on the Hawaiian island. Described simply, each device on the network has a transmitter and, whenever that device has sufficient data to send, it places it in a packet, together with the source and destination address, and then transmits it. On transmission it starts a timer which is used to determine whether or not the packet has reached its destination successfully or been lost or damaged on the way. If another node is transmitting at the same instant, the airways will carry two packets at the same time and the two packets will be corrupted. The receiving nodes will detect errors in the packets by means of the field check sequences not matching the rest of the packet. They will not acknowledge receipt of the packets.

The amount of time lost in transmission due to overlapping packets is illustrated in Figure 3.6. Even though there may have been only a very small amount of overlap, the whole of the two packets are lost and must be retransmitted.

When the sender of a packet does not receive an acknowledgement, it is assumed that the packet must be retransmitted. To avoid the possibility of the same two devices which were involved in the original collision broadcasting at the same time again, the time-out used by each transmitter on the network is random and will therefore usually be different for each device.

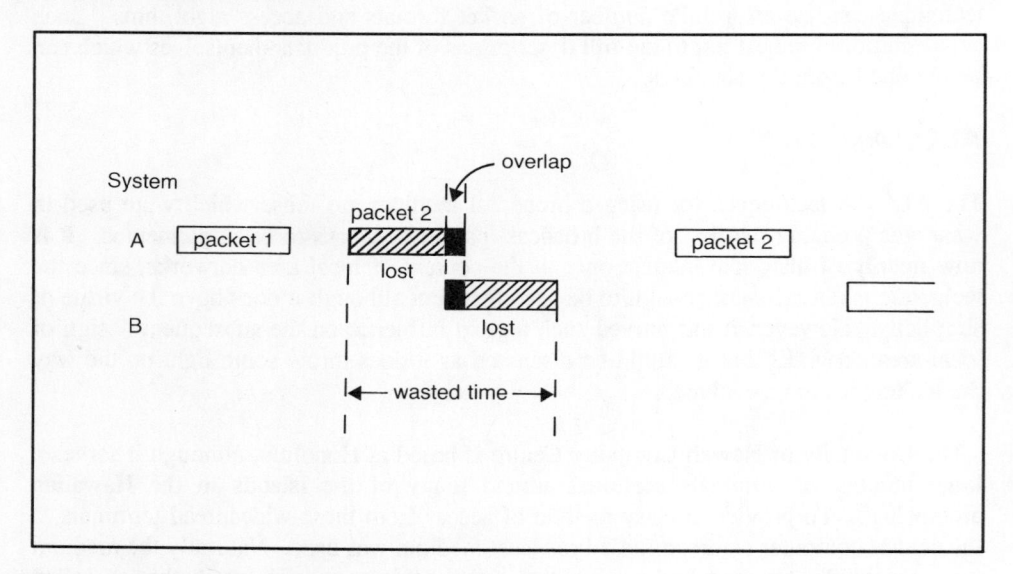

Figure 3.6 ALOHA packet broadcasting

Provided that there is relatively little traffic on the network and the packets used are fairly small, then this technique is reasonably good. The bandwidth is high but the propagation times are significant so there is a very high chance that packets will collide. Also, even when two packets collide, the transmitters have no way of detecting this so they continue transmitting until the whole of the packet is gone. Naturally this is wasteful of the bandwidth. Typically the Pure-ALOHA technique gives an efficiency of around 18.4 percent of the available bandwidth.

One way of improving the efficiency is to remove some of the freedom which is part of the pure-ALOHA technique. The discipline which is imposed by the slotted-ALOHA method is to allow the devices to transmit only at specified times and not whenever they want to. The time is divided up into intervals and the transmitters are only allowed to transmit at the beginning of each time frame or slot. Due account is taken of the time it takes for the transmissions to reach the central computer site in Honolulu so that, regardless of the distance between it and the transmitting sites, the packets all reach Honolulu at the same time. Apart from this, no other discipline is imposed on the users of the network. Thus more than one user may start transmitting packets at around the same time and they will still transmit them in full even though they will be corrupted in transit, but the amount of time between the start of the 'first' packet to be transmitted and the end of the 'last' will be the length of the longest packet, which will be shorter in almost every case than that experienced in the pure-ALOHA system (*see* Figure 3.7).

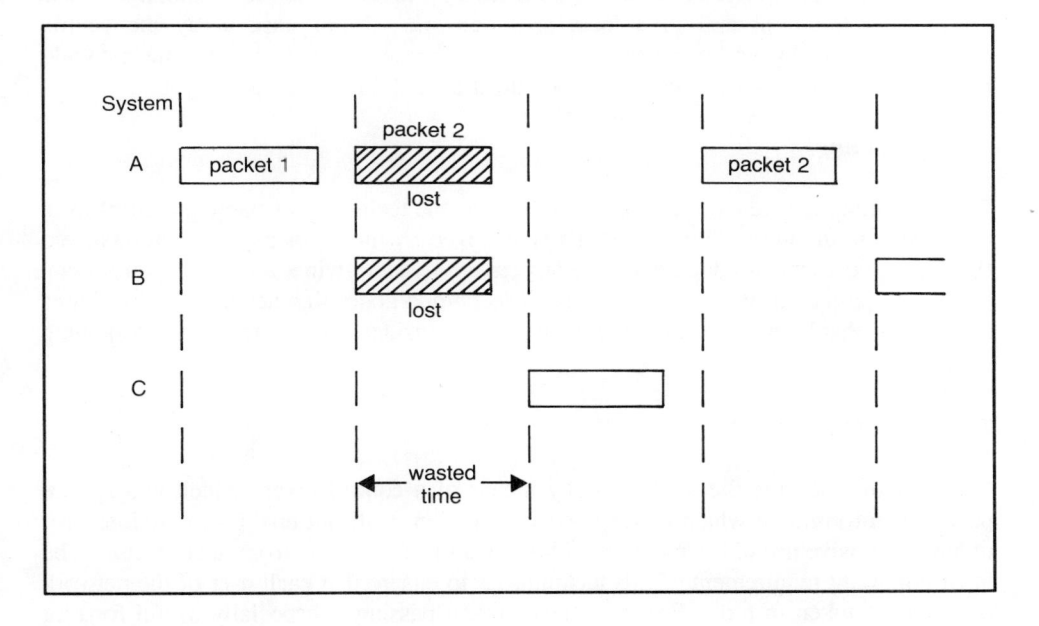

Figure 3.7 Slotted-ALOHA

The slotted-ALOHA technique gives a much better use of the available bandwidth — typically 36.8 percent for large populations of users. Small populations achieve much better figures.

Reservation

Reservation is a blanket term applied to techniques which ensure that the broadcast medium is reserved solely for the use of one node on the network. There are many ways of reserving the network but in this section we will consider just those most commonly used by LANs at the present time.

Time Slots

The network resource can be shared amongst several users by allocating, to each node, a time slot of their own during which only they can transmit information. This is a standard time-division multiplexing technique and was considered in some detail earlier.

Polling

Another way that the network can be shared amongst several users is for some controlling device to ask the other devices on the network if they have any data to send. In other words, each device is polled. Polling requires that special blocks of data are sent to each of the devices in turn, which takes up valuable bandwidth, although this is not usually too important in a local area network. More importantly the central controller must always be working and it must know every device on the network, making it difficult for new devices to be added as and when they are required.

Daisy-Chaining

Daisy-chaining is a generic term used to describe the technique of passing control from one device to the next. Sometimes this is achieved by means of separate circuits from those used to carry the data, and in other cases the same wires are used with special packets to pass control. The most relevant technique under this heading for local area networks is that known as token passing which is considered separately in the following paragraph.

Token Passing

One way of reserving the medium is by means of a control token, which is a special packet of information which conveys no information itself but enables the holder of it to have exclusive use of the medium without fear of interruption from anyone else. The most important requirement of this technique is to ensure that each user of the network is given the token in turn. For this reason, token passing is especially useful for ring topologies (although it can also be used within a bus network) where it is easy to ensure that the token is passed from one node to the next, as data always passes sequentially around the network. Token passing will be discussed in more detail in the section on rings. In this section the particular features of token passing in broadcast bus networks will be considered.

Broadcast Bus Sharing Techniques 85

In a broadcast network, every node can hear every transmission made by every other node and so the token must be explicitly addressed to the next node which is to have control. Generally the nodes on the bus are quite different. Not all the nodes need to be able to transmit but instead can just listen to the transmission on the network, in which case they will not be included in the logical ring for the passing of the token, although they can have normal data packets addressed to them. A typical arrangement of a bus using a token access is shown in Figure 3.8.

The logical arrangement of the nodes on a bus can be changed at any time and in fact a single node can be included more than once per circulation round the 'ring' if it is necessary to give it rather higher priority. Provided that the individual nodes are sufficiently intelligent, it is easy to alter the configuration to take account of nodes which fail.

The operation of the token passing bus is as follows. When a node has a packet ready to send, it waits until it is passed a packet containing the control token by another node. It then transmits its packet of information to the network until either the whole message is gone or until the preset time interval allowed for each node to have the token expires. It then transmits the token, usually to the next node in the logical ring.

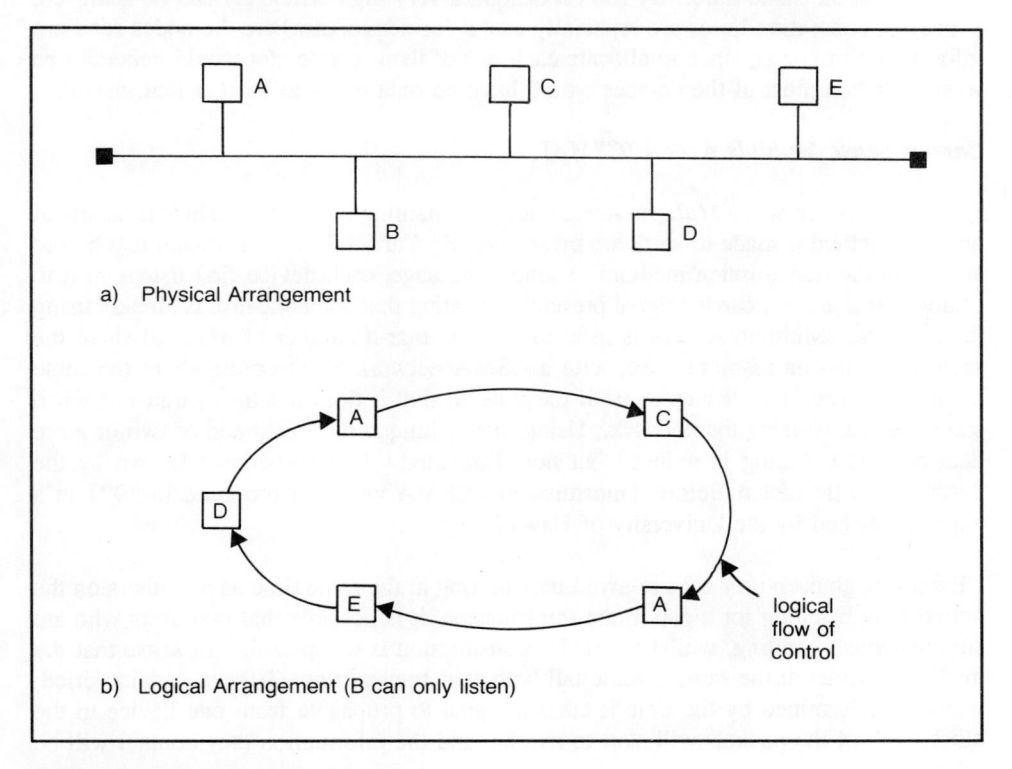

Figure 3.8 Token passing on a bus

86 *Network Sharing Techniques*

However, in some implementations it may be permitted to request an immediate response from the node to which the message was just sent, in which case the token is sent to that node rather than the next one in the sequence. The destination node must then respond immediately with an acknowledgement packet back to the original sender. The token is then passed on to the next node in the sequence.

The token could be part of the information packet which the node transmits. Since every user of the network hears every packet which is transmitted, the same packet can serve two purposes simultaneously: to pass information to another node, and to pass control to the next one in sequence.

Contention Techniques

Another popular way of sharing the use of the medium in a broadcast system is to employ a scheme for obtaining exclusive use of the medium in contention with the other users of the network as and when required. The success of contention networks depends to a very large extent on the design of the algorithms for detecting that the network is free or in use and stopping transmission if there is a collision between two packets broadcast at the same time. By careful design, a very high efficiency can be achieved. Broadcast contention buses are especially useful for networks where the nodes send out information in bursts, since to allocate each one of them a time slot would generally be wasteful when most of the devices would have no data ready to send at that instant.

Carrier Sense Multiple Access (CSMA)

The term *Carrier Sense Multiple Access* needs explaining before the technical details of how the method is made to work are presented. By Carrier Sense it is meant that before accessing the transmission medium to send a message, each device first listens to it to establish if there is a carrier signal present, indicating that someone else is already using the network. Multiple Access is used to indicate that a number of users all share the same transmission resource. So, with a CSMA network all the users share the same circuits and each one listens to it all the time so that it does not try to transmit when someone else is using the network. Using this technique the likelihood of two or more data packets colliding is reduced but not eliminated. It is sometimes known by the descriptive title Listen Before Transmission. CSMA was first proposed in 1971 in a paper published by the University of Hawaii.

Even though each user tries to avoid transmitting at the same time as the others on the network by listening for a gap in the transmission, it is possible that two users who are simultaneously waiting, whilst an earlier transmission is completed, will sense that the medium is quiet at the same instant and both start transmitting. After a certain period, which is determined by the time it takes a signal to propagate from one device to the other, both of the packets will start to overlap and the information they contain will be corrupted.

In the basic CSMA which we are considering now the nodes which are transmitting will continue doing so until the entire packet has been put on the network even though it will have to be retransmitted later when a positive acknowledgement from the recipient is not received. At some point later on, the nodes will try again to send the packets.

This form of CSMA is sometimes called *non-persistent* and *unslotted*. Non-persistent because the nodes do not re-try immediately the network is quiet, and unslotted because each node transmits outside a network time frame rather like the Pure-ALOHA system. Like the ALOHA technique, CSMA can be improved by using a network-enforced time frame in which every node is only allowed to transmit at the start of specified time slots. This does not overcome the possibility of collisions occuring, but it does reduce the time wasted on the network whilst overlapping packets are being transmitted. This version of CSMA is called *slotted non-persistent CSMA*.

Persistent CSMA

In the persistent version of CSMA, the nodes that are trying to retransmit a packet which has been damaged in transit try again fairly quickly after the channel becomes idle.

If the nodes try immediately the channel becomes idle, then the method is called *1-persistent*. In this method, each node listens until the channel is idle and then transmits straight away. This avoids the channel being unnecessarily idle, but it is unsatisfactory in practice since if two nodes are waiting to re-try at the same time, they will both start transmitting as soon as the channel becomes idle and so the packets will collide again.

Persistent CSMA is easily modified to overcome this problem. Instead of re-trying immediately, the nodes re-try only with a certain probability p. In other words, persistent CSMA in which all nodes re-try immediately is where the probability is set to one. In the case where the probability is less than one, and n nodes are waiting to re-transmit in a p-persistent CSMA system, $n.p$ nodes will try to re-transmit as soon as the channel becomes idle. Unless the network is heavily loaded, it is unlikely that very many nodes will be waiting to re-try at any one instant, so the probability of collision is reduced.

Analyses have been made of persistent CSMA which show that a slotted 1-persistent CSMA system is about 53 percent efficient whereas an optimised p-persistent system can have an efficiency as high as 82 percent.

Carrier Sense Multiple Access with Collision Detection (CSMA/CD)

The development of the CSMA technique which is now the one most commonly used in local area networks is the one known as CSMA/CD, where CD stands for Collision Detection. The original specification was known as the DIX (Dec, Intel and Xerox) Ethernet Specification Versions 1 & 2. The IEEE adopted it and improved it realising the IEEE 802.3 Standard (further information on standards can be found in Chapter 7).

88 Network Sharing Techniques

This protocol listens to the network at the same time as transmitting, and the transmission can be abandoned as soon as possible, so saving transmission time on the network. In this kind of technique there is no need to have specific acknowledgement packets since the transmitter can actually hear if a collision is happening. CSMA/CD is also sometimes known as *listen whilst transmitting* as well as listening before, I prefer to call it the *'polite protocol'*. For example, Figure 3.9 shows how it works in layman's terms. First of all, the nodes listen to the line to see if anyone else is transmitting, if there is then it waits a random amount of time. All the nodes are free to communicate whenever they need to without any precedence or order. This means that two nodes could occasionally initiate transmission at the same instant. If this happens, since the messages will crash, both nodes politely apologise to the other and wait again another random amount of time before retransmitting their message.

The main advantage is that time is not wasted transmitting information which will have to be retransmitted because it will not reach its destination unharmed (*see* Figure 3.10). The channel time also saved is thus made available for others to use. Collisions can only occur during the interval shortly after a transmission is started and before the signal has had time to reach all the nodes on the network. This is called the collision window.

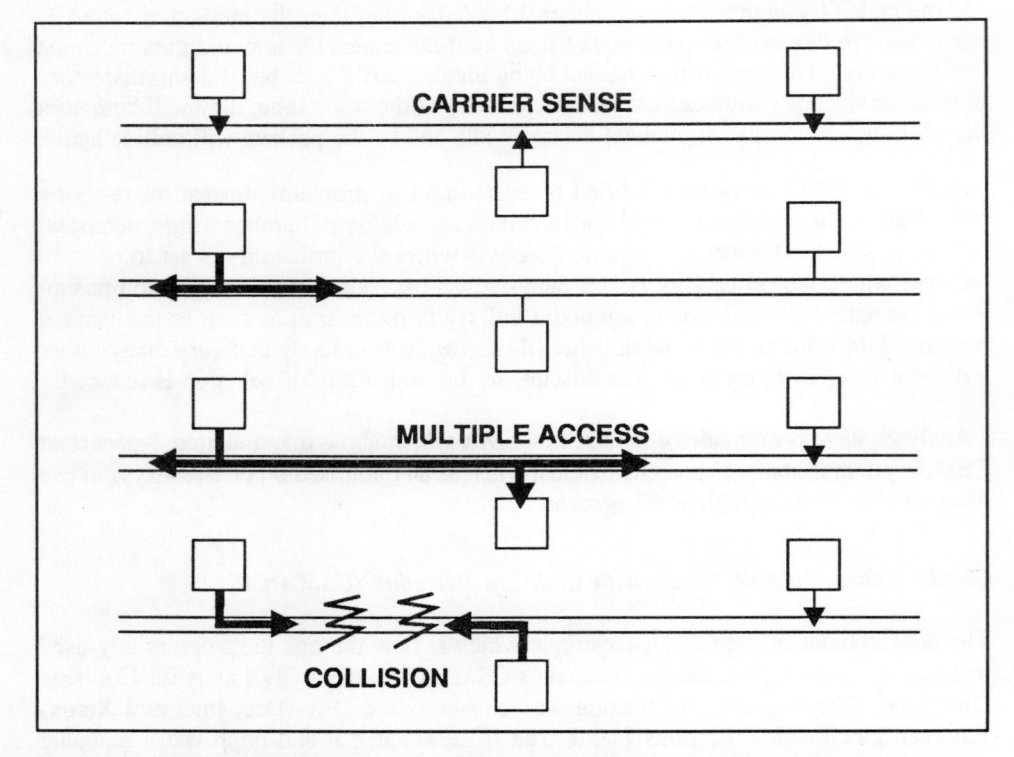

Figure 3.9 Carrier Sense Multiple Access with Collision Detection (CSMA/CD) description of protocol

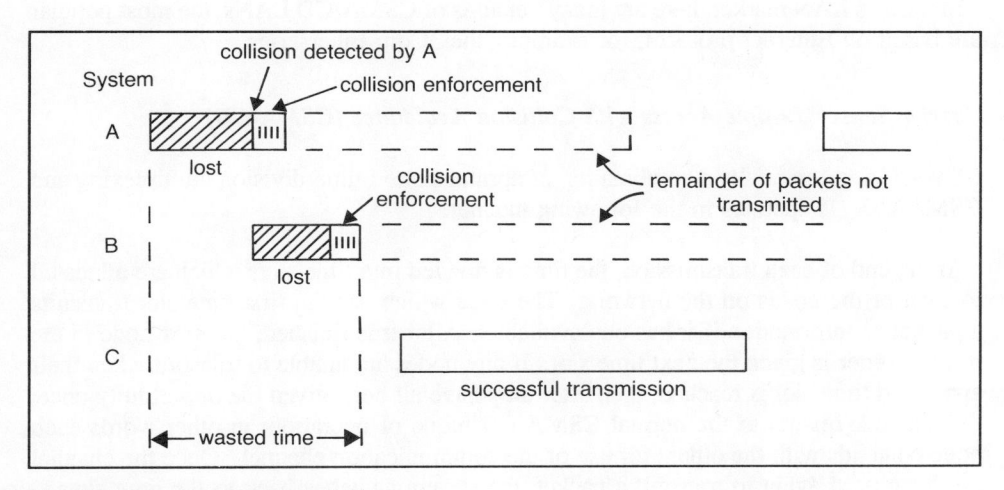

Figure 3.10 CSMA/CD definition

Naturally, for the technique to work properly, each node detecting that its packet has collided with another should not attempt to retransmit immediately, otherwise the same packets will just collide again. The technique which is usually adopted to avoid this problem is for each station which detects a collision to immediately transmit a burst of noise in order that all the other transmitting stations can hear the collision and then to wait for a random interval of time before attempting to retransmit.

If, on re-trying, the medium is busy or another collision occurs, the station backs off for a longer period of time. In this way the nodes using the network adapt themselves to the loading of the medium. When it is lightly loaded, the re-trying nodes will usually find the medium quiet and so the waiting time between transmissions will be at a minimum. As the loading increases, so the waiting time will also increase so that the number of collisions will not rise too high as would be the case if the average period before re-trying was constant.

By means of careful design of the algorithms for re-trying and backing off, it is possible to achieve an efficiency in the use of the bandwidth of over 90 percent.

As mentioned earlier, no explicit acknowledgement packets are required since the transmitting station can itself detect if a packet collides with another. If a packet is damaged by some other means, the receiving node will normally be able to detect this by examining the error check fields in the packet. It is then the responsibility of the destination node to request retransmissions by means of a special packet which says, in effect, that the packet was received in error. If the destination node is not working, the sending node will not receive any response at all, so a higher level protocol is normally used between the nodes whereby a sending node must first determine by means of an exchange of packets that the destination node is there and is in a fit state to receive information.

90 *Network Sharing Techniques*

In today's LAN market there are many versions of CSMA/CD LANs, the most popular are based on Ethernet protocol, for example, the 3Com Etherseries.

Carrier Sense Multiple Access with Collision Avoidance (CSMA/CD)

CSMA/CA is essentially a combination of normal slotted-time-division multiplexing and CSMA/CD. It operates in the following manner.

At the end of each transmission, the time is divided into time slots which are allocated to each of the nodes on the network. The node which has the first time slot transmits a packet of information if it has one available. After it is finished, the next node in the priority order is given the next time slot. If any nodes are unable to transmit when their appointed time slot is reached, then after they have all been given the opportunity once, the network reverts to the normal CSMA/CD mode of operation; in other words each node contends with the others for use of the communication channel. Once the channel has been used again to transmit a packet, the system switches back to the time slots.

Normally there is an extra priority given to certain nodes so that they are given the first time slot of any sequence. Once theirs have been offered and have not been used, the rest are allocated in rotation. The technique is claimed to be very efficient, especially in networks where some nodes need to see the network more often than others and where the overall loading is fairly high.

It should be obvious that the technique can only work well if the nodes attached to the network contain a reasonable amount of intelligence because of the time slot synchronisation and allocation algorithm required, as well as the normal CSMA/CD access methods which in themselves require intelligence.

Similar to the CSMA/CA there are some examples of this type of LAN (although this type of protocol is not as popular as CSMA/CA), for example, Corvus Omninet.

RING ACCESS TECHNIQUES

Local area networks which are arranged in the form of a ring generally require a different type of access mechanism because of the fundamentally different way in which control of the medium is passed from one node to another. In a bus network every node on that network hears every message which is transmitted by every other node more or less at the time it is transmitted, with only a very small delay introduced by the propagation time in the medium. In the case of a ring, the direction of flow of information is always the same and information packets are passed from one node to the next in the ring. Generally the control of the medium also passes along the ring in the same manner as the data. This unidirectional flow of data and control means that a completely different set of access techniques can be devised and, in some cases, far less intelligence is needed in the devices which are actually attached to the network, ie the transceiver or repeaters.

A loop can be thought of as a kind of ring but generally there is a difference in the way the two are controlled. A loop usually has a single device whose task it is to decide which of the other nodes is to be allowed to transmit information at each instant. This may be achieved by means of polling the devices in some preset order or by sending out an empty packet which is available for anybody to use.

The packets of information used in a ring are always passed from one node to the next, after having been regenerated by the node repeater. Unlike a bus system where each packet disappears naturally from the network as the signal dies away, the information circulating on a ring must be removed explictly by a node. Usually the node which originates the packet is the one which is made responsible for removing it since only it is in a position to know what it has put on the network. The destination node is not usually made responsible for this, since there is no guarantee that it will be available and working.

It has been found necessary to include a special purpose node which has the task of removing packets which are damaged in transit and have become unrecognisable to the originator. This node is generally called a monitor station. It must be working all the time that the network is being used but it can be made to perform other functions as well as removing damaged packets. For example, most rings require at the start of their operation that one node generates the first packet which will be empty. The monitor station is ideally suited to do this task and at the same time to check that the ring is complete by looking for its return.

The monitor station can also monitor the number of packets which are in error during operation of the network and it can detect when a node or repeater is producing a higher than normal number of erroneous packets.

All ring access techniques can be thought of as time-division multiplexing methods as they effectively divide up the available bandwidth amongst the users of the network. They generally give every node a fair chance to use the network and do not rely on chance to enable everyone to get access even when the system is highly loaded.

Some ring-based products employ more than one data transmission channel to provide a degree of resilience to link and repeater failure. This naturally makes the design of the repeaters much more complicated since there will then be more than one path between devices, and in some cases the physical order of the nodes on the ring may be different on the two paths.

The following are descriptions of some of the ring access techniques that are met with most frequently. Many other methods have been tried or proposed at one time or another.

Fixed Slot

For each node on the ring, a packet is allocated for its exclusive use. All the packets circulate around the ring continuously and whenever a node has a message to send, it places it in the appropriate packet for the destination node. The destination node reads the packet after it has travelled around the ring and has been relayed untouched by every other node.

This technique is not used very often and no examples of it exist outside the research laboratories.

Pre-Allocated

A pre-allocated scheme works by dividing the time interval up into slots. Each user is allowed to transmit only during his pre-allocated slot. This technique is inefficient except in the case where the network is heavily loaded and each user is sending out information in a steady stream. Such a technique is not used now that more efficient techniques, such as empty slot, register insertion and token passing, have been developed.

Empty Slot

In the empty slot method of using a ring, one or more packets circulate continuously around the ring which can be either in use or empty. If a node has data to send then it waits until it gets an empty packet passed to it at which point it puts its data, the address of the destination node and its own address in it, and then switches a marker to flag the packet as 'in use'. This packet is then passed from one node repeater to the next until it reaches the node with the address given in the destination address field. The node repeater at this location reads the packet into its internal storage, switches a marker to indicate that the packet has been received by the destination node, and passes the packet on to the next node repeater in the ring. The packet is then passed on from node to node until it returns to the node which sent it. This node recognises it as the one it sent out by means of the address field and so it switches the 'in use/not in use' marker to flag the packet as now available for others to use. In general it is not permitted for the same node to re-use the packet which it sent out immediately since this would enable a single node to hog the network and would not give the other users of it a fair chance.

Thus the sending node has exclusive use of a packet for the time it takes that packet to do a complete circuit of the ring. The opportunity to use that packet is then passed to the next node. If the ring only employs one packet which is continuously circulating and each node is waiting to send data, each one will be able to use the packet in turn and there will be no chance that one node will have more turns than any other. This is the way that time-division multiplexing works on a ring which operates using the empty slot technique. The operation of the empty slot ring is shown diagrammatically in Figure 3.11.

Empty slot rings almost always need a monitor station to spot and remove defective packets which are not flagged as empty by their originator. The monitor normally keeps a copy of every packet as it passes through, so if the identical packet passes by more than once or twice it assumes that it is in error and so removes it and regenerates a fresh empty one.

If a destination device is not working, the repeater at that address will not flag the packet as having been received, so the sending node will know that the data has not been read.

One technique sometimes used to detect errors and repeaters or stations which are failing is for each repeater to check the parity of each packet which it relays, as well as those which are addressed to it or which it originates. If a packet which is in error is relayed, the repeater uses the next empty packet which it receives to send an error message to the monitor station. The monitor station can then use the error messages it receives to pinpoint the place where the error occurred and if it is consistently in the same place the person monitoring the system can take appropriate action. Before passing on a defective packet a repeater usually resets the parity so that error messages about the same packet are not sent by every repeater which it passes through.

Since the empty slot method of using rings reached a high state of development in the Cambridge University Computer Laboratory System it has come to be known as the Cambridge Ring. Strictly speaking the Cambridge Ring is a particular version of the empty slot technique in which a particular format of the packet is used, as shown in a later chapter.

The Cambridge Ring also uses two twisted-pairs cables to transmit the data and to provide power for the repeaters. Later versions of the Cambridge Ring have used different packet lengths and formats as well as different methods of transporting the data around the ring.

Register or Buffer Insertion

To implement the register insertion technique of ring access requires that the repeaters include a buffer which can be switched in and out of the circuit as and when required. This buffer is usually a shift register, hence the use of the alternative title.

When a node has a message to send, it places it in the appropriate packet format in a special buffer in the repeater (*see* Figure 3.12(a)). When there is a gap in the information stream being relayed by the repeater, the ring circuit is broken by the repeater. The buffer is now put into the ring and the information it contains is transmitted to the next node. Since it is impossible for the repeater to stop the other repeater which is upstream of it from continuing to send data, the broken end of the ring is switched into the other end of the buffer and the information read into it as the packet originating at the node is read out (*see* Figure 3.12(b)). The buffer remains in the ring

94 Network Sharing Techniques

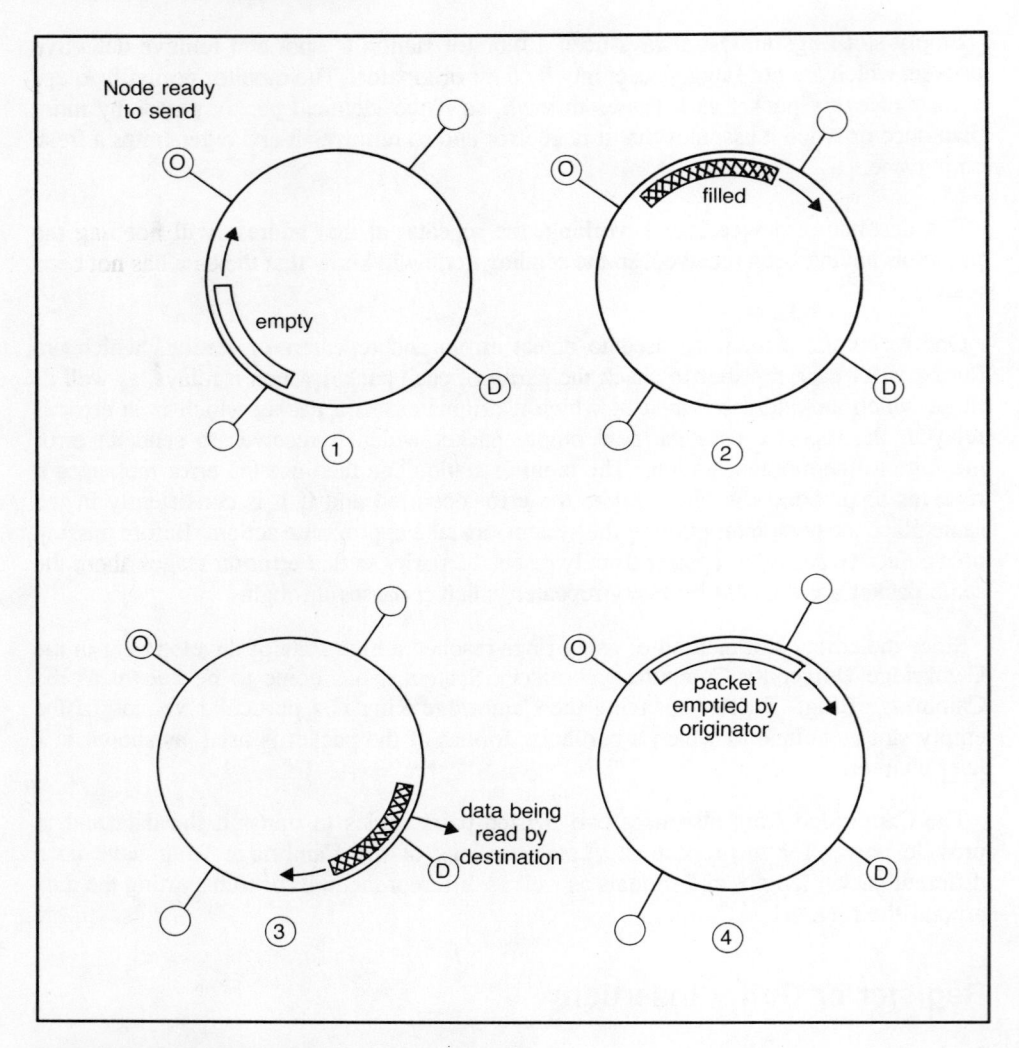

Figure 3.11 Operation of an empty slot ring

until the packet which that node sent returns (*see* Figure 3.12(c)). At that point the buffer is then removed from the circuit (*see* Figure 3.12(d)).

The diagrams show the technique in only an idealised form. In real implementations extra registers and packet detectors will be used because of the high switching speeds required.

In effect the length of a ring which uses the register insertion method increases as each node places its packet on the ring since the ring circuit is diverted through the buffer.

Ring Access Techniques 95

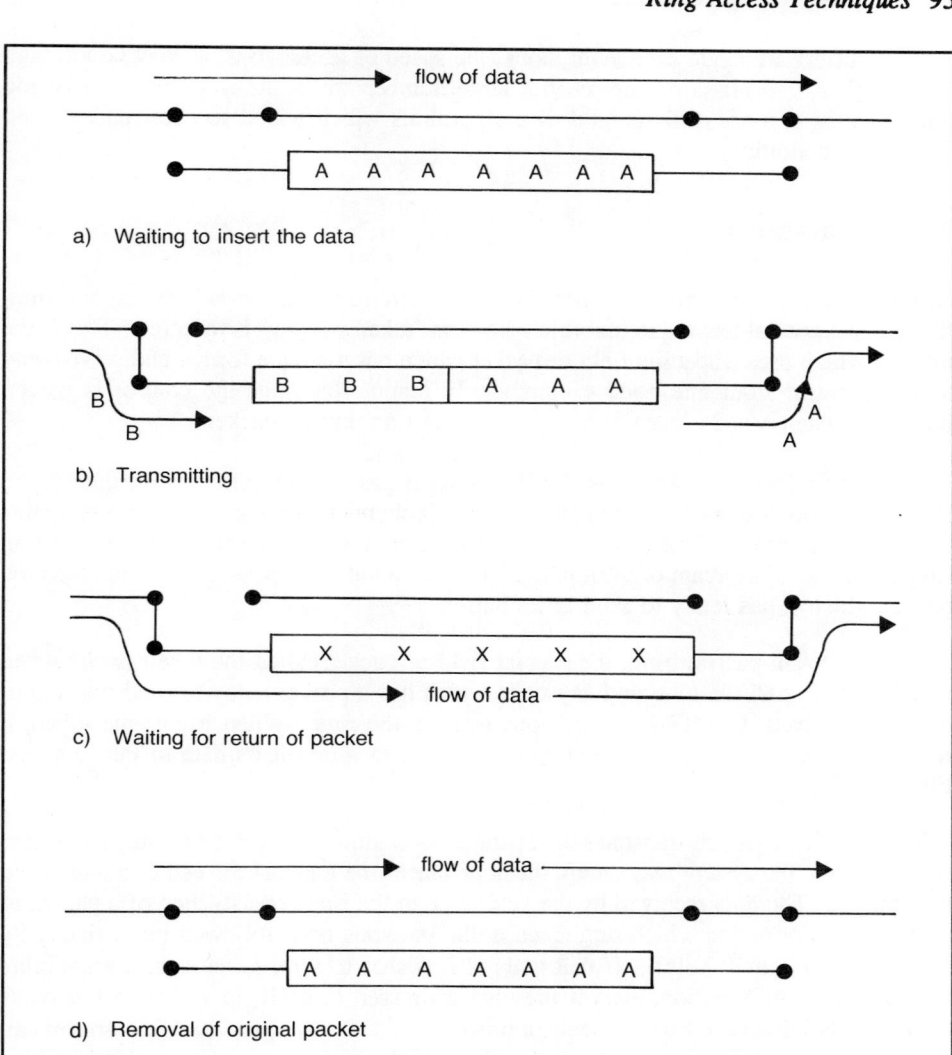

a) Waiting to insert the data

b) Transmitting

c) Waiting for return of packet

d) Removal of original packet

Figure 3.12 Register insertion

This is the way that the capacity of the ring is increased to accommodate the increasing load. As the number of buffers in the ring increases, the time to transport information around the ring also increases and hence the delay in moving a packet from one location to another. The size of the packets which can be transmitted economically on a register insertion ring is limited by the size of the buffer which can be made which will operate in the manner required.

If the buffers are made excessively long, the speed of access to them may be too high and the total transmission time when a large number are in the ring may also be too long, making it more difficult to devise algorithms which will detect lost packets and other error conditions.

Token passing

Although some, if not all, rings are sometimes referred to as token passing schemes, there is one special technique for which the term 'token passing' is reserved. This is the method which uses a specific field or packet which has a unique format and serves only to pass control from one node to another. In empty slot rings the control is passed implicitly when a node repeater has possession of an unused packet.

If that node does not want to use it, the packet is passed on to the next repeater in the ring. If the node has information ready to send, it claims the packet for itself and retains it until it is returned. The only token which can be thought of for a register insertion ring is the end of a stream of information at which point the repeater is able to insert the packet which it has ready to send in its buffer.

In a true token passing ring, the special field or packet called the token is circulated around the ring all the time and any node which has a packet ready to send waits until the token is passed to it by the previous node in the ring. When it gets the token, it removes it temporarily from the circuit and starts to transmit its data to the ring (*see* Figure 3.13).

On completion of the transmission of the information, or after it has spent the time allowed when the system was set up, the node places the token at the end of the data and transmits it. The data received by the next node in the ring consists then of a packet or packets of information which originated at the previous node followed immediately by a token (*see* Figure 3.13(c)). If that node also wishes to send some data, it must relay the packets of information, even if they are addressed to itself, in which case it reads them into its input buffer for subsequent processing, and only when the token arrives can the node remove it temporarily from the circuit and insert its own data as described for the previous node. The resulting situation after two nodes have transmitted information is shown in the figure where two packets of data are being passed around the ring followed by the token.

The string of data continues on its way in this manner with nodes with data to transmit adding their packets of information as they get hold of the token. When a packet reaches its destination, it is normally flagged as having been received by the repeater before being relayed so that the transmitting node knows that the destination has received it.

When the packet is eventually returned to its origin that node removes it from the string of packets. If everything is working as it should then the packet it sent out last will be the first one in the string which is passed to it, as shown in Figure 3.12. However, if a node or its repeater has failed in between sending out the packet and receiving it back again then the packet will not be removed and will circulate indefinitely unless removed by another node such as a monitor station.

The major problem with the token passing method is that tokens themselves may get lost or corrupted and hence become unrecognisable. If a monitor station exists on the ring then one of its jobs would be to always look at the data stream passing by and check that the token is on the end. If it is missing, the monitor would add another. It would also check for more than the specified number of tokens and remove superfluous ones. If there is no monitor station, although this is unusual for true rings, it would be the task of one or all of the nodes on the ring to generate a new token if the one at the end of the circulating data stream is missing.

If there is no information being passed when the token disappears, the monitor or the other nodes will have a time-out mechanism so that they can generate a new token if none has been passed to them during the set interval. With a monitor station to take charge of this there is no real problem, but without one it is possible that more than one node will generate tokens at around the same time and so more than one token will exist on the ring. Node repeaters are generally configured to remove extra tokens if they can detect them. They would do this normally by transmitting a packet and then receiving another token before the packet they have just sent out is returned to them. The chance of more than one node generating a token at the same time is minimised by the adoption of a random time-out delay.

Token passing is claimed to make very efficient use of the available capacity of the network. It is adaptable to broadcast bus media as well as sequential configurations such as the ring, although the exact way the two operate is slightly different due to the requirement of the broadcast medium to specifically address each packet and the token itself. However, in the broadcast bus case the information packets are sent direct to the destination even though the control may be sent to another node. The nodes in a ring pass the packets of information from one to another as well as the token.

PBX APPROACH

We have already discussed several popular LAN sharing techniques, however all these have one major component in common, that is that they are all devised from the use of a specialised algorithm that controls every aspect of the network. Another way of sharing a network is by using existing telephone equipment, and here is where the PBX comes in. (Note several years ago these machines where either termed PABX or PBX, however today all are automatic, hence all are termed PBX).

Most sites already have a very widespread analogue and digital communications network in the form of their telephone lines, so why not use this as the basis for a data communications network as well? At the centre of every telephone network is a telephone exchange which is capable of providing many more functions than is usual in a voice network.

In most instances the telephone cables are grossly under-utilised since each is only used for a very small proportion of the day. The corresponding circuits and equipment in the exchanges are also not fully used. If the function of those cables, which have been installed over the years at a considerable cost, could be extended then this would appear to be a new ideal solution to local data communications needs. Since the lines and equipment are already used for speech it may seem that extending their use to include data could aid the integration of voice with data communications in the office: a long-term aim of many researchers into office procedures.

A local telephone network is built around a local exchange so it is essentially an example of the more general star network described in Chapter 2. To put the PBX network into the context of data communications, the general star network will be discussed first, followed by how this configuration fits into the local area network arena.

The Star PBX Configuration

A star-shaped network is well known both as a typical computer network (as described in Chapters 2 and 5 and in Figure 3.13(a)), in which the centre of the star is a computer system performing processing on information fed to it by the peripherals, and as a telephone system (*see* Figure 3.13(b)), in which the central hub (the PBX) is a switch which interconnects the different users on the network. The first example illustrates the suitability of the star topology for a many-to-one approach, the second its use for interconnecting pairs of devices. It is less suitable where several spokes require concurrent access to a device on another spoke.

If we take the view that local area networks exist to provide on-site communications between computer-based devices, then the star network is by far the most dominant class today, since most existing computer systems have on-line access facilities to one or more central computers. However, local area networks are typically thought of as providing interconnection between all the devices on the network, something which is not always present with the traditional computer-based networks. These networks typically operate via a device at the hub (which may be the computer itself or, more likely, a controller dedicated to handling terminals and peripheral devices) asking, or polling, each device in turn to see whether it has data to send. Only when the hub gives its permission can the devices on the spokes send the data.

If the data is intended to go to another terminal, it is usual practice in such systems for the computer to process the information at the hub and then send the message, rather than just switching the incoming line to that of the receiver so that messages can pass through without being processed by the hub.

a) Star Computer Network

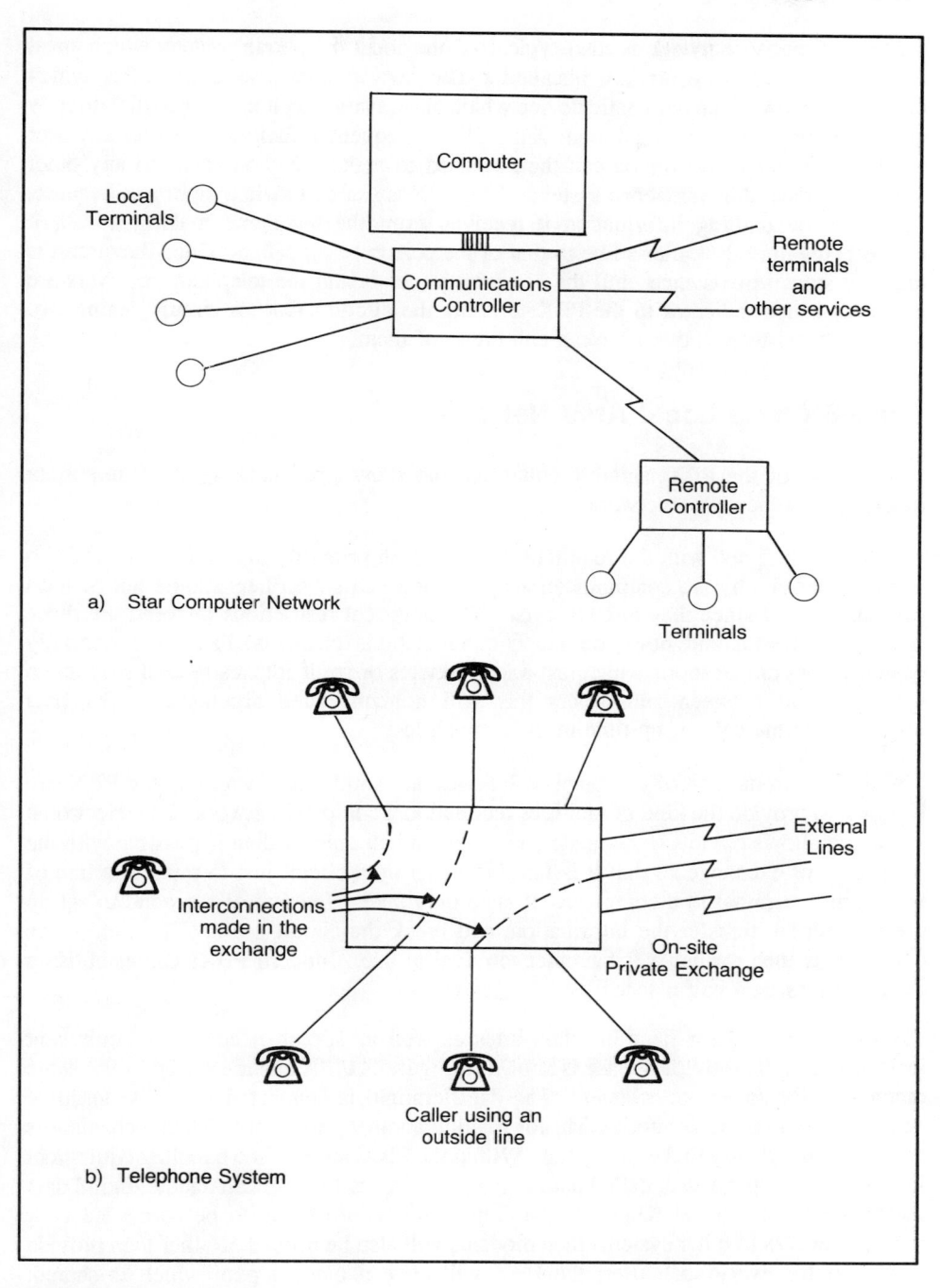

b) Telephone System

Figure 3.13 Star networks

The star-shaped network is also typical of the local telephone system which most offices and sites have already installed. The hub in this case is the PBX which nowadays is always an automatic device which allows any telephone user to dial directly any other telephone connected to the same PBX. Frequently, facilities exist for any user to dial an external line which can then be used to make telephone calls to any other number on the public telephone systems. The PBX is a circuit-switching device because, based on the dialling information it receives from the telephone making a call, it connects together the caller's line to that of the person being called. Once the circuit is made, it stays in existence until the conversation ends and the telephone receivers are replaced, which indicates to the PBX to break the circuit. Once a circuit joining two telephones exists, no other user can call either of them.

The PBX as a Local Area Network

In the guise of the PBX, suitably enhanced, the star-shaped network is an important topology as a local area network.

PBXs are designed with the requirements of speech primarily in mind, but there is no obvious reason why the communications paths between subscribers should not be used for data as well since they already exist. The only real restrictions imposed are those due to bandwidth and noise on the communications channels. PBXs are normally designed for conversations which last a few minutes or so; if it takes several seconds to set up a call between subscribers this will be considered acceptable. For data requirements the call set-up time must be much less.

With the introduction of computer techniques and solid state switching, the PBX can be made to provide the kind of facilities required in a computer network. Fast electronic switching allows circuits to be made and broken much quicker than is possible with the older type of exchange so that it is feasible to set up a circuit just to transfer a line of text from a terminal to a computer. It need only take a fraction of a second to set up the connection, transfer the information, and break the circuit again. The link to the computer is then available for another terminal to use. Modern PBXs can establish a circuit in less than half a second.

A PBX designed for handling data lines as well as speech needs extra equipment installed in it. The simplest case is shown in Figure 3.14. Calls are set up in the same manner as for speech telephones. The data terminal is connected to a data terminal adaptor which has some mechanism for dialling another subscriber. The mechanism is generally an ordinary dial or a keypad. Within the PBX, special line handling equipment for data circuits is needed, called data line units. Generally these can handle digital data transmission rates of 64 Kbps. If the data terminals are going to be connected over public networks to other systems then modems will also be needed. Rather than provide a modem for every such user, the PBX will have a modem pool which is shared. Whenever a data terminal requests an outside line, a modem from the modem pool will be selected by the PBX and switched into the outside line.

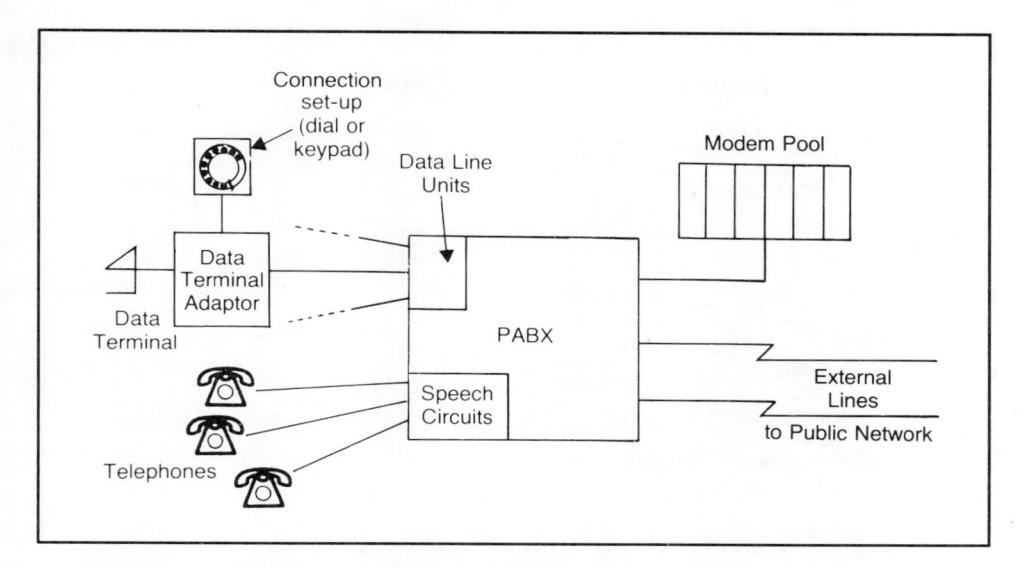

Figure 3.14 A PBX capable of handling data lines

Another, more advanced, implementation is shown in Figure 3.15. In this the data terminal adaptor and the data line unit are enhanced to remove the need for a separate dialling unit. The connection to another subscriber is achieved by the data line unit itself using commands sent by the data terminal user.

In both the examples just discussed the main part of the PBX is essentially the same as would be provided for handling speech only.

Modern digital PBXs can handle remote concentrators and multiplexers, each of which in turn serves several subscribers. Figure 3.16 shows an example of a modern in-house telephone system which has the additional facilities to handle data on the same line as the speech (subscriber multiplexed). The subscriber on one link can use both his telephone and the data terminal at the same time. Each device is handled separately at the exchange, so the data terminal could be connected to a computer service, for example, whilst still allowing the telephone to be used in the normal way. This has led to the evolution of ISDN, described further in Chapter 10.

The technique of employing remote devices to concentrate the information flow from several subscribers on to a limited number of exchange lines can be extended to handle remote networks. Figure 3.17 shows how the remote multiplexer/concentrator could be replaced by a local area network node which acts as a gateway between the PBX network and the local area network. Depending on the type of local area network employed, this node could be a network controller or just a gateway.

Although circuit-switching is the traditional technique employed for the hub in the PBX type of network, it is possible for it to operate as a packet-switching exchange.

102 *Network Sharing Techniques*

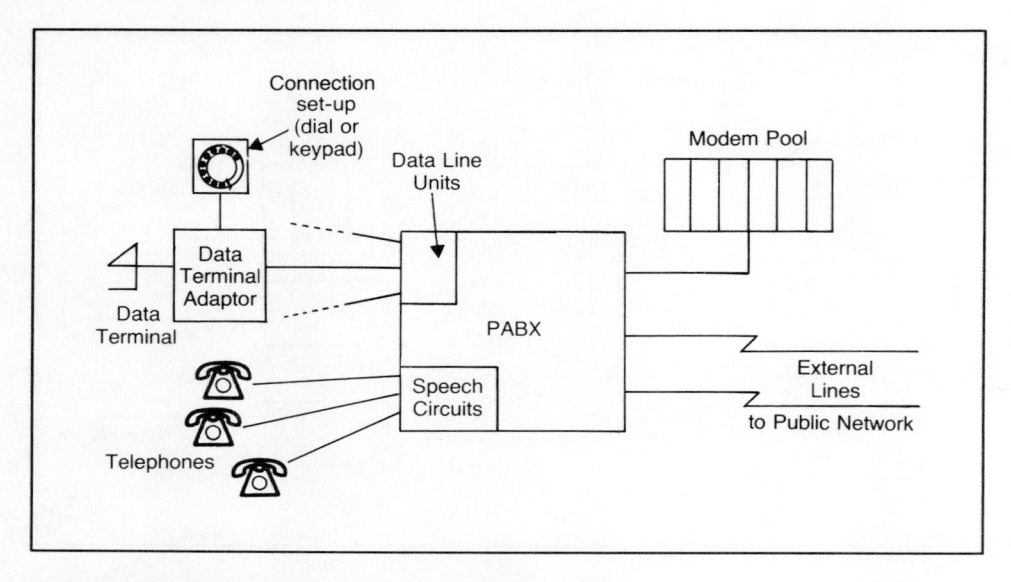

Figure 3.15 PBX network with enhanced data handling

The PBX at the centre of a network can perform functions other than normal line or message-switching. For example, the PBX can provide conversions between the data transmission speed of the sender and that required by the receiver. The sending and destination devices may also operate using different communications protocols and character sets. The PBX can act as a protocol converter so allowing a terminal from one manufacturer to work successfully with a computer system from another. Protocol converters can be services shared by everyone connected to the PBX.

One of the most significant aspects of a star network is the fact that much of the intelligence needed to control the network can reside in the one place and be shared by all the devices in the system. This enables dumb terminals to be used directly in the network, with each one operating at any speed it likes. No special logic is required to gain access to the circuits since each of the links is usually dedicated to the one device. It is conceivable, although not frequently encountered, that different media could be used for the links between the devices at the end of the spokes and the hub. For example, twisted-pair cable could be used for some links, coaxial and ribbon cables for others, and even fibre optic cable if the application demanded it.

The hub software could also provide a high degree of security protection to prevent unauthorised persons from using the network, or unauthorised terminals from accessing certain computer systems. If a link or end device develops a fault, it is easy to identify which spoke the fault is on and report it to the network supervisor and disconnect it if necessary. Addressing is also simplified as each spoke corresponds to a particular device.

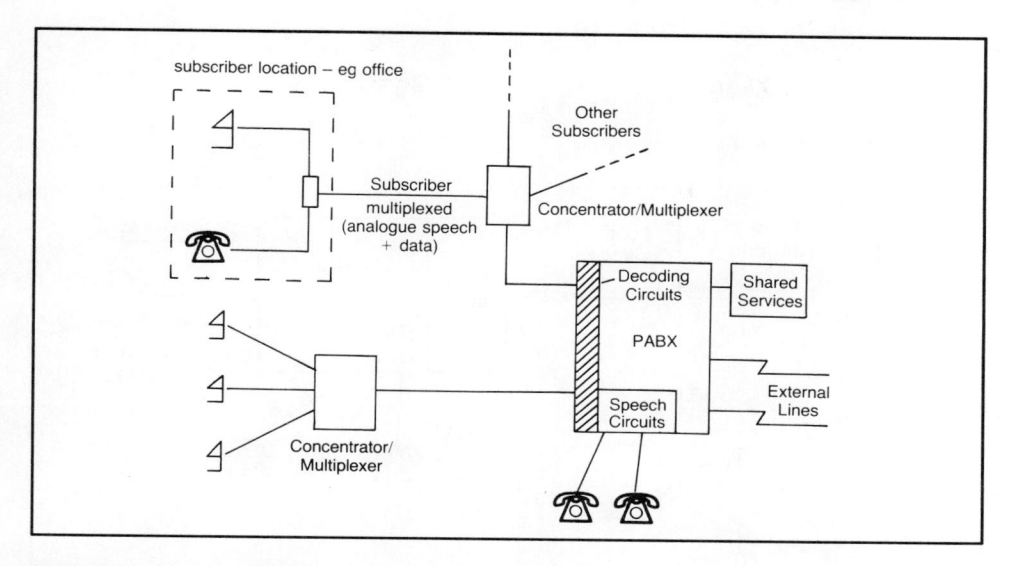

Figure 3.16 Advanced PBX network with multiplexing

The typical facilities offered by a PBX are that:

- a call can be automatically redirected to another number if the dialled number is engaged, does not answer, or if the person associated with it has moved to another number;

- extensions can be dialled directly;

- certain numbers can be restricted;

- extension numbers can be changed easily so that a person can retain his own telephone number even when changing offices;

- traffic can be measured and recorded;

- fault location and diagnosis facilities can be provided;

- telephone conferencing with more than two subscribers being involved is possible.

In addition to these facilities there are various advantages for making a PBX handle data traffic, for example, the data terminals and computers can see the cables and ducts provided for the telephones.

However despite this, the installation of a PBX controlled LAN may not always be the best solution. The PBX itself, by virtue of the intelligence it requires to control even the

104 Network Sharing Techniques

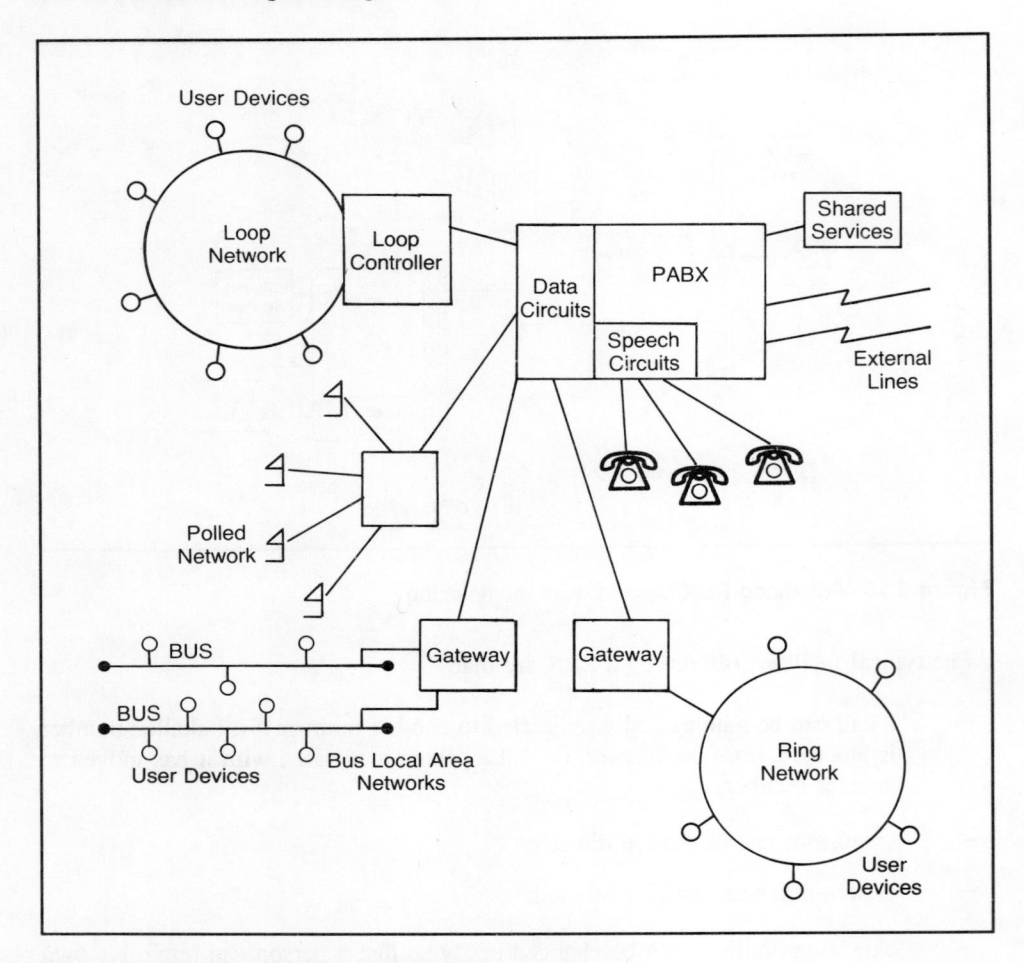

Figure 3.17 Integration of LAN into PBX network

simplest network, is going to be quite a costly item. If there is an adequate PBX already installed for the telephone services it could be difficult to justify its replacement with a PBX for both voice and data, or indeed the installation of another for data alone.

The PBX is also quite vulnerable to failures since it must contain significant quantities of software to perform its functions properly. Advocates of the PBX approach point to the high reliability required and achieved for normal PBXs, and reason that the computerised ones will have to be as good if they are to replace the existing ones. However likely the hub PBX is to fail, the possibility of it happening is sufficient to deter many users who have the need for a very reliable data transmission network. Failure of the hub, whether this is a computer system, a circuit- or packet-switch, will stop the system performing as a network. If a network is being heavily loaded, the central control circuits and software can also become overloaded causing significant delays in setting up a call.

The cable network required by a star network is simple to visualise but generally difficult and costly to install when a large number of devices are being served. If the existing telephone cables can be used to handle data devices at an adequate speed without preventing the telephone itself from being used at the same time, then this problem is not serious. If new cables are required then each device will need a separate line to the centre.

Summarising the features of the star-shaped local area network based on the PBX, the following are the main advantages and disadvantages.

Advantages:

— ideal for many-to-one configurations;

— suitable for dumb terminals as well as intelligent ones;

— mixed transmission media and speeds can be used on the spokes;

— each spoke is independent of the rest;

— high security is possible;

— easy fault detection and isolation;

— addressing is easy, and is centrally controlled;

— cost can often be justified for voice alone;

— integration of data and voice (integration of office information handling) is possible;

— total network bandwidth can be very high (several hundred Mbps);

— a fairly large area can be covered (up to 3km between device and hub).

Disadvantages:

— vulnerable to central hub failures;

— complex technology required at the hub - hence expensive;

— ports are needed at the hub to handle all the lines - either on a one-to-one basis or shared;

106 *Network Sharing Techniques*

— laying cables and altering their routes can be expensive;

— the data rates which can be handled are generally slower than ring or bus topologies due to the hub processing required — 64 Kbps typically, per channel.

WHICH ACCESS METHOD SHOULD I USE?

This is a rather difficult questions to answer as it depends on many issues. The following flowchart may help you analyse the type of LAN environment you have and hence guide you into deciding what type of access method is the right one for your environment.

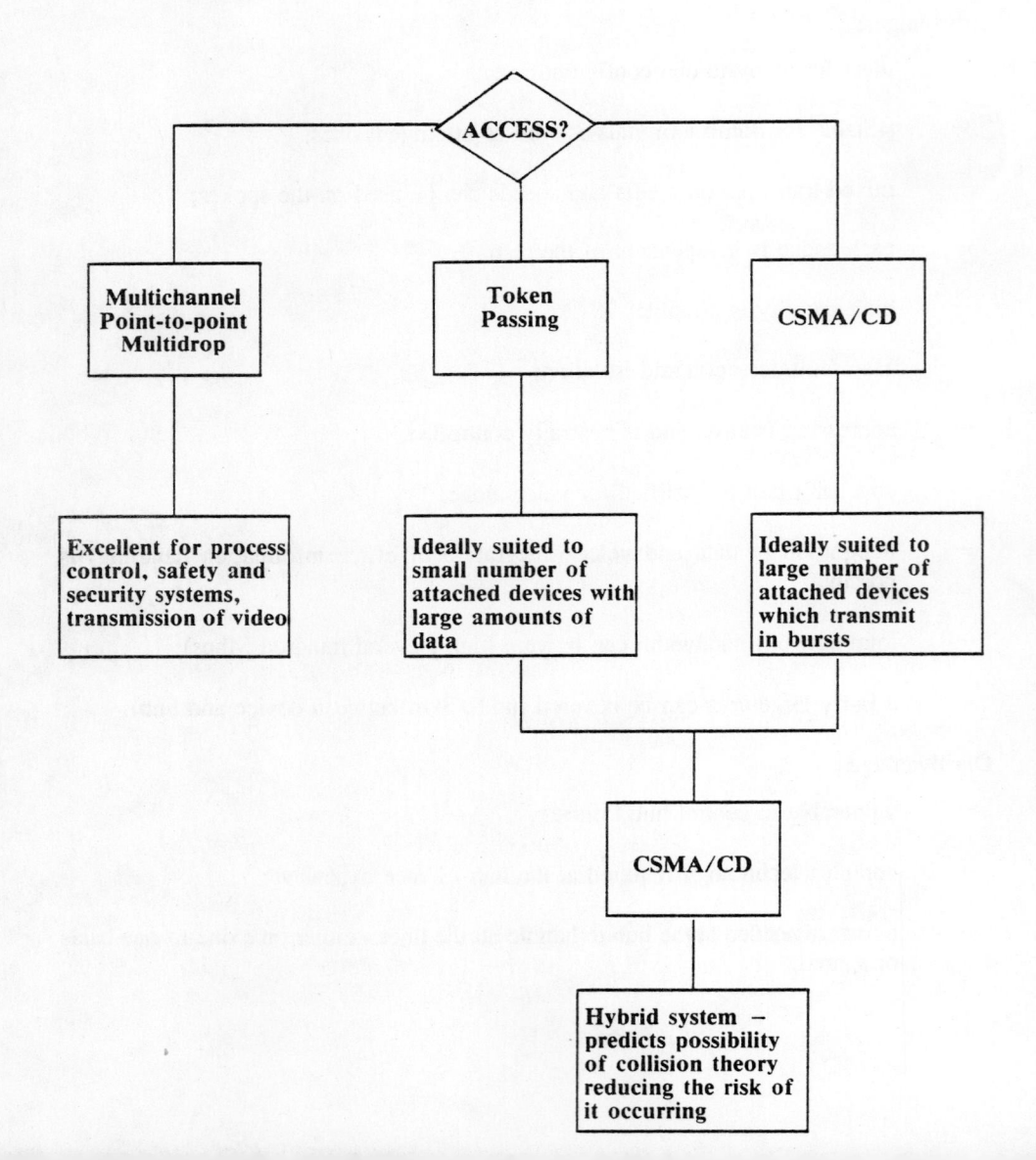

```
                    ┌─────────┐
                    │ ACCESS? │
                    └────┬────┘
        ┌────────────────┼────────────────┐
        │                │                │
┌───────────────┐   ┌──────────┐    ┌──────────┐
│ Multichannel  │   │  Token   │    │ CSMA/CD  │
│ Point-to-point│   │ Passing  │    │          │
│ Multidrop     │   │          │    │          │
└───────┬───────┘   └────┬─────┘    └────┬─────┘
        │                │                │
┌───────────────┐   ┌──────────────┐ ┌──────────────┐
│Excellent for  │   │Ideally suited│ │Ideally suited│
│process control│   │to small      │ │to large      │
│safety and     │   │number of     │ │number of     │
│security       │   │attached      │ │attached      │
│systems,       │   │devices with  │ │devices which │
│transmission   │   │large amounts │ │transmit in   │
│of video       │   │of data       │ │bursts        │
└───────────────┘   └──────┬───────┘ └──────┬───────┘
                           │                │
                           └────────┬───────┘
                                    │
                              ┌──────────┐
                              │ CSMA/CD  │
                              └────┬─────┘
                                   │
                           ┌───────────────┐
                           │Hybrid system —│
                           │predicts       │
                           │possibility of │
                           │collision      │
                           │theory reducing│
                           │the risk of it │
                           │occurring      │
                           └───────────────┘
```

CASE STUDIES

In the previous edition of this book, the author placed Ethernet as a research topology. Although this was fine for that edition, things have moved on and Ethernet is now a well established environment, out of the research laboratories and into the business environment. Therefore, this publication has taken the view that this area requires a 'Case Study' approach.

This section will endeavour to investigate briefly two of the most popular and main local area network topological environments in existence today. The main objective is to explain the origins and how the environments work in terms of its network sharing technique.

Ethernet

The original Ethernet system was installed on an experimental basis in the Palo Alto Research Centre of the Xerox Corporation in California during the early 1970s. Its purpose was to connect office workstations to expensive computing resources or other office machinery so that they could be shared by everybody with a workstation.

The main design objectives were:

- to design a communications system for an office environment which had the potential to grow smoothly with increasing demand;

- to accommodate several buildings containing personal workstations, computers and other computing facilities;

- to provide a communications network that would be cheap to install and run, since the workstations were to be fairly cheap;

- to provide a reliable network;

- to concentrate control of the network in one location or device;

- to achieve very low overheads in maintaining and running the system;

- to provide a network that would be suited to handling data traffic in bursts.

It was decided that reliability and cheapness could best be achieved by making the network as simple as possible. The requirement to handle traffic in bursts meant that normal techniques for polling and time-division multiplexing would not be the answer. It was decided, therefore, to adopt the University of Hawaii's approach, used in their ALOHA network, of distributing control of the network to every user, but adapting the

108 Network Sharing Techniques

technique to minimise wasted transmission time caused by two or more users sending a message at the same instant.

The medium chosen for the network was coaxial cable because it was easy to obtain and connect devices to, was capable of carrying high speed transmission and was comparatively cheap.

The topology used for Ethernet was an 'un-rooted' tree in which only one path must exist between any two points; otherwise, packets would reach the destination by several routes and consequently be out of synchronisation due to different path lengths.

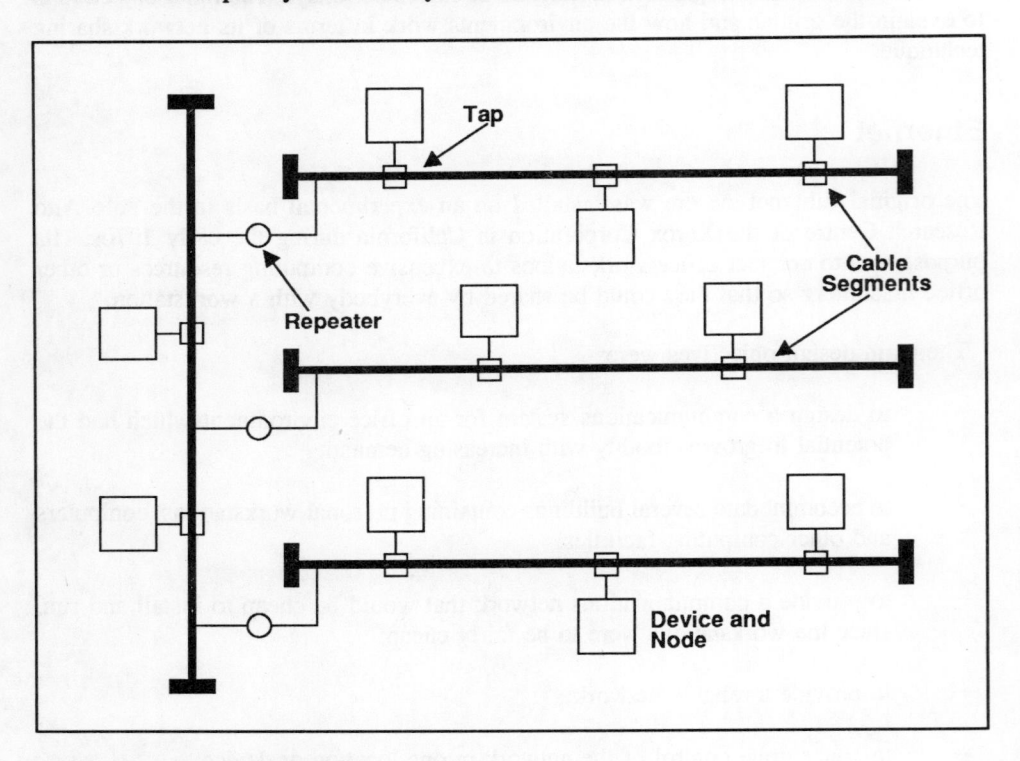

Figure 3.18 Ethernet topology

The key to Ethernet is not the medium nor the technology, but it is the way the medium is used. The medium is shared by all the users and each may transmit packets of information at any time. Each packet contains a header which specifies the address of the destination but every other user listens to every packet transmission. The sender relies on the intended recipient hearing the transmission and reading it into its own store for subsequent processing. The other users of the network should ignore the transmissions which are not addressed to them, and they should not transmit whilst someone else is using the network. There is no automatic acknowledgement that the packet has been successfully received built into the technique. Higher levels of protocol are needed to send back explicit acknowledgement packets, or requests for retransmission if an error in the packet was detected by the recipient.

Ethernet uses a development of the Carrier Sense Multiple Access/Collision Detect (CSMA/CD) technique. The designers recognised that packets in transit on the network are very likely to overlap with one another and therefore they made specific provision in the design to handle collisions.

The capacity of the Ethernet network is fairly divided amongst the users only if they all abide by the same rules. Stations can take unfair advantage of the technique by various means, for example, not waiting before attempting retransmission after a collision has occurred; not adjusting the interval after two successive collisions; and sending large packets. The responsibility for fair use of the network lies with every device using it.

The Ethernet technique has been the subject of many investigations in an effort to make it fair, but in practice the system has worked well. Some of the criticisms that are normally discussed are:

— no upper bound on the maximum number of collisions which can occur;
— collided packets are discriminated against by delaying them; this means that devices which experience several successive collisions are made to wait for an unreasonable length of time;
— there is a wide variation of waiting times.

The most favoured techniques for reducing these inefficiencies are so-called 'slotted' Ethernet schemes (*see* Chapter 3 for a discussion of slotted schemes in the ring access environment). Here the CSMA/CD technique is normally used, but after collisions occur, the channel is allocated to different users on a slotted basis, so avoiding another collision with the same packet.

Token Ring

In October 1985, IBM announced its Token Ring Local Area Network. Since then Token Ring has become one of the cornerstones of IBM's communications standard and strategy. The Token Ring architecture, in its initial implementation, defined a 4 Mbs ring using a star wiring topology, that supported up to 260 attached nodes. (*See* Figure 3.19). Discrete rings could be connected together with bridges (*See* Figure 3.21).

The main design objectives were similar to Ethernet but using different access techniques and equipment, these are:

— the interconnection of computers and devices within a building;

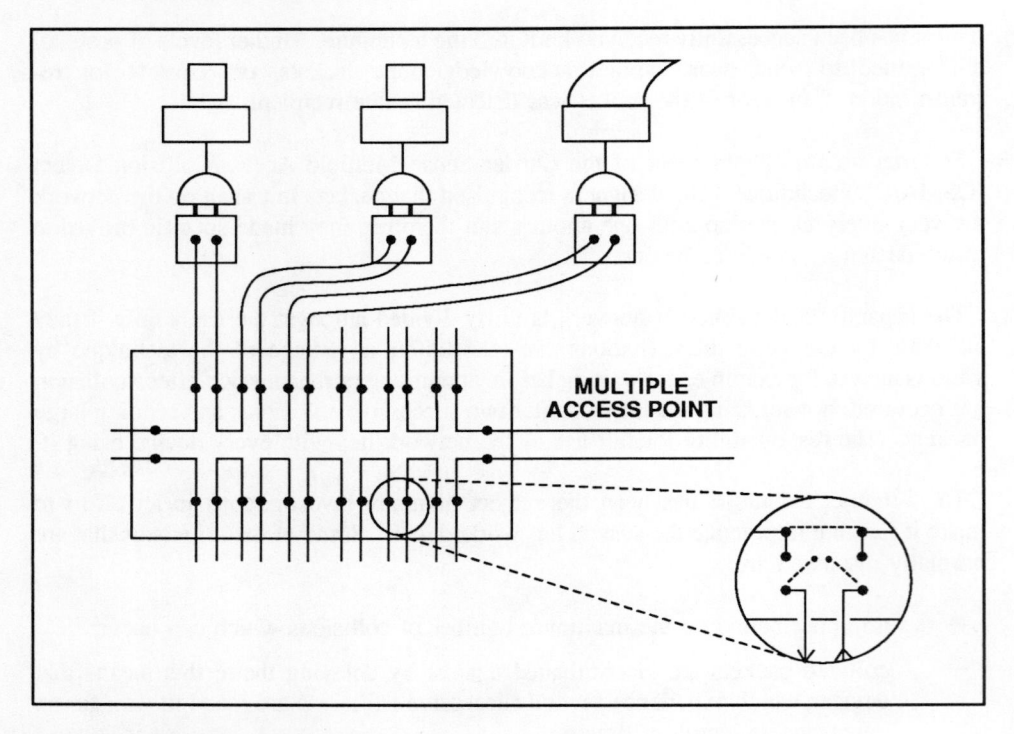

Figure 3.19 Token ring cabling

- simple design and implementation;
- low cost (although from the user point of view in terms of using the IBM cabling system this is not the case);
- good reliability and error handling characteristics;
- baseband transmission capabilities;
- deterministic logic.

The general format of transmitting data on the ring is called a frame, shown in Figure 3.20.

The data portion of the frame is variable in length and contains information that the sender is transmitting to the receiver. All the other fields within the frame are control entities dealing with the integrity of the whole frame.

The control mechanism for regulating data flow in a ring topology is normally based on the use of permission fields in the form of 'free tokens' passed sequentially from node to node around the ring. The free token, as can be seen in Figure 3.22, contains

Case Studies 111

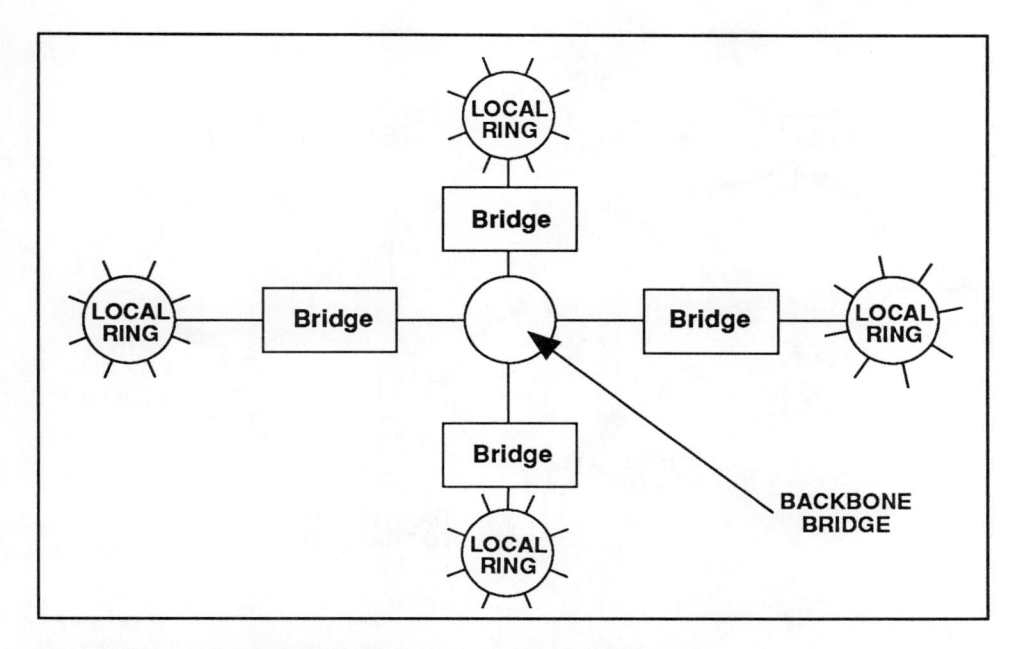

Figure 3.20 Token format in comparison with packet format

TOKEN FORMAT

Size	1	1	1
Field	Start Byte	Access Control	End Byte

Token bit: 0

PACKET FORMAT

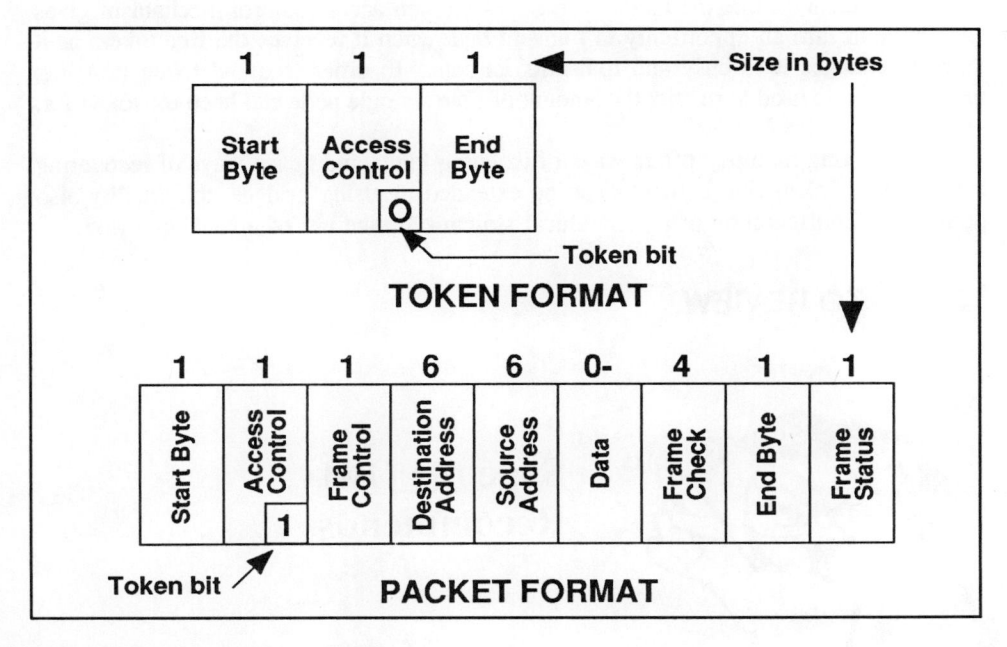

Size	1	1	1	6	6	0–	4	1	1
Field	Start Byte	Access Control	Frame Control	Destination Address	Source Address	Data	Frame Check	End Byte	Frame Status

Token bit: 1

Size in bytes

Figure 3.21 Token ring backbone

112 *Network Sharing Techniques*

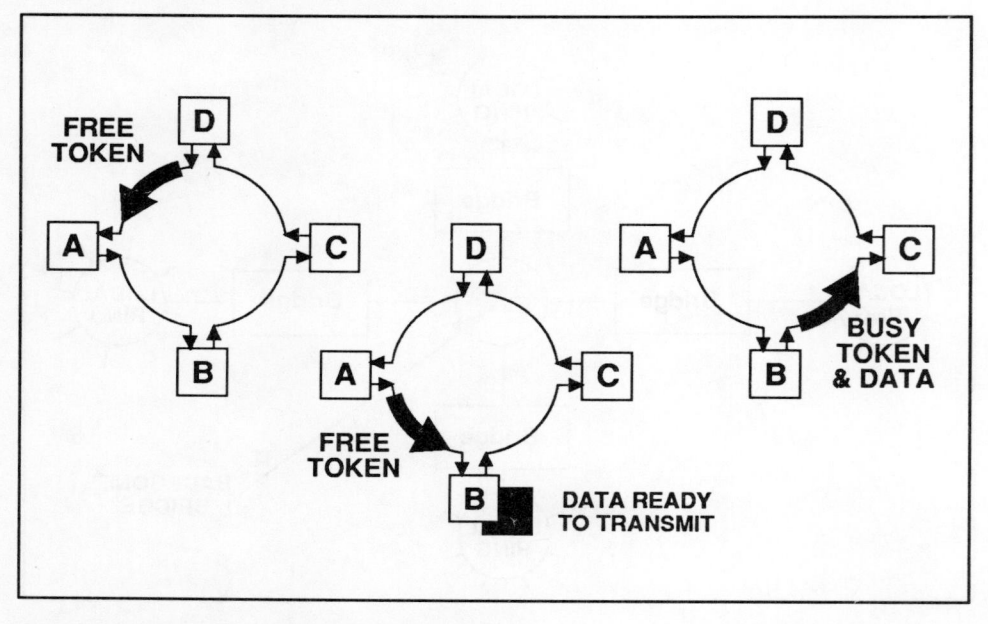

Figure 3.22 Token ring local area network

a one-bit indication that the token is free. This token access control mechanism gives each node in turn an opportunity to transmit data when it receives the free token, as it takes it, changes it to busy and transmits its data. In order to avoid token hogging, mechanisms are used to restrict the amount of time a single node can keep the token for.

The token ring topology offers ways of isolating faults and hence ways of recovering from them. Token ring networks can be extended by using bridges, this facility also permits the configuration of a hierarchical structure by the use of a backbone ring.

TERMS TO REVIEW

Sage the Owl Recommends

- Multiplexing
- Time-Division Multiplexing (TDM)
- Statistical Time-Division Multiplexing (STDM)
- Frequency-Division Multiplexing
- Polling
- Bus
- Packets
- ALOHA
- Slotted-ALOHA
- Reservation
- Token Passing
- Contention
- Carrier Sense Multiple Access (CSMA)
- CSMA with Collision Detection (CSMA/CD)
- CSMA with Collision Avoidance (CSMA/CA)
- Ring
- Star PBX Configuration
- Star
- Ethernet
- Token Ring.

4
Application Areas

INTRODUCTION

LANs are sometimes described as an ideal union of data, text, image and speech 'on a single line'. However, experience shows that a significant number of private networks are used purely for data processing and in most cases have integrated mainly data and word processing. However, although this situation is still predominant in today's private networking environment, it will undoubtedly change in the future to encompass the real definition of LANs. Figure 4.1 shows some of the existing and future applications of LANs.

After ten years of evolution, there are many types of LANs, some which already supply the users with a wide range of facilities. The main aim of all networks, whether LANs or not, is to provide a communications facility between two devices, usually computer related. Some of the LANs provide, in addition to the communications facilities, an integrated set of services, like voice and data, which can be applicable to many business environments. Others concentrate solely on the communications facility, for example, file transfer, which the user can utilise when required.

The growth in the use of LANs has to a large extent been guided by the following two LAN characteristics. In the office environment the requirement has been to integrate office tools like mail, word processing, telex, fax, telephone, etc, into one entity; while in the IT market basic data communications network and processing is a necessity.

In general most of the devices used by LANs will normally be based on, or related to, a computer processor. These may be traditional computer systems which have a powerful processor supported by on-line storage media and I/O devices. They can also be mainframes, minis, micros, terminals (either intelligent, dumb or multi-function — like an ISDN terminal that integrates digital telephony and PCs), peripherals, electronic office products such as word processors, telephony apparatus like fax and telephones, and all manner of equipment which incorporates microprocessors. The amount of equipment which fits the description has become enormous, and is increasing very rapidly. The one common feature of the equipment applicable for use with LANs is that all the devices are able to communicate with others on the same network or other networks via an internetwork facility.

116 Application Areas

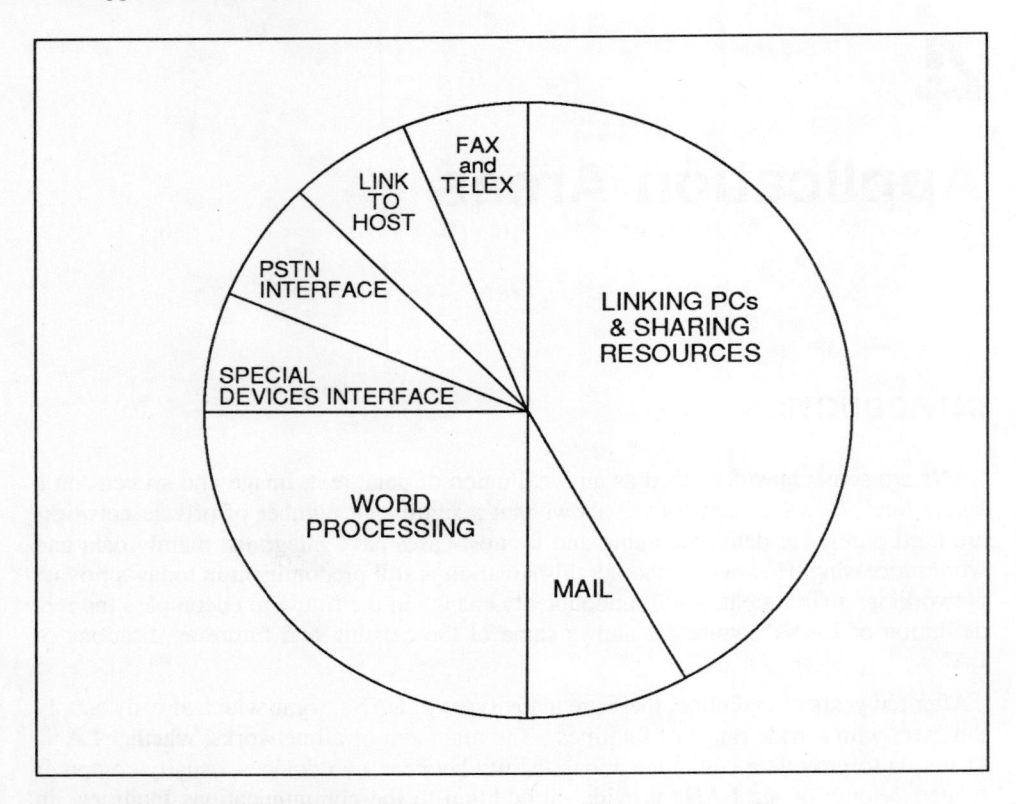

Figure 4.1 Networking applications

A LAN can represent a sizeable investment and before any full-blown implementation is undertaken the decision to use a LAN must be accompanied by the decision of what you expect from your LAN, immediately and in the future. Initially, most LANs are implemented to move and share information across a workgroup and therefore it can be argued that a relatively low-cost LAN linking everybody together would have considerable appeal.

Having widespread interconnection of devices will give the users the potential to do many things which would be difficult or impossible in any other way. For example, in a network for distributed processing there is often a need for back-up in case one of the processors fails, or a link between them becomes unusable.

Local networks give their users easier access to a wider range of facilities and services such as shared storage, shared computer power, etc. New applications can be developed, such as the use of video or PC conferencing, which really demands a large number of users all on the same network and the use of digital technology.

Introduction

Users of older computer systems benefit from on-line access from terminals. Users of distributed processing networks benefit from sharing resources such as expensive peripherals, like a laser printer, and by allowing terminal access to several different computer systems. LANs make interconnectivity of IT devices a reality.

The networking industry realises that price is an important part of any purchasing decision and due to the proliferation of PCs has had no choice but to make simple LANs accessible without needing any heavy investment. This means that within an electronic office employees have immediate access to a workstation (ie a PC or a dumb terminal) which can perform many routine office functions and which in turn shares network resources. Linking the workstations has many immediate advantages since much of an office worker's time is spent sending, receiving and dealing with information.

The mere existence of LANs and integrated systems has brought about many changes in the way people and systems work. Office automation, for example, integrates a variety of services, like PCs, databases, word processors, and electronic mail to carry out a multiple of corporate, departmental and personal tasks. Communications networks are vital in establishing integrated systems. Once LANs are installed, it is conceivable that they will bring about new work patterns within offices and factories. It is unlikely that a new method of working would be thought out first and then a LAN installed to serve it.

LANs can be justified in terms of their existing uses. The technology also exists to develop them to handle voice and visual information as well as data. In many cases the cost of the network could be justified for any of these on their own. In this chapter, we will look at some of the known applications of LANs (computer and terminal networks and the electronic office) and speculate on some of the areas which could be developed once the communications infrastructure exists.

The main obstacle to the implementation of future communications devices is paradoxically the need to replace obsolete devices. Few companies are able to afford large scale replacement since starting from scratch (which could be much easier to construct a more effective and efficient system) can be expensive. Most companies today have some sort of IT technology installed and hence have already both invested heavily in IT and have made the decision to use IT to improve their competitiveness. What this means is that unless the economy is buoyant and, more importantly, the business is profitable most companies cannot change from what they have installed already and have to proceed from where they are. This is one of the reasons why the move over to open systems is so difficult, most companies have already committed themselves to a proprietary system, for example the use of IBM's SNA communications architecture.

COMPUTER NETWORKS

Distributed processing and computer networking simply mean that different independent systems having their own local processing power and memory, need to communicate by being able to access and store information. Note a system is a physically distinct object, for example a computer, that contains one or more applications. This means that an application in this definition is anything capable of sending or receiving information, for example, a database or electronic mail facility.

These various elements are linked together by some means, usually telecommunications circuits. Processing of user applications may be performed at several places in the network, in which case it is often referred to as a distributed computing system. This definition is the forerunner to the much talked about 1990s concept 'Client-Server' architecture. In a client-server environment a database application, for example, would be split into two parts. One part deals with processing and data storage and the other acts only as a front-end to the system. For further information on client-server *see* Chapter 5.

Alternatively, the network may exist to allow users, over a wide area, to access a central computing system by means of various types of terminals. The network in the latter case may contain some processors but these will perform functions associated with data transmission and not with application processing of user-supplied information. The particular requirement of terminal networks from the point of view of a LAN is considered later in this chapter.

As already discussed, there are many types of networks, many of which extend over several sites which are linked by the public telephone network or by circuits which are leased from the public authority, namely WANs (wide area networks). In this environment LANs are only used to link equipment which is contained wholly on one site and which does not require that the public authority, or anyone else, be involved. To make the maximum use of LANs in situations where the complete computer network also extends over more than one site, or where access from the outside world is needed, provision must be made for linking LANs with normal computers or WANs. This is usually accomplished by means of special computers, called gateways (*see* Section headed 'The Use of LAN Servers', Chapter 2 for further information on gateways), which perform protocol and speed conversion and which act as an interface between networks.

Computer networks come in a variety of forms, each one having been built to serve the needs of the organisation to which they belong. Some organisations want a main, central computing and storage facility which controls all the rest of the equipment in the network. The outlying computers exist to serve the central system although they may perform some processing themselves which would be inappropriate or inefficient to be performed centrally.

Other organisations have placed the responsibility for running applications with the departments that generate or use the data; in which case central responsibility is retained only for program and system writing and maintenance. In other cases the need to have computing capacity always available is so crucial to the organisation that the network has been designed to provide a degree of back-up in case of processor and telecommunications link failures.

Some applications, notably in the industrial production area, for example, Just-in-Time (JIT) Inventory Control, require many computers to cooperate to perform a task. Computers which monitor and control production processes in a factory often fall into this category. The failure of one part of the production process will affect both those processes which supply the materials to the failed process, and which use the products of it. To respond quickly enough, and to provide back-up computing power in case a control computer fails, often requires that the computers are linked.

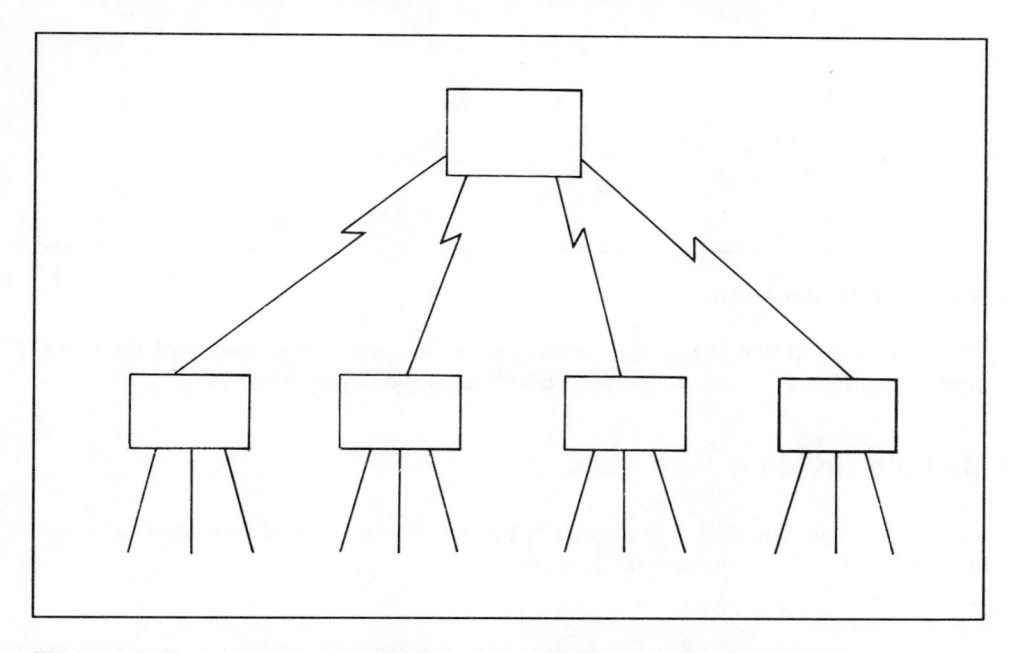

Figure 4.2 End-users or other computer systems hierarchy of star networks

To meet these many and varied requirements, computer networks have developed in a number of ways. The topology is the most obvious variable. A centrally based network, with links to devices feeding it with information and allowing users to access the results is in fact a hierarchy of stars, as shown in Figure 4.2.

Other network topologies frequently encountered are the mesh network (*see* Figure 4.3), in which a number of nodes are connected together but where information from one sometimes has to pass via a third party to reach its destination because no direct link exists; and the fully interconnected network (*see* Figure 4.4), in which each node is directly connected to every other one. Another topology is the bus, illustrated in Figure 4.5, and the ring or loop, shown in Figure 4.6.

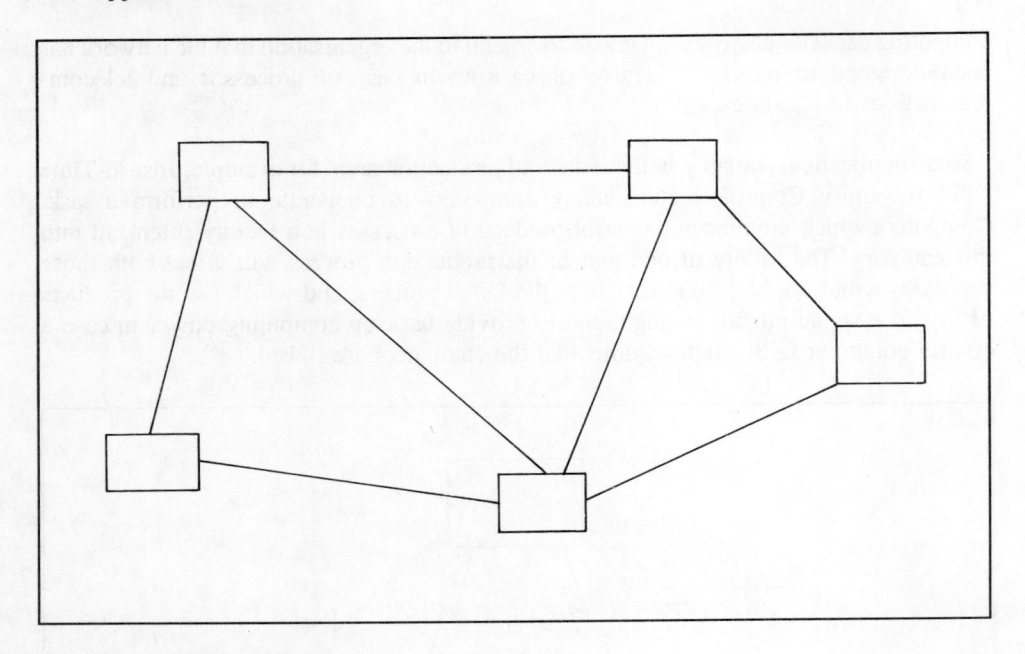

Figure 4.3 Mesh network

To service the different network topologies and different requirements of the users, there are various facilities, which will contribute to the design of networks.

Multiple routeing

Information from one device to another in the network may not always need to follow the same route. There are several schemes:

Fixed routeing

Here a route is selected for each source-destination pair of nodes in the network.

Flooding

This technique requires no network information at all. A message is sent by a source node to every one of its neighbours. This technique contains two important properties. All possible nodes are tried and since all are tried, at least one copy of the message to arrive at the destination will have used a minimum route.

Random routeing

This technique has the simplicity of flooding but with far less traffic. With this method, a node selects only one outgoing path for retransmission of an incoming message. The

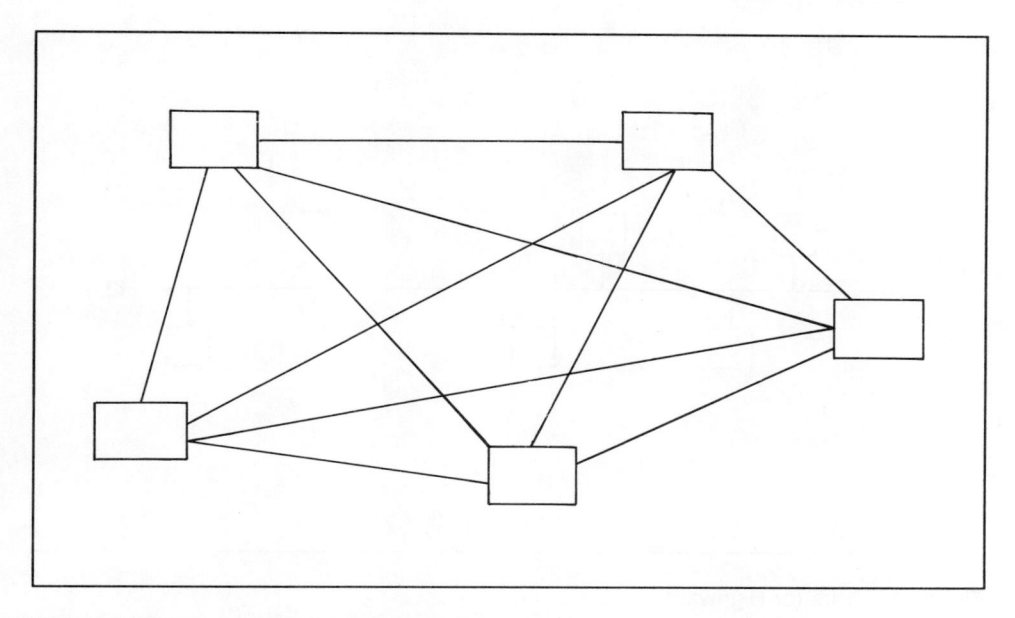

Figure 4.4 Fully interconnected network

outgoing link is chosen at random, normally excluding the link on which the message was received.

Alternative routeing

Where information normally follows one route between any two nodes, but it can be made to take another if the network or link fails or is overloaded, or the network supervisor decides to alter the traffic flow for some reason.

Adaptive routeing

With this technique the network as a whole keeps track of the state of traffic on each link and decides at the time of transmission of a message, or any separate part of it, which route it should use at that time. This routeing strategy reacts to changing conditions within the network environment. Thus a message which is split into three blocks for transmission may reach its destination by three different routes.

Such a system enables the network to function without attention even when links or nodes fail. the system of alternative routeing described earlier, requires some outside intervention to change the routes. There are two major advantages to this type of routeing, first, this strategy can improve performance and secondly, it can aid traffic control.

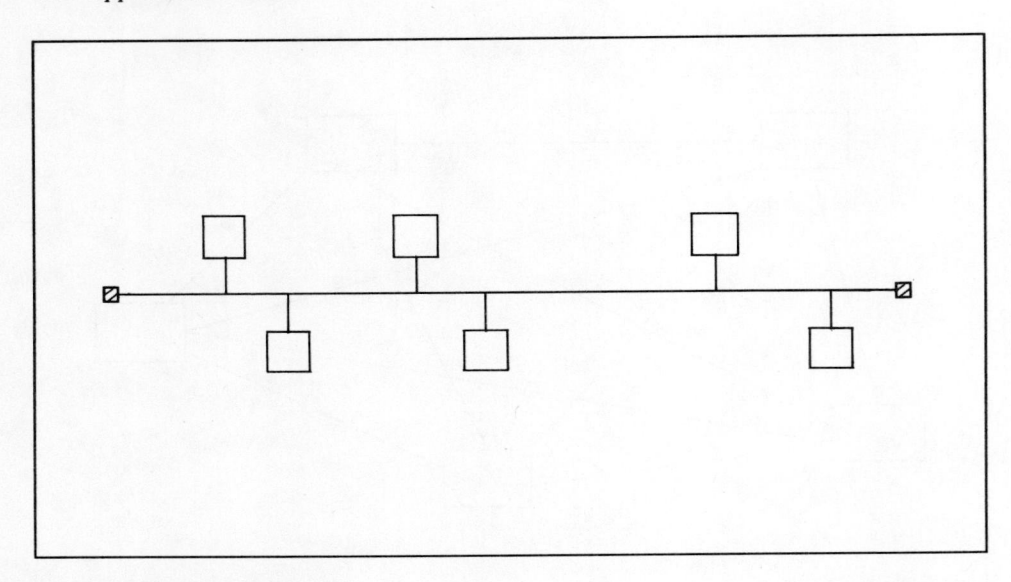

Figure 4.5 Bus (or Highway)

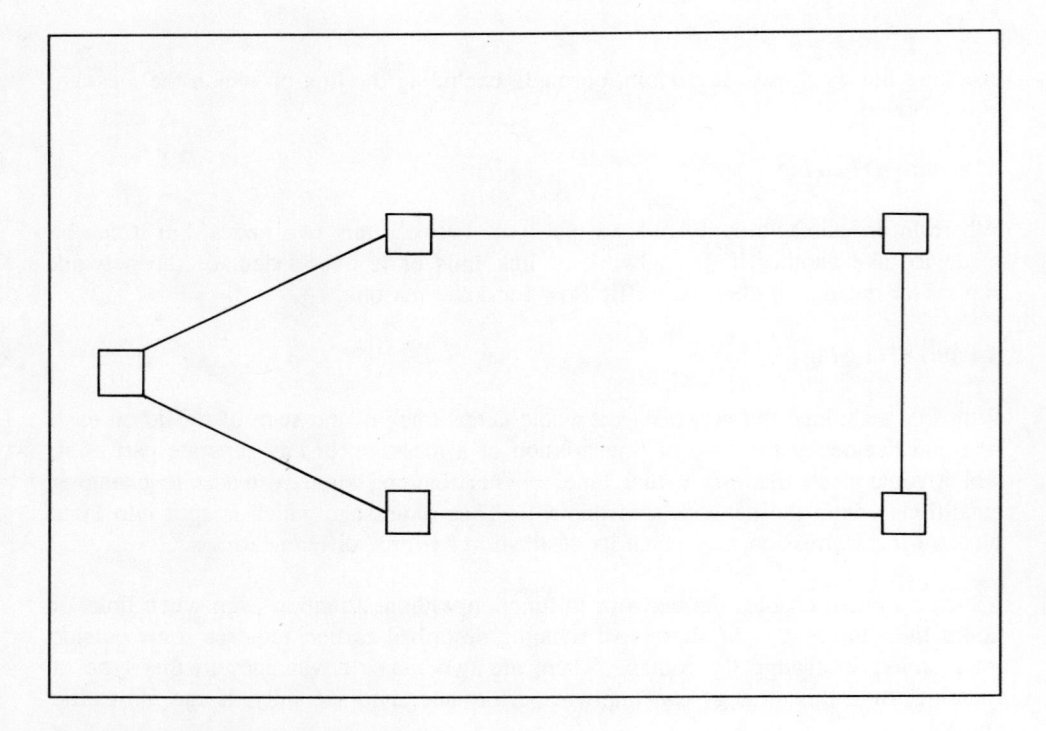

Figure 4.6 Ring or loop network

Computer Networks   123

In all the routeing cases described, the least-cost criterion will probably be used, this will minimise the number of 'jumps'.

Remote Access

A vital element in the success of most networks is for a terminal or computer system in one location to be able to access and work with another system on another part of the network as they would if they were local to each other. This requires that all intermediate nodes are transparent to the users. In this type of environment, the nodes are usually located at a considerable distance from the host. Application programs, computer systems, files, databases and peripherals should all be accessible remotely; most network suppliers go some way towards this.

Telephone lines with special equipment such as modems, Packet Assembly-Disassembly (PADs) devices, multiplexers, FEP or concentrators are used to connect the remote
         nodes. The main element in this configuration is normally the use of a dial-up service and maybe gateways into other LANS or WANs.

File Transfer

In systems where several computers are linked it is often advantageous to transfer all or part of a file from one system to another so that it can be accessed or updated locally rather than remotely. Moving files can be difficult if the source and target systems are not matched. However, the requirement is considered to be so important that the problem of file transfer is addressed by many suppliers. In addition to moving files, users sometimes want to manipulate (update, delete, copy, archive, etc) them from a remote location. This can pose similar problems to those inherent in transferring them.

To be able to carry out these tasks, systems need to use a File Transfer Protocol (FTP). This defines how a file or portion of a file will be moved from one system to another. The FTP must at a minimum transmit the data plus the file structure. The file structure usually contains, a unique filename, file size and definition of structure.

Job Transfer and Manipulation

Users of mainframe computer systems often use a special terminal and software commands (for example, Job Control Language (JCL)) to enter a job in one place to be run on the computer in another location. The requirement is very important for distributed processing systems because one computer on the system may itself transfer a job to another location, the system must permit access to all the files it requires, regardless of their location, and the operator or user must still be able to control its execution. The output should also be produced in the correct location.

Resource Sharing

Networks based on minis often 'grew up' because of the need to share relatively expensive peripherals and storage systems amongst all the computers on the network. Frequently only one or two high speed printers and hard disk files were provided for a number of computers. As already discussed in Chapter 1, the introduction of micros into the office environment, has increased the requirement for sharing resources.

In the LAN environment it makes a lot of sense to share a high capacity hard disk unit, rather than each system being supplied with low speed, low capacity floppy disks.

Database Access

An organisation which uses a corporate database needs a network which is capable of providing users with access to that database. Some organisations may profit by parts of the database being kept or updated in different locations whilst still retaining the overall unity of the structure. This requirement can be viewed in relation to two distinct scenarios.

First, the LAN-mainframe; most corporate databases are usually kept at a central location and since the size and processing power required of this database is high, it is normally stored on a mainframe. Within this environment a LAN link to a mainframe is essential. Control and integrity of the database is still maintained at the mainframe end but access and manipulation can be achieved via a PC or LAN link.

Secondly, the Client-server; the client-server concept has already been mentioned and will be discussed further in Chapter 5. It is enough to say that in relation to a database environment a relational database server can be implemented which supports a distributed approach to database processing.

The above are just some of the services which are provided from normal computer networks today.

A significant feature of the more traditional computer system is the rather slow data transfer rate which is supported. A rate of a few thousand bits per second can severely hamper data transfer between computers although it may be more than adequate for terminal transactions. Linking computers by circuits which operate at speeds significantly lower than the computers' ordinary operating speeds can cause difficulties unless the computer systems themselves have made special provision for such links in the form of communications hardware and software.

It was against this background that some LAN technologies were developed, notably the Cambridge Ring, designed for use within the University of Cambridge Computer Laboratory — for further information on this ring *see* Chapter 2. The ring was designed to link several different computers and terminals in order that the equipment and files could be shared amongst all the users. At the same time it was to provide the communications sub-network to help with research into distributed systems.

The Cambridge Ring was designed to operate at speeds comparable with the internal computing speeds of the machines on the network. 10 Mbps was chosen as the raw transmission speed which gives in practice a point-to-point transfer rate of over 1 Mbps because of the way the network is accessed and shared. The ring is simple in concept and easy to implement in practice, and it affords a convenient and cheap method of interconnecting all the devices. Terminals can thus access all the computers using the same wires, rather than a separate link to each being needed.

Since its installation in the mid-1970s, the Cambridge Ring has proved ideal for its purpose. It shows that a very useful distributed system which looks like a fully interconnected network to the user can be constructed and operated easily.

In a normal fully interconnected network each node requires *(n-1)* links and ports, if *n* is the total number of devices (*see* Figures 4.7 and 4.8). In the usual LAN, only one port is required to connect to the network interface device or repeater, which are the devices responsible for sending and receiving information to and from the network.

In common with most other forms of LAN, the Cambridge Ring removes the problem of having to control several I/O ports at each node whilst still enabling information to be sent to any other node without the need to pass through intermediate computers.

A more common situation is illustrated in Figure 4.9. Here three computers serve a number of terminals. These terminals are connected to their local computer systems, through which they can access other systems and the shared resource located on system P3. Schematically the network is shown in Figure 4.9(a). In practice the system would be wired up something like that shown in Figure 4.9(b) where terminals in the office have individual links to the computers. Installing a LAN using the corridor as the route for the wire, we can get the simple situation shown at Figure 4.9(c). The multiplexer used for the terminals in the big office can be dispensed with as well as simplifying the wiring in the rest of the system.

Once the basic LAN is installed, new services and features can be added to enhance the system for the user since many of the interconnection restrictions can be removed. Typically, a mailbox and shared file facilities can be provided and, if the interface units can be suitably designed, protocol and code conversions may be provided to enable otherwise incompatible devices to work together.

Thus we can see that LANs can provide significant advantages for computer networks when these are wholly within one site. If the networks cover several sites, the provision of a gateway device to interface between the LAN and the WAN is essential. Where the network incorporates a computer system which is capable of interfacing to WANs, this system itself could be made to perform as a gateway.

126 *Application Areas*

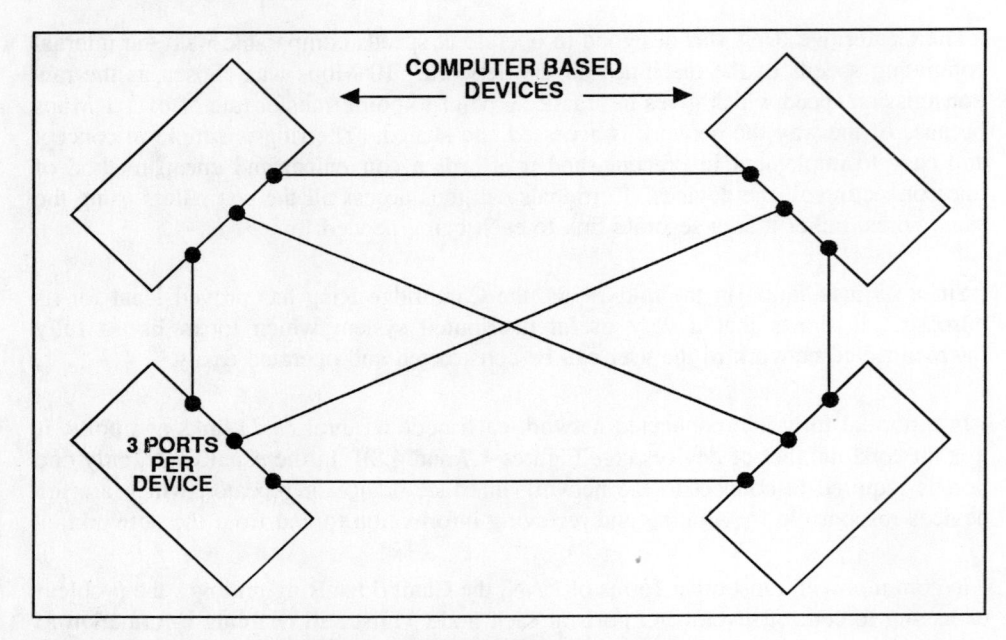

Figure 4.7 Interconnected using separate ports and links

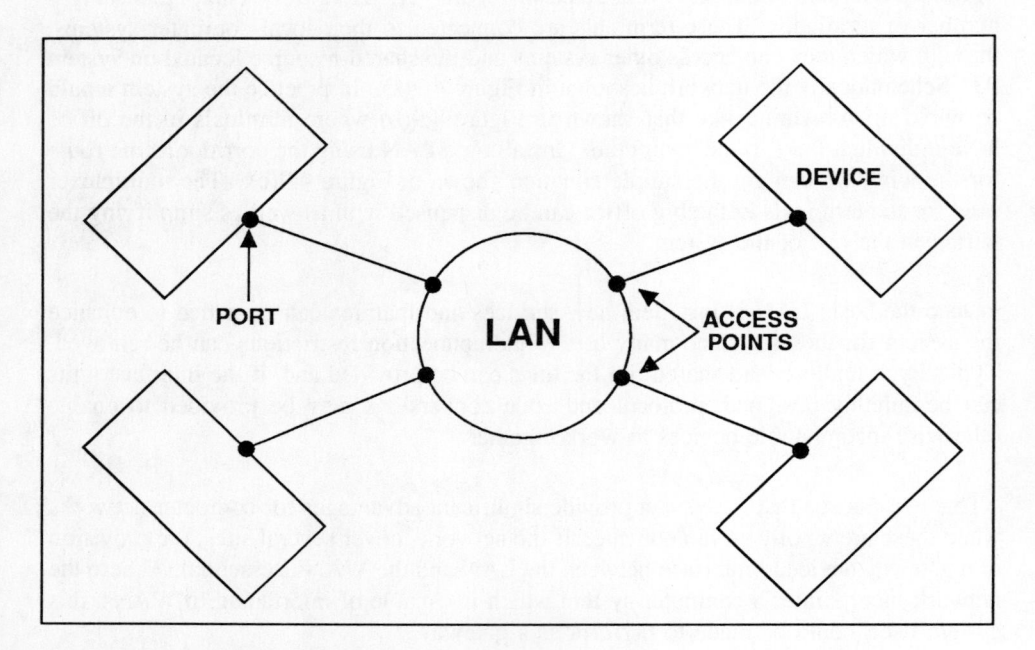

Figure 4.8 Interconnected using a local area network

TERMINAL NETWORKS

There are two classifications of terminals, dumb (these offer limited functions) and smart (these offer extended functions, such as editing and formatting data entry). Note, although some terminals are called 'intelligent terminals', they are not 'terminals' in the true sense of the word as they are programmable and may even have local processing power — hence I would define these as computers in their own right.

The bulk of terminals in use are still relatively 'unintelligent' devices and require terminal controllers or specialised circuits in computers to control them. The network which serve these terminals are essentially stars, possibly multiple stars or hierarchies. In the centre is the computer system which includes most, if not all, of the computing resources, data storage, printers and other peripherals associated with serving the end-user. A typical example is shown in Figure 4.10.

The processing unit is connected through a communications controller to the terminals. Sometimes terminals are connected directly to the computer, although these are usually restricted to those with special control or speed requirements, such as raster graphics terminals. Remote terminals are generally connected through public or private lines or a data transmission network to the communications controller. These generally operate at a low speed because of restrictions imposed by the line quality. Local terminals can use different techniques and transmission facilities which, combined with the limited distance over which they operate, mean that higher data transmission rates can be supported.

Where clusters of terminals exist in a remote location, it is common to connect them to the central system through a terminal controller which is local to them. The terminal controller can often be connected to the communications controller through relatively high speed lines of good quality. The terminal controller performs the dual purpose of handling the terminals, which are usually 'unintelligent', and sharing the high speed line capacity amongst them.

It was from this type of system that the early distributed computing systems developed. The remote terminal controllers are capable of performing end-user applications themselves and this can very significantly reduce the load imposed on the links to the central system. Reduced transmission load means that poorer quality, and hence much cheaper, circuits could be used, more than say the cost of the extra intelligence required.

In the early systems, the terminal controllers performed simple user-related tasks, such as data format checking. Their capabilities soon increased with the advent of cheaper processors and on-line storage. Thus the terminal controller was able to perform many of the data editing and even some full scale applications itself, with minimum reference to the central system.

128 *Application Areas*

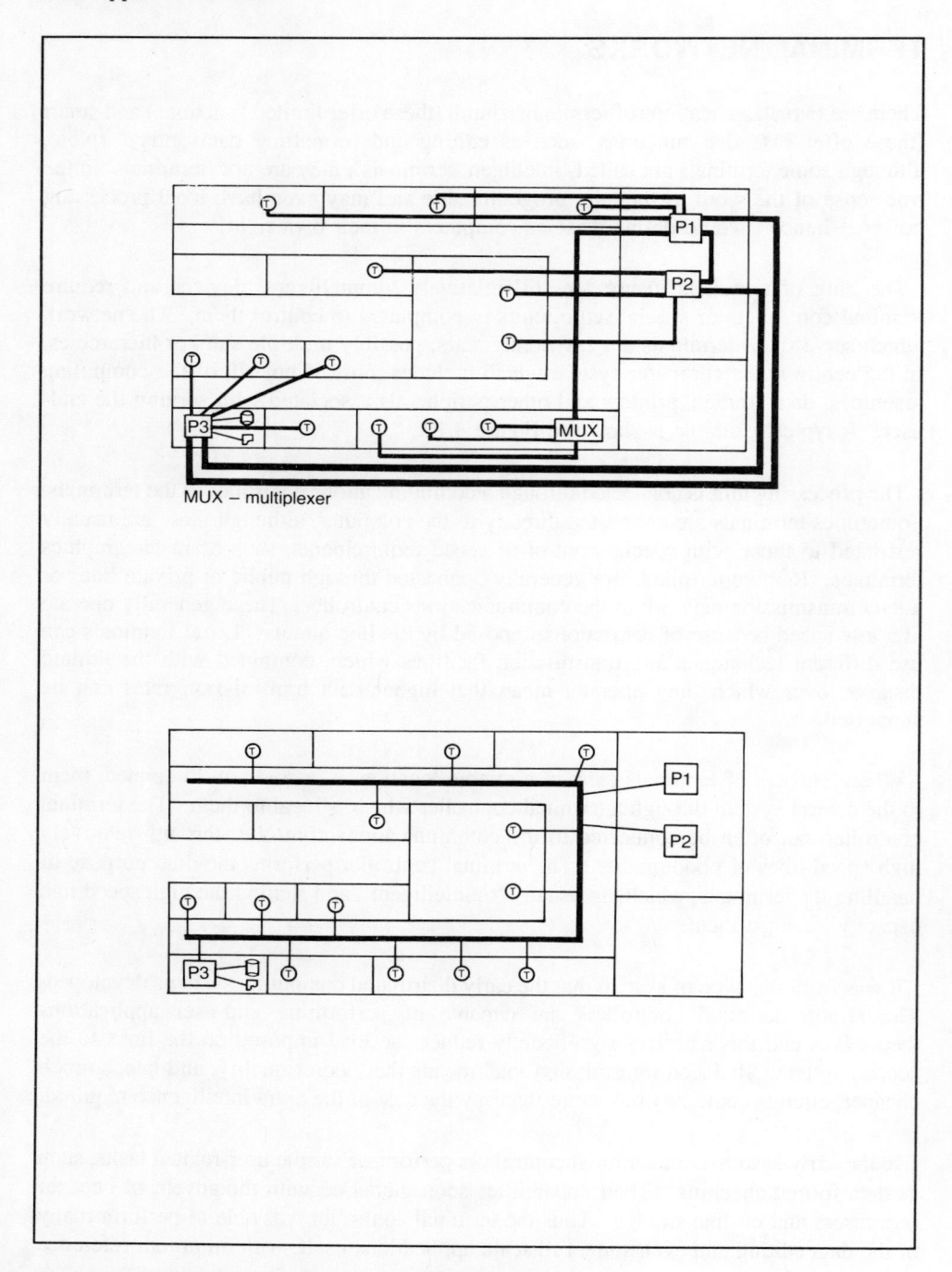

MUX – multiplexer

Figure 4.9 Computer network in office environment

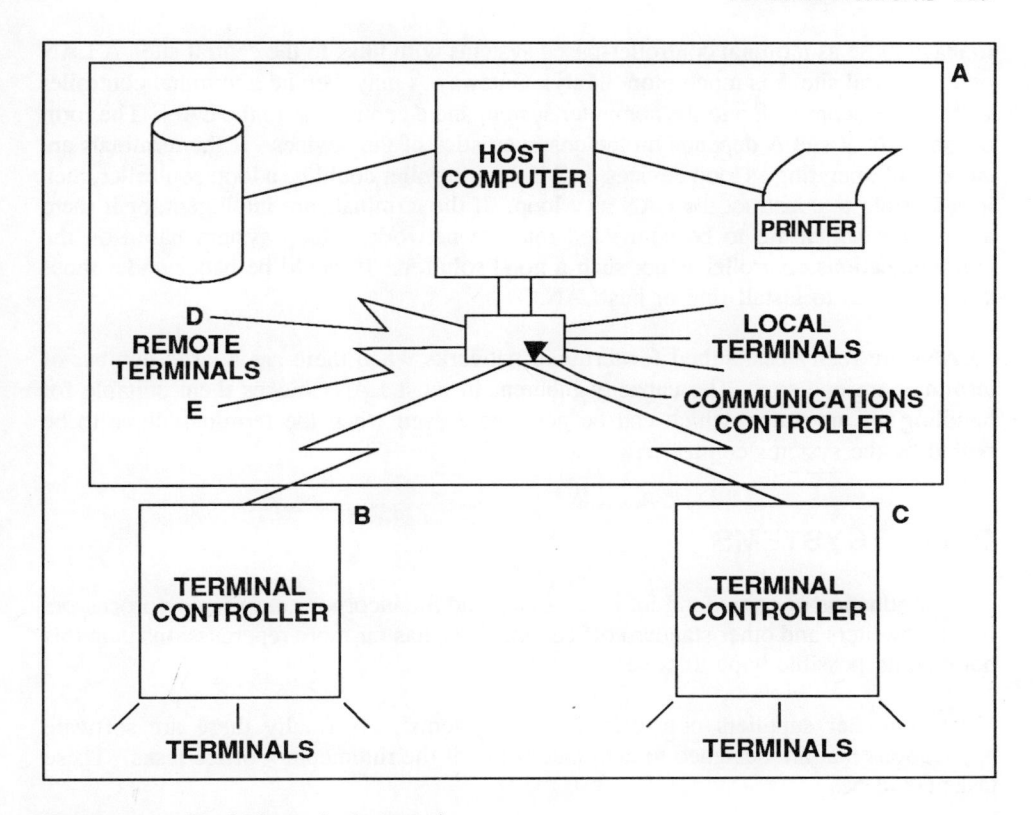

Figure 4.10 Typical terminal network

How can the basic form of a computer network be adapted for use with LANs? The first thing to realise is that the network shown in Figure 4.10 is in fact, when considered in the light of local areas, three interconnected networks, one network at each of the locations A, B and C. The remote terminals represented at the separate locations D and E are outside each of the other local systems and cannot sensibly be incorporated into any LAN. Thus the network can be redrawn as in Figure 4.11 to show how LANs could be incorporated.

Notice that the communications and terminal controllers have gone and have been replaced by gateway devices. These gateways are devices common to both the LANs and the public networks, or WANs made up from circuits leased from the public telecommunications authority. The function of the gateway is to provide facilities to convert between the procedures used in the local network and those required by the public authority.

Although the solution just described is possible, it is unusual at this time to put LANs at locations B and C if there is no processing capacity there as well. It is more common to leave these as terminal controller-based systems with links to the central site. A LAN on the central site A is much more likely. Gateway A may then be a terminal controller with a direct connection to the computer system and a connection to the LAN. The form of the LAN at site A depends on the characteristics of the devices. If the terminals are capable of operating as loop devices, and if the controller could be a loop controller, then it is feasible to construct the LAN as a loop. If the terminals are intelligent, or if there are micros which are to be connected into the network, a loop system based on the communications controller is not such a good solution. It would be better under those circumstances to install ring or bus LANs.

LANs are really best suited for terminal networks when there are a large number of terminals on one site. The capacity inherent in most LANs makes them suitable for handling all the traffic which can be generated, even when the terminals have to be polled by the systems controller.

OFFICE SYSTEMS

The introduction of computing into the office, and the incorporation of microprocessors into typewriters and other standard office machines, has far more repercussions than this book could possible hope to cover.

Most computer suppliers now offer 'office systems'. Normally these are software applications that are designed to automate some of the rudimentary office tasks. These tasks could be:

— *document preparation:* typing, updating and correcting documents, including taking dictation and copying the final results;

— *message distribution:* telephoning and mail;

— *personal information management:* use of filing cabinets, in/out trays, diaries and planning charts;

— *information access;* reference to corporate information, reference documents, libraries, bibliographic services, etc.

Office technology with its generic office tools has enabled most users to become more efficient, however this increase in the use of technology has not closely been linked with other corporate data processing (DP) applications.

The advantages of combining electronic computing and communications technologies makes office tasks easier to perform, and therefore they can be carried out more efficiently. With the use of these office systems, information is easier to access, which in turn gives the worker more up-to-date information. This obviously can be done more quickly than with a manual system. With the use of, for example, an electronic messaging or mail system your business colleagues and associates are more accessible; if the recipient of a message is absent or unavailable, then the message can wait in his electronic 'in-tray'. Furthermore, files can be shared, making it much easier for two or more people to work on one document and removing the requirement to duplicate documents.

Office systems are intended to help the individual with the normal filing and retrieval tasks associated with office work. Documents should be easy to retrieve from the electronic 'filing cabinet' and there should be no possibility of a document being replaced in the wrong section - a major cause of lost time with manual systems.

Above all, office systems in theory should free the users from many of the mundane administrative support tasks. The time saved can then be spent more profitably on the major job.

All these office systems' characteristics have been offered by various suppliers since the mid 1980s. In the early days the offering was 'business and office information systems' which tried to tie together both the office and DP environments. Their offering has mainly contained the following main components:

— *A workstation* which is a device for accessing and using the files and services provided. It is suitable for both experienced and naive users and is similar in appearance to the normal computer VDU terminal, but should have local processing power and access to a printer and personal file storage. Preferably, the keyboard should be suitable for text handling rather than program and data input. In an ideal world there would be one workstation for each user. However this is probably still not happening in many businesses, as users share access to a workstation. As price continues to drop for this technology (especially the PC) there will come a day when a workstation will probably be on every desk.

— *Shared facilities* — these are facilities that are expensive to buy or which any one user does not use continuously. A high speed printer, a good quality laser printer and high volume data processing facilities are examples of facilities which are needed only occasionally for a single user. High speed disk storage, archiving facilities and service programs are examples of facilities which are needed by all users but which are expensive to provide on an individual basis.

— *Communications facilities* - to link the workstation to all office systems services and, of course, other workstations. There are several ways this can be achieved, for example, via a central computer system with links to all the workstations and services or a central switch similar to a telephone exchange which will provide the links between the workstation and the service the user requests, or even a LAN. Telephony is also an important element for communications and this can be integrated with the data handling functions by using, for example,

ISDN technology. Overall the communications facilities should be easy to connect to, easy to add new devices to, and be high speed.

- *Access to external facilities* — the normal office worker does not work in a vacuum and needs to communicate in various ways with the outside world. To do this, there is a need for access to specialised services and databases, information services, libraries, patents information, data networks and possibly electronic mail services. These should be accessible from the office worker's desk.

The current thrust in the office systems technology has moved on from the 1980s word processing systems to multi-media and document imaging. Multi-media systems integrate together most of the normal office tasks, from word processing to communications, but with the added facilities of images and sound. For example, you could have a database picture gallery system where you could search for a particular painter and year and it would present the painter's drawing and explain through its voice-synthesizer the history behind the picture. For a discussion on document imaging. *See* Chapter 4.

Word Processing is still the workhorse of most office systems, and even if some systems are beginning to be used for more advanced office practices, the word processing role is still conserved. This is mainly due to the fairly cheap cost of word processing and to the relative user acceptance.

Apart from word processing, other services should be available in the office environment, for example:

- *Telex and teletex* — external national and international electronic mail services using either a dedicated network in the case of telex, or various networks in the case of teletex services. These services are still required even though their use is now diminishing.

- *Facsimile* — electronic transmission of images which typically are not text, such as pictures, drawings, annotated documents, etc.

- *Information* — corporate and external reference files and databases as well as personal information.

- *Electronic messages* — memos between users on one site take up a significant amount of time. Sending electronic memos from one user to another can be quicker than any other method.

- *Conferencing* — there are many forms of conferencing including voice (provided by some private telephone exchanges), computer conferencing and various levels of video conferencing.

— *Data processing* - ready access to data processing facilities and to the files and services available on the company's corporate computer system should be available.

LANs, in one form or another, are a vital element in linking together the components of the electronic office. In particular they are essential to provide the user at a workstation with access to all the other workstations and services which can be provided in a shared resource system. LANs can provide the catalyst to the integration of these different services and the media for communication (voice, data, text, visual, facsimile).

In addition, the problem of linking very large numbers of workstations and other office machinery together demands that a fresh look be taken at communications between computer-related devices. This was one of the forces behind the development of the Ethernet LAN. The concept of Ethernet is simple; provide a single data highway to which a very large number of devices can be attached all of which can then address each other. The concept has proved so successful that a large number of Ethernet systems are now installed.

A LAN for the office environment permits a large number of users to be connected to it, and also supports a wide range of equipment. The cost of connecting each device to the network must be low compared with the cost of each device.

Ideally the local area network should be capable of transmitting information in a variety of forms: analogue voice, digitised voice, data, text and video. The different information types demand different network responses since some types of information, real-time colour video, for example, cannot afford to wait for a convenient place to transmit, otherwise the picture judders and voice conversations become difficult to follow.

In the office environment the provision of user-oriented services by the network is very important. Electronic mailing within the office or site is something which should be provided as part of the network rather than provided by a separate computer-based device which the other users can access. Similarly, traffic and usage statistics should be gathered by the network for performance and usage monitoring.

DOCUMENT IMAGING

In the previous section we have discussed an office environment where computers and communications technology together are being utilised to make office conditions as productive and effective as possible. The main elements within the office to be used are documents and information, from telexes, fax, databases, etc. All these documents contain some type of information whether in text or graphical form.

As technology has developed, the need for higher definition and clarity in images has been paramount, especially when it comes to computer aided design (CAD) documents and image processing. With the advent of higher quality facsimiles, desktop digital

134 Application Areas

scanners, bit-map VGA displays, laser printers and high density digital storage devices (for example, write one optical storage devices), document imaging processing (DIP) has grown in popularity. The application areas that have benefited from DIP are publishing, contract and official document management (for example, cheques and insurance policies), engineering and CAD. However, what do we mean by DIP?

Depending on the application, users have seen DIP systems as a way of overcoming some of the limitations of traditional paper-based and computer systems. DIP offers a potential for capturing images accurately as they come into an organisation and then allowing the user to manipulate the image as he likes.

Therefore we can describe a DIP system as containing the following stages:

— *Input* — this is the capturing or creation of new documents. Here a page image could be scanned and digitised and the resulting image stored;

— *Storage* — here the document and associated file structure definition and index data record (this is used for fast and easy search and retrieval) would be stored on magnetic or optical disk storage devices, depending on the volume, performance requirements, and length of time the document needs to be held.

— *Retrieval* — the software provided would facilitate search and retrieval procedures to locate and identify relevant documents.

— *Communications* — this can be seen as an extended electronic mail facility that allows users to assemble files of page images at a workstation and place them in an envelope and forward them to a named recipient. This facility will also comprise links to facsimile, host storage and server systems, expensive laser printers, high quality scanners and special imaging devices. *See* Figure 4.11 and Figure 4.12.

This is just a brief description of DIP as the scope of this publication does not permit any further elaboration. The reader is referred to NCC/Blackwell's *'A Technical Introduction to DIP'* by A M Handley, for further information.

OTHER APPLICATIONS

To date there are many applications that would be too difficult or too expensive to implement without the use of IT communications technology. In this section other existing uses of LANs are discussed, together with some possible future uses.

Electronic Mail

This is probably the oldest LAN application and has already been mentioned in this

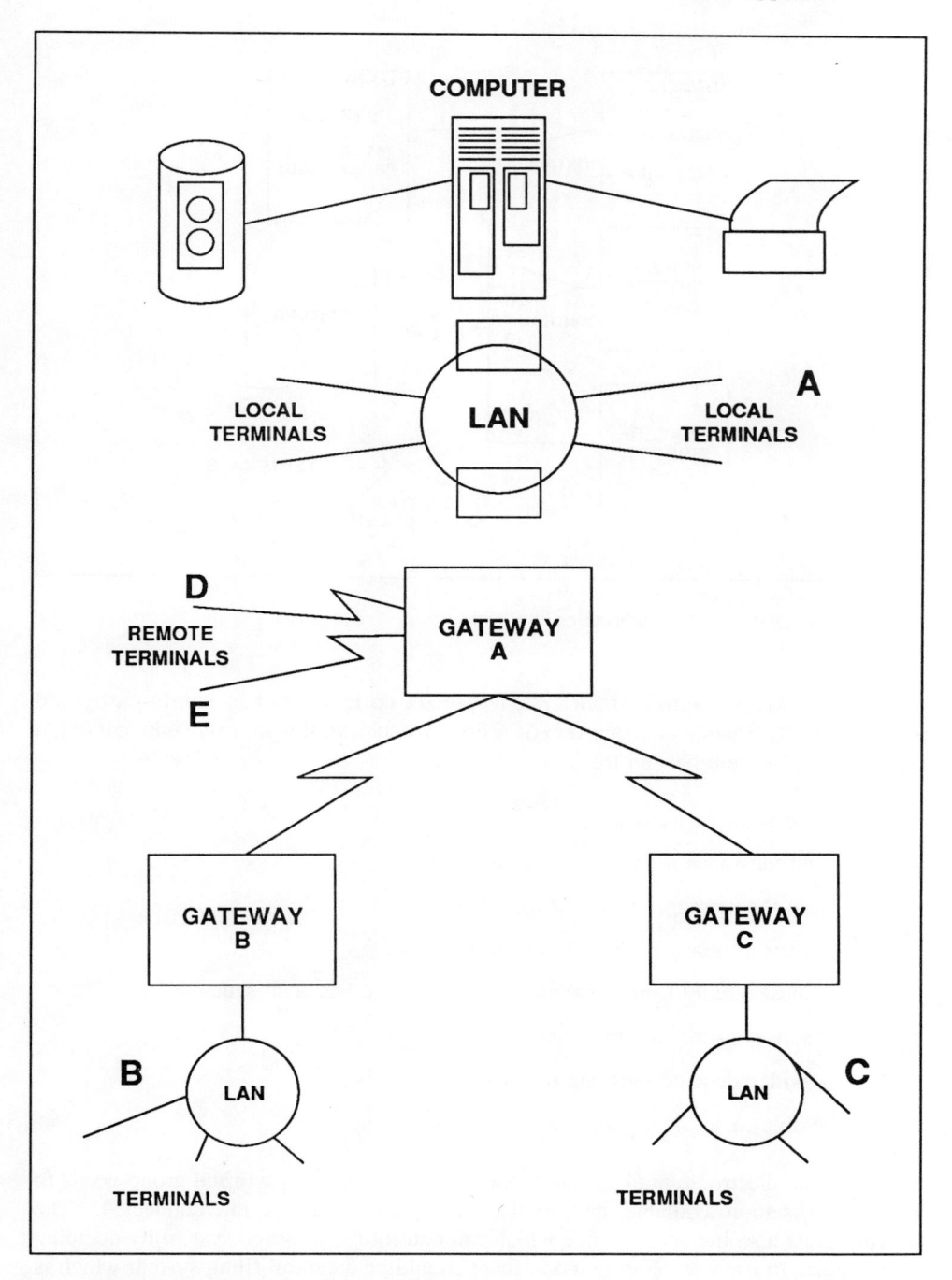

Figure 4.11 Terminal Network using LAN

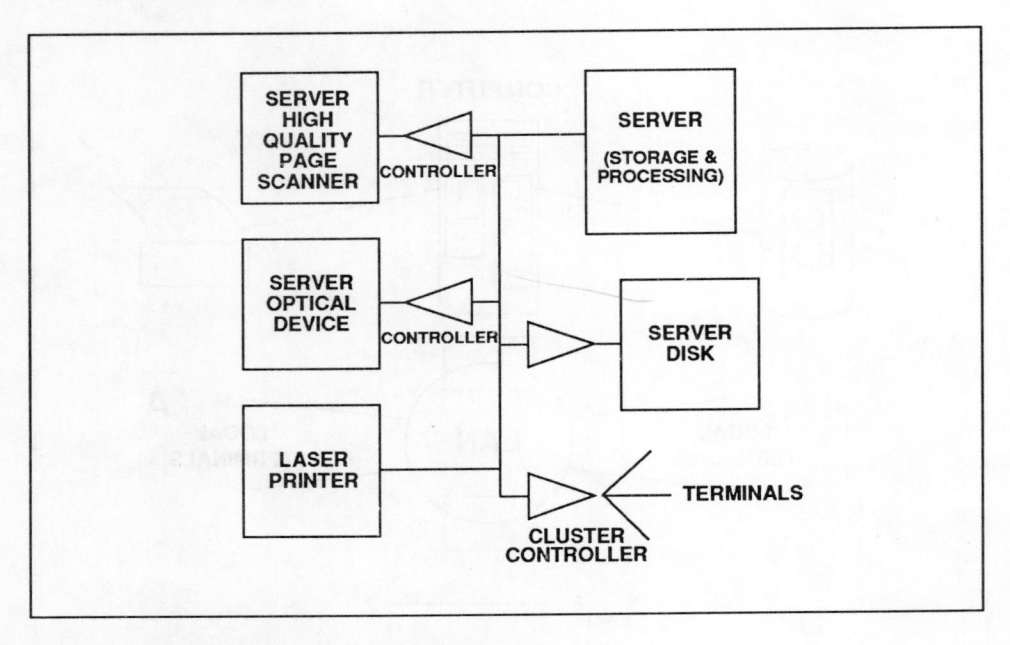

Figure 4.12 DIP communications configuration

publication. Most electronic mail systems are set up to transfer messages easily and quickly between members of a group of users. To achieve this in a sensible manner, a range of facilities are needed to:

— write and edit messages;

— send messages to one person or a group;

— store the messages sent and received;

— answer a message which has been received;

— request a reply from someone after a message has been sent;

— ensure confirmation of delivery;

— provide adequate message privacy;

— be able to set an urgent message priority.

To make an electronic mail system work effectively, each user in the group needs to have a workstation available, and all the workstations must be interconnected. The network must also include a device which can control the message system by deciding which routes to use, etc. Furthermore, there should be a central filing system which is used to store and control the messages.

In most organisations this type of messaging is normally maintained within a local group on a single site with the odd possible message to remote users. The network must provide full interconnectability between all the workstations and the message-handling system. In the early days of electronic mail, speed did not seem to be a critical factor as network reliability and availability was a more pressing need. Although these two criteria are still very important, speed has also become an important issue, especially if, for example, the electronic mail application is being used within say a bank dealing room.

An electronic mail system can easily be constructed without using a LAN by installing a central mail server which performs the message store and forwarding. Adding new workstations to a star system of this character is not always easy (*see* Chapter 2 for further information on the star topology) and there may be a relatively low limit on the number of users permitted. Computerised private telephone exchanges may be suitable in this role.

Using a LAN based on a ring or bus generally offers some advantages. Typically, new workstations can be added without much trouble wherever they are required (provided, of course, that the network is accessible from that location). Large numbers of workstations are easily supported on most LAN systems and the initial installation is usually quite inexpensive.

In situations where there is a need to send and receive messages electronically to and from other sites, (for example, electronic data interchange - see last applications discussed in this section) the LAN must be equipped with a gateway device for the public system.

Information Management

Information management is associated with handling and accessing both corporate and personal information. By corporate information I mean data which is used by the organisation as a whole and which requires central integrity control. It can cover information related to the trading performance of the organisation, and reference data needed for individuals to carry out their work (catalogues, directories, datasheets, timetables, library services, personnel records, etc). Personal information is that information required by an individual to organise work schedules effectively, for example: diary details, details of meetings, lists of names, addresses and telephone numbers, are all types of personal information without which the average office user would find it difficult to work efficiently - note this generally has been based on a PC system.

The requirement here is to provide an information handling mechanism to all the workforce. Naturally, each user must be able to access relevant corporate and personal information. An individual user should be positively excluded from accessing confidential files or information personal to other members of the organisation, unless explicit permission is granted.

Corporate information will normally be held on central storage devices (although recent events have indicated that distributed processing could distribute corporate information across a multitude of sites — see Chapter 5.) often associated with the company's main computer system. Personal information could be stored on a personal floppy disk. Another system would be to set up a specialised file handling system on the network, which is shared by every user, but which has the necessary security locks to prevent unauthorised access to another user's data.

To meet both the corporate and personal information handling requirements, each workstation must be on a network which includes the appropriate databases and files. The network should be highly reliable, especially in circumstances where no paper copy of the information is easily accessible in case of failure of the network. LANs are particularly suited to the handling of personal information where all the users share a high speed, high capacity data storage device. This has very obvious advantages when more than one person is associated with handling a piece of information, such as writing a report. By using the same shared-file storage system, all the users involved can access the same version without separate copies having to be made although this raises the computer security problems associated with unauthorised change to an individual's work..

Accessing a corporate information database, where this is stored on a company central computer system, is also possible with a LAN, provided the computer system itself is connected to the network. This is normally achieved through a type of gateway (for more information on gateways read Chapter 2) where each terminal or PC on the LAN can access the shared gateway which supplies them with a link into the central computer system.

The link is normally an emulation of the central computer operating environment. For example, in an IBM environment where the central mainframe system is an IBM mainframe running the Multiple Virtual Storage/eXtended Architecture (MVS/XA) operating system under a System Network Architecture (SNA) communications protocol, and where the user is trying to use Application System 2 (AS2), then the gateway would tell the IBM mainframe that the connecting node was a normal IBM terminal and the gateway would make the PC behave like an IBM terminal. Note that a PC could be directly connected in this manner by using an emulation card which connects the PC via a coaxial cable directly to the host Front End Processor (FEP).

A LAN is not essential to the installation and running of a management information system. However, its existence does make it much easier, and the user can have access to a wider range of services than would be economically possible with any other way.

Facsimile

This service has been available for many years, but has not been fully utilised in the past because of lack of standardisation and the limitations of the analogue telephone network. This is now beginning to change and the facsimile machine is becoming a piece of standard office equipment.

Today there are two main facsimile standards, namely Group 3 and Group 4. The standard you should use depends on the level of definition you require and the type of communications technology you use. Group 3 (using digital transmission with a resolution of 200 x 200 pels/inch, taking about one minute to transmit) is the oldest and therefore the most widely used, while Group 4 (using digital transmission with a range of resolution from 200 to 400 pels/inch, operating at about 10 to 20 seconds for an A4 page) is gradually becoming a more utilised standard.

In general, facsimile is the transmission and reproduction of paper images (ie graphics, hand written and printed material) between two or more locations. Facsimile is generally employed for images which are not easily codeable for transmission in any other way. For example, text is easily codeable with each character being given a unique code. The code is transmitted and can be interpreted by the recipient and the original text reconstructed. If, on the other hand, the sender and recipient wished to transmit a handwritten text exactly as written - possibly for signature verification - then the picture of the text must be transmitted and not the code corresponding to the text. Facsimile is usually employed for photographs, drawings, annotations, etc.

One of the restricted features of facsimile transmission is the need for external communications, for example, when transmitting from one city to another. Therefore, the use of WAN communications (in this case the PTT's WAN) is a must. This means that although you could use your LAN with a facsimile gateway into a WAN this is generally not the case, facsimile machines are still in general stand-alone devices. Possibly using one stand-alone PC to help in the collection and transmission of multiple facsimile documents.

A LAN is normally used when a workgroup need to transmit and to have their own private facsimile machines would be too costly, especially when using Group 4 devices. In this situation it is sensible to place a facsimile device on the LAN, so that the workgroup can be fully integrated.

Voice

Without doubt, voice communication is still one of the most important mediums in both business and social environments. The telephone is still an essential device and is the one 'terminal' which is accessible to the majority of workers, whether in an office or factory.

140 Application Areas

The move towards the digitisation of voice communications has been going on for some time. Most European public telecommunications network providers have in the past five years undergone a highly costly and future-proof digitisation process as a commitment to the European Communications 1992 — Memorandum of Understanding. This upgrade to their analogue communications has meant that many physical telecommunications switching devices and cabling had to be changed. This digital service was called Integrated Digital Access (IDA) in the UK and has now become the well known acronym ISDN (Integrated Services Digital Network). For further information on ISDN please read Chapter 10.

The reasons for using digital technology are clear; digitised voice can be transmitted without severe degradation and distortion. Digitally controlled telephone exchanges can operate much faster than their older analogue counterparts and can link the caller with the destination very quickly. Digital exchanges can also be programmed easily to provide alternative numbers, voice conferencing, etc, and a user can move offices whilst still retaining the same telephone number without any wiring alterations being needed.

In the LAN environment the move towards digital voice communications has also had an impact. Until recently the integration of voice on to a LAN had been the main obstacle to an integrated digital LAN.

To handle good quality voice traffic requires a transmission capacity of 64 Kbps in each direction. This is easily achieved within the capacity of normal LANs, but compared with the transmission of data, voice communications is relatively insensitive to errors but is sensitive to transmission delays.

If we think of a normal telephone conversation, any significant gap in the conversation is disturbing to the listener. He finds it difficult to follow the speech and may think, momentarily, that the link has been broken. Even worse would be the case where individual words were punctuated with gaps. In transmitting data, gaps in the transmission are not usually important, provided they are not too long. The computer or terminal will usually wait for a reasonable length of time before deciding that the link has been lost. Even a line being printed in segments is not very disturbing to the user of a terminal. With data, however, it is essential that all the information received and passed on to the user or the computer system is correct, with not a bit out of place. Data communications protocols must be able to cater for errors introduced in the transmission. The human ear is much less demanding of accuracy if a word is distorted or even lost in transmission, the listener can often reconstruct the meaning by examining the rest of the phrase. If a portion cannot be interpreted, the listener has only to ask for it to be repeated. Thus, speech traffic must be promptly delivered, even if it has errors, and there should be very few delays in transmission so that unacceptable gaps are not introduced between the speaker finishing a phrase and the listener hearing it.

LANs are suitable for voice transmission since now they have the necessary bandwidth to handle speech without distortion. Converting voice to digital signals has normally been achieved by using specialised telephony techniques like Pulse Code Modulation (PCM). This is a time-division process that can transmit analogue signals over a digital medium at high speeds. However over LANs, this technique has required very large bandwidths. Therefore another technique had to be used. There have been several pilot techniques used but the most popular one has been the packet mode LAN.

In a packet mode LAN the voice signal is broken down into independent packets (with each packet being addressed individually) before it is placed into the LAN and transmitted. In order to reduce packet transmission overheads, a silence suppression technique is required to eliminate empty packets which occur when a person is silent.

Furthermore, packet mode LANs can have other problems. For example, if the same node is dialled by two others at the same time, the recipient must be able to accept one call and reject the other. One solution is for a special node on the network to act as a controlling device, this special node can say whether the called number is engaged, not answering or ringing. If another caller then tries to access the same node, the controller will be able to say that it is engaged.

Some networking techniques are more suitable than others for ensuring that speech is transmitted quickly and without noticeable gaps. In particular network access techniques, which ensure that every node is given the opportunity at regular intervals to send information, are generally better for speech than those which rely on contentions with other nodes to give a reasonable, average level of use, especially when the latter are carrying a lot of traffic.

LANs which provide voice-handling facilities should also provide the ancillary services needed to ensure that the network is used most efficiently. We need, for instance, the equivalent of a dialling and route-making device. On a local network, unless it is star-shaped, all the nodes share the same physical communications channel and each message or packet can be heard by the others.

The above techniques are based on what is sometimes referred to as 'voice over LANs', but you could also use your existing telephone communications devices to create a LAN-based telephone system.

The Private Branch eXchange (PBX) is the most obvious candidate for adapting to handle voice and data traffic as a LAN. Such networks are sometimes called integrated service networks. The same physical lines joining the telephone to the PBX can also be used for data simultaneously, with the PBX differentiating between the two channels and routeing them accordingly. This has the obvious appeal that no new wiring is needed, since telephone lines of adequate quality are already available to most offices.

However, on further examination, it can be seen that, as far as handling data is concerned, the idea has some disadvantages. For example, normal telephone lines are usually unable to handle high data transmission speeds, which makes them generally unsuitable for bulk data transfer or for use with devices which incorporate processors. Also computers and some other devices need to be in dialogue with several devices simultaneously and this can be difficult to handle in what is essentially a circuit-switching PBX.

As well as the fact that new wiring is not generally needed, the PBX approach can have other advantages. One is that the PBX needed to handle mixed data and voice will also be able to handle the more advanced telephone routeing functions: multiple users involved in calls if required, automatic redirection, truncated numbers, hold on to busy numbers and call them when free, etc. The cost of a new PBX to provide these facilities can often be justified for speech alone, and the advantages are more easily quantifiable than for a new LAN.

In the fully integrated electronic office, voice and data transmissions will both be handled but the decision today for using a PBX or a shared-media LAN will probably depend on business issues rather than technological ones. It seems likely that the digital PBX will become another node on a LAN, thereby allowing information to pass from one to another. Incoming calls which cannot be connected, for some reason, to their destination could then be redirected to a file storage device on the LAN where a message would be stored, much like an answering machine.

A note would be placed in that user's electronic in-tray to the effect that a telephone message is waiting. (Voice messages can be used as alternatives to text messages.) The user could then dial the device where it is stored using a normal telephone to listen to the message. This, and other new facilities, will become available when voice and data are properly integrated.

Note: PABX (Private Automatic Branch eXchange) is not used within this publication as it is assumed that all exchanges are (in the 1990s) already automatic.

These two methods of voice transmission over LAN-based technology still have the main drawback of not having adequate bandwidths to cope with integrated telephony systems. With the introduction of broadband LANs, operating at speeds of up to 100 Mbps, support for large numbers of both voice and data channels will be introduced. For example, investigations are now underway with ANSI Fibre Distributed Data Interface (FDDI), which specifies a 100 Mbps token passing physical ring using fibre optic cable. FDDI will provide high speed local connection of computers together with backbone support for multi-media performance LANs. For further information on PBX read Chapter 3 and for FDDI read Chaper 10.

Video

The transmission of visual information, other than facsimile, is becoming more widespread. If moving colour pictures of television quality are required, bandwidths of around 6 MHz are necessary for transmission and circuits with this bandwidth are expensive to obtain, especially when the distances involved are large. In the early 1980s experiments were made which combined real-time black and white pictures and voice communications devices. This was the first time that the use of such a system was seen as having a business value.

The main benefits for such an application include:

— enhanced executive productivity;
— improved speed and quality of decisions;
— cost savings on travel (this is only applicable if the LAN connects to a WAN);
— augmentation of the overall level of communication within a group of professionals;
— reduction of the number of face-to-face meetings.

What has resulted from these trials is that users who are in voice communications often would like to supplement the information they are conveying with simple graphics. For example, transmission of a line drawing would be perfectly adequate, either as facsimile or by means of graphics terminals. Transmission of facsimile has already been discussed. It usually takes quite a long time to transmit a complete page as it scans and digitises each line in turn.

In the cases where the pictorial information to be transmitted is composed of line drawings, graphs or diagrams, the information can be coded much more easily and transmitted quickly to the other end using normal digital data transmission speeds, where it is reassembled by the receiving terminal into a copy of the original. Both these facilities are possible now using transmission lines of normal bandwidth. Once a picture is sent, it does not need to be sent again until a change is made, unlike real-time television pictures.

By developing the idea of transmitting simple images, an electronic 'sketch-pad' or 'blackboard' can be envisaged in which both the sender and receiver can alter the image and then transmit it to the other. By these means, two workers can discuss and amend a drawing, or any other pictorial information, using a telephone suitably enhanced by the addition of a low speed graphics terminal.

The applications just discussed are of most value where the two people involved are too far apart for a face to face meeting to be feasible. It is doubtful if there is very much need for video transmission within a single site, unless it is very large. At present, because video and graphics terminals are much more expensive to provide than simple workstations, most organisations will be unwilling to provide a bulk set of such facilities for all their users. This limited cover of the potential population will also limit the amount of use which is made. Ironically, the latest developments in LANs are ideally suited to the transmission of video information.

LANs almost always have a high data transmission rate and can therefore support the rather larger capacity required for visual information better than the traditional low speed links.

Those local area networking techniques which require all the users to share one data communications channel are not suitable for real-time video transmission for two reasons. First, the bandwidth available is only just sufficient for real-time colour pictures with sound, but this leaves little extra for the other users. Second, real-time traffic demands that capacity is available the whole time and transmission cannot be interrupted for more than a fraction of a second at a time. Even a single conversation of this type is sufficient to load the network almost to its full extent and special priority must be assigned to it to prevent other conversations from fragmenting the information flow. If the visual information transmitted is of the graphical or blackboard type, or if slow-scan television is used, the load will be considerably less and a fragmented dialogue will have no noticeable effect on the quality.

Broadband LANs are based on technology which originated in the cable television market and hence represent a perfect solution to transmitting real-time colour pictures. The techniques used by broadband transmission will not be discussed fully in this chapter, but suffice to say that a considerable number of video channels can be shared within a single coaxial cable. Data channels can also use the cable but need much less bandwidth. In this way, a number of simultaneous video conversations can take place on a broadband LAN without interfering with, or being interfered with by, the data transmissions also taking place.

Many observers claim that the broadband technique for LANs is the one which will become the norm because of its advantages and enormous bandwidth — 300 MHz — compared with around 20 MHz of other techniques.

Thus, we can see that the technology supports video transmissions. It remains to be seen whether there will be the demand within a single organisation on a single site, and whether the equipment needed to meet the demands will be developed.

PC Conferencing

As an addition to video, work has progressed in recent years in the multi-media integration of the workgroup. As already stated video conferencing via a LAN, although the capacity is there, is not really recommended. However, PC conferencing takes the philosophy and benefits behind the use of video conferencing and integrates PCs, its applications and its users into a conferencing unit. This type of conferencing will permit concurrent voice and data calls between various PCs. Its main benefit is to support the sharing of information between a group of people who have difficulty in meeting face-to-face. Thus providing a discussion environment where topics can be raised, opinions considered and conclusions reached.

The characteristics of such a system are:

- automatic screen image transfer, where every PC sees the same document, no matter where it is located;

- background file transfer. This is useful in terms of being able to share files and messages that may or may not be associated with the conference;

- transfer of keyboard/screen control. Here the conference proceedings can be controlled by a chairperson. Note the role of the chairperson is to ensure that the purpose of the conference is understood and that it is kept in order. Furthermore, this facility can be very useful in training situations;

- interface to different sources of data, for example, scanners, facsimiles, etc.

PC conferencing gives an organisation the opportunity to maximise the use of its experts. PC conferences can be used to form task groups to address issues affecting the company as a whole. For example, a group of designers could benefit by using such a facility to discuss concerns over a forthcoming product.

Data Processing Services

Within most business environments, access to data processing resources is essential. The requirements are very varied and can range from the ability to run computer programs from a remote location, or enter them into a job queue for later running, to accessing a centrally maintained database to read the information contained in it (this has already been discussed earlier in Information Management). As the processing capabilities of the terminals and workstations scattered around the site increase, the number of data processing services needed by a network will also increase.

The oldest requirement is remote job entry. This facility permits a user to enter a job for processing on a computer system in another place. The printed output either appears at the device at which the job has been entered, or a message is sent to it to the effect that the job has run and the output can be obtained from a central DP area or printer server location. In networks where several computers are linked, different jobs may be run on different computers without the user necessarily knowing which.

In addition to the above, the following services may also be required:

- remote access to central computing facilities;

- personal computer — each manager and professional, with a workstation in a network, may want to use it as a 'super' pocket calculator;

146 *Application Areas*

- file transfer and file sharing — moving files from one computer to another, and the use of a shared-file storage device;

- terminal access to other users and computers;

- access to external services provided by other networks and organisations.

Most LAN technologies are able to support the above requirements in terms of the transmission speeds and carrying capacity which they offer. The services which they provide are usually of lower level than those required. These have to be added on to the network once installed.

The only service which may prove a strain on the LAN is the transfer of large quantities of information from one computer to another, since the speed with which a computer can output data is of the same order as the network transmission speed itself.

The requirement to link to externally supplied services means that a gateway or bridging device is needed between the local network and an external system. This is required whether we are considering a LAN or an on-site computing system. Most suppliers of computer-based networks provide facilities to link to external systems, either in the form of a public telephone network interface, a device for a public packet-switched system, or the ability to use leased circuits. Most LAN products when they appear on the market, will have these facilities.

Electronic Data Interchange (EDI)

EDI has become synonymous with effective and efficient business practices. EDI is a general term defining the transmission of business information in an agreed structured, electronic format from one computer application to another.

For example, the direct transmission of a standard bill of lading (formatted according to the Transportation Data Coordinating Committee (TDCC) standard) to a carrier's computer system. This would eliminate the need for printing, mailing, and rekeying, consequently reducing the cost of the transaction, as well as cutting down on the number of errors.

There are various benefits for using EDI and they can be classified as follows:

- *direct (the easiest to identify)* — this means that the information is sent electronically from one application to another thereby reducing direct costs of transactions.

- *indirect (the greatest benefit)* — this is the use of EDI to enable the technology to change the way an organisation does business, for example, EDI can help change inventory policy, such as a move towards the use of just-in-time (JIT).

- *strategic (the hardest to measure)* — the use of open communications and the sharing of information (eg demand schedules) with suppliers and customers can lead to a long-term, low-cost producer market position and therefore create a move towards the production of products developed from customer demand.

With these benefits in mind, it is obvious that the communications vehicle used must address the three main elements of document processing, namely confidentiality, integrity and availability (CIA). It is not the aim of this publication to discuss the security and business philosophy behind the use of EDI, the reader is referred to NCC/Blackwell's publication *EDI and Security* by Mario Devargas. For further information on CIA please refer to Chapter 6.

However communications availability is obviously of paramount importance and therefore how are these documents transmitted?

Once the business document is formatted according to a set standard (ie the de facto standards used today are either ANSI X12 used in the US or the UN's EDIFACT standard used mostly in Europe) there are two ways of delivering them electronically.

Direct communications between one computer and another

This can be achieved in various ways:

- physical line link from computer A to computer B (only if closely situated);
- the use of a telecommunications carrier (PSTN or Packet-Switched Data Network (PSDN)), where computer A dials (or uses a direct circuit like BT's kilostream) computer B's telephone number.

Indirect communications between one computer and another

This is achieved by using a third party network, for example, a Value Added and Data Service (VADS). With a VADS there is no need to have a direct link with a trading partner, as the VADS acts as the middle man (ie a store and forward house) between the trading partners.

EDI Gateway

In terms of using a LAN, it is obvious that the most cost-effective method of using EDI within a LAN would be via a EDI gateway so that everyone that is permitted to transmit documents to trading partners is able to do so via the LAN. This gateway could act as the central corporate transmission point for EDI documents. Note that the documents could be formatted locally on the workstations or via a server, either way the user would only see a transparent transmission via his terminal, and hence could believe that he is transmitting the document himself.

The LAN would only be used as another vehicle to the outside world, and therefore the EDI tool would only be seen within the LAN as just another application.

CONCLUSION

LANs can be used in many areas of IT and the electronic office. Indeed it is not an exaggeration to say that some applications could not be developed to their greatest extent without them. The integrated electronic office is just not possible without some form of LAN.

The question which should be asked is how many services should the LAN provide:

— Should it be a highly reliable, available, and fast transmission service only?

— Should it be capable of handling different makes and types of equipment?

— Should it provide some central shared storage facilities?

— Should it provide electronic messaging, word processing, personal information handling services, archiving, etc?

— Should access be provided to corporate information services?

— Should it provide printing and copying facilities?

— Should there be access to external services?

— Should voice and data be integrated?

— Should data processing and personal computing facilities be provided?

— How many video services should be provided?

— Is a telephone answering and voice message storage facility required?

The answers to these questions are dependent on the requirements of the individual organisations and the availability of suitable products. As with everything else, the more facilities a LAN possesses, the more it will cost to buy, run and maintain. The trade-off is between the cheap and simple local communications facility upon which the purchaser has to build the required services, and the costly developed network which will be inherently more difficult to adapt at a time when the requirements are still a bit hazy.

Common to many requirements is the need for a gateway device to link the LAN to the outside world. Its precise functions depend on the exact requirements and the outside networks which are to be used.

To take two examples, firstly *local area network to public switch system*. The public network can be used to access remote computers, terminals, networks, services and other organisations. These can also access the LAN if they have permission; and secondly *local area network to mainframe computer network*. This would allow devices on the LAN to use facilities in the computer network. The requirement is for a gateway to emulate the terminal protocols acceptable to the mainframe.

TERMS TO REVIEW

Sage the Owl Recommends

- PBX
- ISDN
- PSTN
- EDI
- DP
- DIP
- Star
- Mesh
- Remote Access
- File Transfer

- Facsimile
- Routeing
- Resource Sharing
- Database Access
- Office Systems
- Workstation
- Conferencing
- Electronic Mail
- Information Management
- Voice
- Video
- Telephony
- Electronic Office
- Office Automation
- Node
- Terminals
- Word Processing
- Digital
- Analogue.

5
Client-Server Methodology

INTRODUCTION

Cooperative computing and distributed systems as a philosophy (and maybe in some instances a reality) has been around for many years now. However, most IT systems are based on one single unit (normally a central computer) facilitating all the resources and power required by the rest of the community of computers or terminals. This means that this central unit must be able to deal with any request given to it as quickly as possible. Most central computers do not have infinite resources to call on when required. Their finite resources will deal with a fixed amount of work efficiently but when asked to do something over and above this it is always going to have difficulty. For example, if a central computer works at its optimum with 20 terminals or computers hanging from it, when you attach another it is obvious that its performance is going to deteriorate.

The philosophy behind client-server computing is based on the effective division of labour between two or more computer units that are able to share the workload between them. In the client-server environment, for instance, an individual application could be subdivided into different tasks, where each task would be run on different computers. Therefore, the client (or front-end) computer runs those tasks that present and manipulate the data (eg, accepts input, prepares and issues a request to the server), while the server (or back-end) computer runs those tasks that store, retrieve and protect the data.

In this example the capability of the computer used will dictate what task will be assigned to it. Therefore in such an example, a mainframe type computer could be allotted the tasks of storing, retrieving and securing the data (traditionally these tasks have been some of the main strengths of the mainframe environment) while a PC could be assigned the tasks of presentation and manipulation of the data (in this environment the obvious graphical capabilities of the PC would be of great benefit).

This combination of processing capability means that the user will get the benefit of both worlds, a friendly graphical user front-end that he is accustomed to and the processing power of a mainframe.

152 Client-Server Methodology

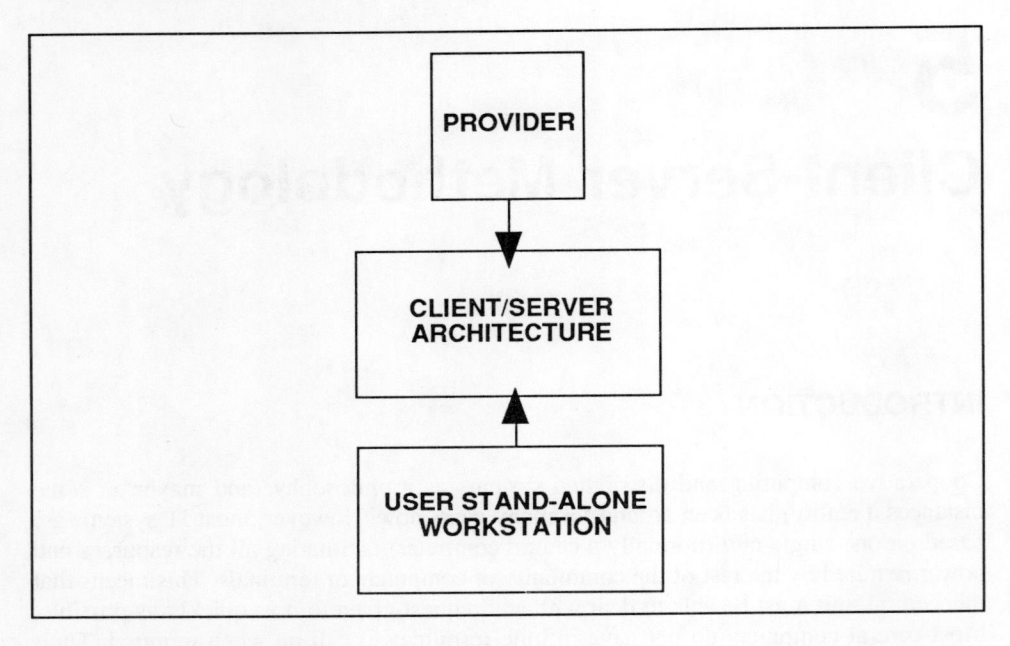

Figure 5.1 Client-server environment

This can be seen in Figure 5.1, where the service provider, a mainframe, mini or super PC runs or contains:

- sophisticated multi-user, multi-tasking environment;
- centralised data processing facility;
- advanced administration and security features;

while on the user end it probably has:

- sophisticated graphics capabilities;
- easy to use applications;
- the flexibility for expansion.

EXTENDING THE WORKGROUP'S CAPACITY

We have seen how the use of local area networks has extended productivity, from a stand-alone PC to the ability to share data and software. This can be further extended when we expand the LAN environment into supporting the client-server philosophy and therefore opening up the full potential of LANs.

Extending the Workgroup's Capacity 153

In the local area network environment the nodes are connected together and normally through the use of application software and specialised servers can share the network and its data.

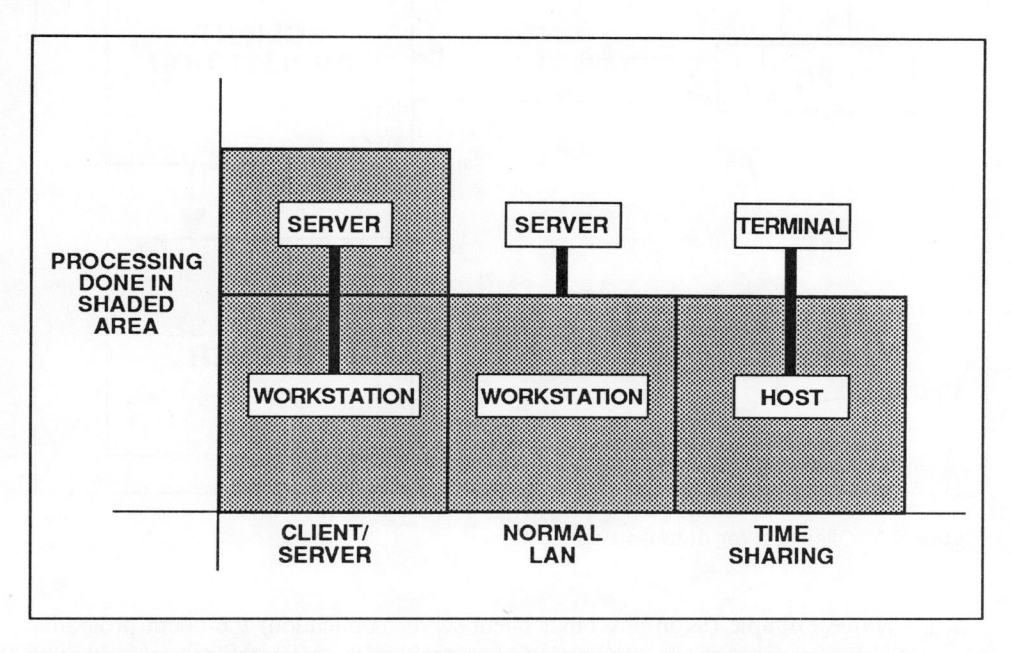

Figure 5.2 A comparison of volume of processing achievable using various network types

Client-server computing describes the strategy that is used to share work, much like the division of labour philosophy. This means that in terms of the workgroup environment, not only can users share the network (and all its applications) but every node whether a user or a server can share the resources, ie the servers can themselves call on other services and thus become clients as well as servers.

However, this philosophy has some ambiguities in the LAN environment. We have defined earlier in this book that the job of a server is to serve and hence by implication the job of a client (or user) is to receive a service. In the client-server environment this changes and some sort of definition of 'division of labour' must be applied. As already discussed, the usual divide is that anything that is specific to the functioning or presentation of an application to the user is the job of the client, while anything that is common across users is the job of the server. The obvious example of this is a database management system, where every user needs to access data, hence a database server is required, while the users may also wish to represent their data via his high resolution screen running a graphical user interface, and hence a present-day PC is required, (*see* Figure 5.3).

154 *Client-Server Methodology*

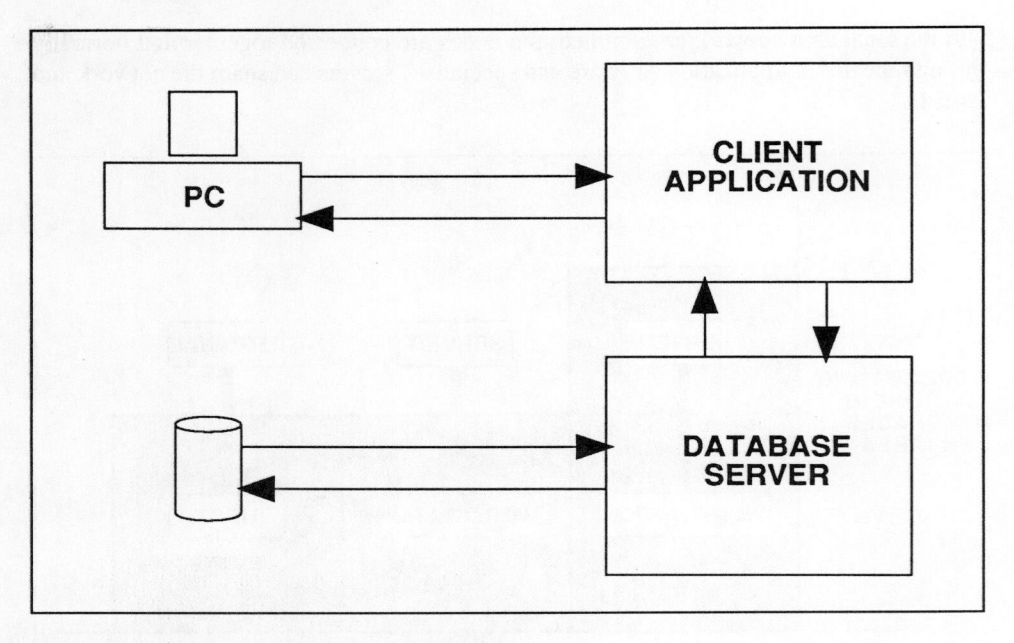

Figure 5.3 Client-server database application

In the above example (as in any other client-server application) the client programs consist of the portion of the application that enables the user to interact with the computer. The server programs perform all the processing required of the database. Hence on a typical database transaction the following would occur:

— the user makes a query to the database via his application on his personal computer;

— this goes into the server that processes each query (for example, searches for a particular record);

— once the server has an answer, whether positive or negative, it returns the result to the client application;

— the application then, with the help of its graphical user interface, presents this information in whatever format the user has initially set up, to the user.

A typical client-server database could be based on, for example, the relational SQL environment. Figure 5.4 describes such an environment. Here the SQL server uses client-server methodology to allow multiple front-end applications (ie, accounting, sales administration) access to the same database.

The use of Networking and a Relational Database - an example 155

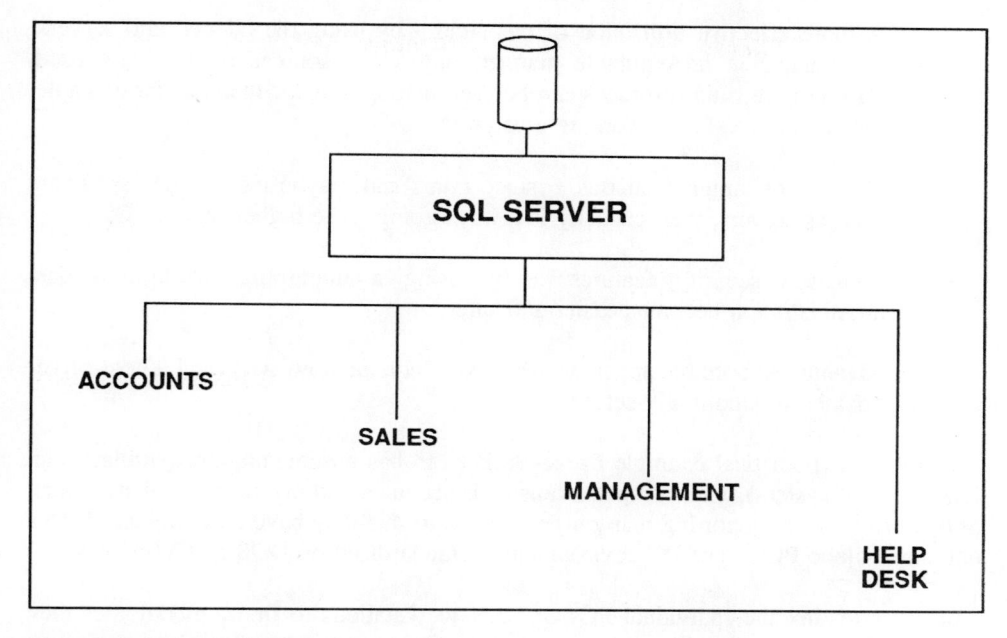

Figure 5.4 SQL environment

This approach reduces the amount of data that is transmitted down the line (as compared to a normal local area network request, where the processing is usually done via the individual workstations themselves and in the majority of instances an entire file is sent back and forth across the network). This will obviously increase the overall speed of the application and its related transactions, leading to a more cost-effective IT environment.

THE USE OF NETWORKING AND A RELATIONAL DATABASE — AN EXAMPLE

Client-server computing offers various advantages over the traditional LAN solution for a typical database application. These can be summarised into the following:

— Cost effectiveness - PCs and simple LANs are relatively inexpensive, the use of these devices offers a higher price/performance ratio than does traditional mainframe time-sharing;

— Increased speed of data access - since processing is divided amongst all the available resources, the users should see a marked improvement when retrieving data;

- A more effective utilisation of resources - by using the clients' and servers' intelligence in an equitable manner, only the resources required are used. Furthermore, said resources can be used in a specialised manner, for example, the use of RAM as a working area only;

- The use of larger databases — since minis and maybe mainframes are being used as servers, their capacity is always going to be higher than a PC;

- Increased security features — by using a mainframe workgroup data administration becomes easier and safer.

These advantages become apparent when we look at how a typical client-server relational database is normally set up.

To take a hypothetical example Bread-Basket Ltd has a minicomputer (similar to an IBM AS-400 system). This computer runs their accounts and inventory database via an SQL environment supporting many users. Added to this they have several small LANs and stand-alone PCs. The PC environment is standardised on DOS and Windows.

In order to link the individual PCs or LAN workstations to the minicomputer they presently have to emulate the minicomputer operating system. This gives them a window into the minicomputer where the users can access the SQL database as if they were linked directly to the minicomputer. If they wish to extract any information and place it on the PC for future use or further analysis they need to execute a file transfer transaction. This means that an entire file is transmitted either across the LAN to the workstation or directly to a PC.

A more effective solution to this problem would be to implement a client-server environment, with the minicomputer acting as their database server and each workstation or PC acting as the client. This environment will also help them implement a just-in-time inventory control system, with delivery of materials being placed as they are needed rather than warehousing large quantities.

The implementation of such an environment involves three design phases. Firstly, the database which already runs on the mini needs to have some design changes made to it. On top of the existing central control already exerted by the mini, the database should also take into account the total integration of (standard across the company) PC-based applications. Furthermore, by creating this environment the number of simultaneous users will increase, this means that it must perform equally well with the increase.

Secondly new data entry forms need to be designed. These entry forms will be used to input inventory changes. Finally, since more data is going to be available to the user, he needs to have the right tools to analyse it. Hence, a real-time PC-based graphical system would be ideal here.

With this implementation we now have a division of processing and an increase in the amount of benefits that can be attained from the centrally held inventory database. However, how would it actually function? As parts arrive into Bread-Basket Ltd, the people accepting receipt would enter the new inventory items directly into the SQL database. As the part is required by an employee, he would update the database of this (this could be done automatically for example, by bar-coding each part and as it is taken out of the warehouse, passing it through a reader). This information is then fed to the relevant authority so that a decision can be made on when to order more parts.

The main benefit to this implementation of a client-server environment is the ability to have instant access to up-to-date inventory information, and hence reduce the levels of inventory held and of course costs.

TERMS TO REVIEW

Sage the Owl Recommends

— Client
— Server
— Front-end
— Back-end
— Workgroup
— Database
— Processing (Where is it Done?)
— Division of Labour.

6

Local Area Network Security

INTRODUCTION

We have seen in the previous chapter how LANs can increase the level of productivity of virtually any workgroup. There are numerous advantages to networking in terms of speed of response, accessibility to data and availability of information. Local Area Networks' main philosophy is to share information and resources across distributed systems. This philosophy is in direct conflict with basic security principles, ie the control of access to information and resources. In other words, networking supplies general and flexible access while security imposes limited access using rigid control mechanisms. This may seem an unreconcilable contradiction to solve, however I will endeavour to harmonise both requirements and show that one cannot function without the other.

Today's business has become highly dependent on information technology systems for their day to day operation and even their future existence. Allied to this is the recognition that information is the life-blood of any organisation and as such must be protected from harm. This means that like any other risks, IT systems and especially networks need to be reviewed so that cost-effective measures can be taken to reduce the risk to an acceptable level. Therefore what exactly do we mean by security in IT?

SECURITY THEORY

Information technology security is the protection of information and associated resources from accidental or intentional harm. This can occur through unauthorised disclosure, modification, destruction or the inability to use that information or resource. Its basic premise can be defined in terms of loss of *confidentiality, integrity and availability (CIA)*. Confidentiality defines the need to restrict information (or access to information) from prying eyes and systems resources from unauthorised users. Integrity determines how a system's resources are supposed to behave and also requires that information should not be altered or damaged by an unauthorised source. Availability means that a resource is accessible to a user whenever it is required.

Therefore in general the security of any IT system could be measured against the four 'A's. *Authentication* (ensuring that the identity of a user is ascertained and confirmed before the user is granted access to the system, for example, via the use of passwords), *authorisation* (defining what actions and access is allowed to the user), *accountability* (the recording of events via, for example, an audit trail) and *assurance* (what level of confidence does the system have? — Is it as trustworthy as claimed?).

In order to keep these four 'A's we need to maintain CIA. CIA can be enforced by using physical (this aims to ensure that the systems resources and information are neither removed or physically damaged), procedural (this provides clear methods of how employees should do their work) and logical methods (concerned with the use of software mechanisms for the provision of security).

However even with all these security precautions, it is still up to the user himself to enforce them and to consider how much security he really requires. Before implementing some, if not all, of the above security measures it is advisable to follow the eight introductory security procedures below.

— Formally create an organisation-wide *Security Policy* (normally a short document) supported by the highest levels of management. This policy should describe the directions for security and give guidance. Supporting documents should identify the risks, describe cost-effective measures and how they should be implemented. User, management and IT personnel responsibilities should be clearly defined and described in these documents.

— Formally assign *Security Responsibility* to some member of staff. This individual should be a high-level security manager with authority to act for the entire company. He or she is responsible for directing and co-ordinating implementation of security policy and procedures.

— *Classify all levels of information.* Ownership should be assigned to different types of information, this ensures that all information is accounted for and therefore receives the required protection. Furthermore, by assigning ownership to information, it is far easier to define who is authorised to do what with particular types of information.

— *User Awareness* needs to be taken seriously. All employees must comprehend the importance of security and therefore be alert to the need for it. This awareness campaign must come from top management and through the proper training of all employees. Unless staff are persuaded into using the appropriate security precautions, security measures are unlikely to be effective. Training and awareness will convince the users that security is not an obstacle or inconvenience to their daily work. On the contrary, it can help them, for example, in the recovery of lost work.

Furthermore, once users are properly trained you can then formally proceed into creating a clear statement of accountability, where everyone will have some level of responsibility assigned to them.

— Formally implement *Disciplinary Measures* and if someone is found to breach security, act against them. A statement of discipline which is not used will be taken for granted. Legislation can be used to enforce your measures, for example, the Computer Misuse Act defines three offences: unauthorised entry to an IT system, unauthorised entry to an IT system with the intent to commit an offence and unauthorised entry to an IT system with unauthorised alteration of the contents of the system. However, successful prosecution under this Act will only be possible if proper security measures have been taken by the company.

Note when transmitting information across a network this Act seems to be lacking, therefore, a formally established company-wide security policy is still the most effective method of protection against computer misuse.

— Many frauds, thefts, etc usually occur due to the lack of thought given to the types of jobs within the business environment. For instance, implement a *Division of Labour* policy where no one person is able to control completely a process or transaction. Try as much as possible to remove the opportunity for fraud, theft or whatever. The logging of every important event (and making sure that everyone is aware that it is being logged) will help in this.

— *Risk Analysis*, although in many areas a difficult concept to implement, is imperative. Vulnerabilities and hazards will differ from one organisation to another and hence it is advisable to perform an individual risk analysis to analyse your own unique exposures to loss. This analysis should help you design a contingency plan.

— Your *Contingency Plan* must cover every conceivable loss that you think could affect your business. Loss of power, fire, theft and many others can have disastrous effects on your network systems. Note: Contingency Planning ensures a continued processing capability for systems in the event of an unexpected computer or network failure.

NETWORK SECURITY

Network Security can be defined as the protection of the integrity and availability of data in a networking environment. Its main objectives are to ensure that the information transmitted across it, is received at the destination as it was intended, to with nothing added, removed or changed. To do this it must also guarantee that all the components of the network (eg terminals, modems, data links, telecommunications lines,) function as required (and on demand) and are only accessible to authorised personnel. Furthermore it must also have the correct mechanisms for authenticating transmissions (ie the recipient of the data can verify that the person from whom the communication appears to come from is really the person who sent it and that the sender can verify that receipt has only been made by the authorised recipient). Finally it must protect the whole networking environment from outside intervention, so that the information cannot be observed, tampered with, or extracted from the network by some unauthorised person.

These networking security objectives can also be defined in terms of CIA, examples of types of threats could be:

— *Confidentiality*: hacking, tapping, masquerading, eavesdropping;

— *Integrity*: corruption due to line noise or to deliberate intervention, repudiation of transactions;

— *Availability*: line failure, power failure, equipment failure.

With these basic requirements and objectives for network security we can now evaluate the types of exposures and threats that LANs are subjected to. Remember that the main object of this exercise is to implement some type of security control mechanism against anything happening to your network that could expose your business to threat. As with any other business decision, budgetary constraints and organisational requirements will always play an important part in the decision making process.

Exposures

The biggest exposure is normally due to errors and omissions caused by honest employees who make mistakes. This is followed by fire, natural disasters and floods. Dishonest or disgruntled employees who take advantage of one loophole or misuse their authority follows closely.

External threats are a small risk in this environment, although these threats tend to hit the press with more frequency due to the 'stardom' accorded to hackers. However, even though this is a small percentage of all threats it still cannot be ignored.

Due to the very philosophy of local area networking, of sharing both information and resources, it is difficult to implement some security measures. However simple common sense should always be used when designing and installing LANs in order to avoid exposing your network. For example, printers are normally more susceptible to loss of confidentiality than are visual display units. With a shared resource such as a printer, confidential information should *not* be printed on it, printouts usually stay near the printer until collected, sometimes hours later.

Furthermore, most PC users are not normally educated in simple security techniques. Users still have problems with the elementary procedures of back-up. However in order to reduce the level of exposure in terms of human error it is of paramount importance to educate your network users, not only concerning their workstation but also how they affect the network. For example, most PC users have got into the habit of leaving their applications running on the PC — some with confidential data which should not be left even on a stand-alone basis. If this continues within a networking environment this exposes your network to anyone. If this habit cannot be changed, then it is advisable to install software to suspend the application after a certain amount of idle time. Furthermore, the user should be prompted to re-enter his/her password in order to gain access to the server again.

Vulnerabilities

Any device that has been designed and created by man will always have some element of vulnerability. IT systems have evolved from a big mainframe device serving many naive users (where its vulnerability mainly came from the fact that if it failed everyone was affected) to the personal computer (where if it fails only its user is affected). However with the use of networking techniques and the consequent dependence on servers, gateways and bridges the personal computing environment has also become a fairly vulnerable environment. An individual that wishes to breach security within a LAN can do significantly more damage significantly faster on the LAN than on a stand-alone personal computer.

One of the main increases in vulnerability as a result of the use of LANs is as a consequence of the reliance that has been placed on them by businesses. There are various reasons for this.

- Larger Security Boundary to control and monitor, a LAN has to be considered as one contiguous system that needs to be protected from harm. This increased area of control can be difficult to maintain due to its span of activities. For example, what one manager considers sensitive in one department may not be so important in another. However since all share a common communications system, LAN security managers must have total responsibility and authority to manage the whole span of the network.

- One of the most common methods of attack on a network is via the use of dial-up services. This facility should be implemented with great discretion and should only be given when absolutely necessary.

- Local area networks are sometimes implemented without proper care and attention as to how the cabling is connected and where it is placed. Accidental damage can occur when people tread on or pull the cables from their sockets. This occurrence will of course lead to the loss of availability of the network. Therefore all cables should be protected and if possible placed within conduits.

Cabling is also the most vulnerable area in terms of malicious intent. Most local area networks use copper cables, some of these cables are unshielded twisted pair and can be tapped very easily.

This vulnerability can be reduced by the use of structured cabling techniques (discussed in Chapter 2). With structured cabling users do not share a cable, they each have their own cable from the desktop to the patch panel. Future developments in the use of fibre optics, specifically Fibre Distributed Data Interface (FDDI) will also increase the level of security in terms of the cabling used.

— It is difficult to implement a consistent networking security policy. This is due to the diversity, rapidly changing environments, and dynamic interface characteristics of the LAN. Furthermore with the increased span of the network across many departments within an organisation (and sometimes across companies) there are technical and political concerns with distributed security controls. In other words how does a network manager implement a cohesive security policy across all the networking boundaries?

A lack of a specific security policy can leave the network open to many occurrences, whether malicious or accidental. One of the main problem areas is the introduction of malicious logic otherwise known as viruses, this is discussed later on. However without the relevant security policy in place throughout the whole networking environment, this type of threat cannot be successfully controlled. People could input these into the systems unwittingly by using 'pirate' software or games.

Threats

The threats to a networking environment are numerous and need to be controlled (or at least known about ie accept the risk of it occurring). Threats normally fall into two categories: unintentional (errors, equipment failures, etc) and intentional (theft, fraud, sabotage, etc). The following list is by no means exhaustive but indicates the type of intentional threat that LANs can be subjected to.

— *Illegal use of the Network*; A stand-alone PC seldom requires the need to authenticate who is using it, if you own a PC then its yours to do what you wish with. However with networks the issue of who is using it is very important. Therefore to control this type of threat you need to have some type of user authentication and access control mechanism in place. Within the LAN environment there are two types of access control mechanisms that need to be investigated and the one you use depends greatly on the type of applications that you are running on your LAN. First, there is the traditional access method used on mainframes, where access on to the network is controlled by the server via the use of passwords. However once inside the server you could implement different levels of passwords for different applications or areas of data.

This type of access method is suitable for those devices that are not going to be doing any local processing of the server data. However on a normal PC environment this is not the case and hence further security is required.

Therefore the second access method would be more suitable here. The second access method is based on distributed processing methodology. Here a two-phased access control mechanism is required. The PC is first protected, so that no one can use it without the use of another password or key to unlock the device. New technology is being developed to help in the protection of these devices, namely Smart Cards. Without the use of such a device the PC would be inoperable. For further information on Smart Cards the reader is referred to NCC Blackwell's publication *Smart Cards and Memory Cards* by Mario Devargas.

— *Passive Tapping*; Confidentiality is threatened by the passive tapping, or eavesdropping, of traffic. The degree of threat varies with the type of media used, for example, fibre optic is very difficult to tap without detection while copper wire is easier. For this reason cables should be housed within conduits. This will make accidental damage less likely and will discourage deliberate tapping.

This type of threat can be minimised by the use of encryption. Encryption provides for the protection of data from unauthorised disclosure and against message interception. The normal way of achieving this is by both parties sharing common secret cryptographic keys (algorithms) which are used for both encrypting and decrypting messages and data.

Within a local area networking environment the most common method of passive tapping can be achieved by using common LAN protocols and operating system features. For example, any workstation can listen to the LAN traffic and secretly search it for information. An attacker can also use a LAN network analyser to determine locations and identity of communications hosts and consequently attack the servers and hosts directly.

— *Active Tapping*; The threat of message modification is often referred to as an active tap. It is not as difficult to detect as passive tapping but is potentially more dangerous. An active tap is one in which the information in transit may be modified as well as extracted. This could include the alteration or deletion of part or all of the information. It can also include the insertion of new information and the re-ordering/re-routeing of messages on a network.

Active tapping can also result from the inherently insecure protocols used within the local area networking environment. Most use either logical bus or ring access methods where all the data is broadcast to everyone on the network. This assumes that only the station that is supposed to receive the data is going to read it. This means that there is no way of stopping a workstation eavesdropping.

— *Repudiation*; This threat refers to either the denial of transmission or reception, or to the fabrication of a false message by one of the parties involved in communications. This situation usually occurs when communication is between two separate organisations. For example, in an Electronic Document Interchange environment, where two companies LANs are inter-networking.

— *Denial of Service*; This is defined as the inability of the network to provide the required level of service and/or functionality. This threat can cause the loss of messages, delays or the loss of the complete network. Such a threat may come from either intentional or accidental means, from a software bug or a blown fuse, to a terrorist bomb.

There is no direct method of totally avoiding this threat. In the event of such a threat occurring a contingency plan should be put into action which restores full network services as soon as possible. Small interruptions to the network can usually be tolerated, however longer ones may only be allowed if they are planned in advance. Contingency plans will need to be invoked if the loss of service goes beyond this and will certainly be required after a major disaster.

— *Malicious or Benign Logic*; These are what are more commonly known as viruses. Benign viruses (or worms) are those that cause some disruption but no serious damage, while malicious (or malignant) viruses or trojan horses, destroy data or the integrity of the data. Viruses are software programs that are capable of replicating themselves, some include malicious code to damage its immediate environment. Trojan horses are programs which appear to be normal, performing a useful function but they also carry out some secret function.

Worms are similar to viruses and are a form of logic bomb, causing problems by generating spurious data.

Network managers must be aware that viruses represent a real threat to networking. Therefore a company must review its vulnerability to these viruses both in terms of who has access to the network and in policies governing what constitutes an acceptable source for software.

There are many viruses out today, most act on a stand-alone basis, however some are appearing that are potentially harmful to networks, for example, the MILNET virus, although not a true virus but a worm that infected over 60,000 machines. Therefore it is advisable to follow these basic rules when it comes to protecting your network against viruses:

- Test all software on an isolated machine;
- Use add-on boards and Smart technology to protect access to hard disks;
- Perform frequent back-ups, not only of the individual personal computers but of the network servers also;
- Install vaccine programs;
- *Do not* use bulletin boards if not required as part of your business need;
- *Do not* accept or allow the use of pirated software;
- Educate your users.

RISK ANALYSIS

Every local area network is different and therefore its security requirements are obviously going to be unique. To adequately examine the security requirements of a LAN, a qualified security consultant should perform a risk analysis. The ultimate purpose of risk analysis is to help in the selection of cost-effective safeguards that will reduce risks to an acceptable level. Risk analysis requires experience and knowledge which most IT personnel do not possess and therefore it is recommended, where possible, to always have a lead risk analysis specialist to conduct your network risk evaluation. However, do remember that this person cannot perform this task on their own, he/she requires the assistance of users, operations staff and most importantly senior management.

Risk analysis is the cornerstone of risk management and control. It is a procedure used to estimate potential losses that may result from network system vulnerabilities and the damage from the occurrence of certain threats. It tries to identify not only critical assets that must be protected but considers the environment as a whole.

In terms of a LAN environment risk analysis should determine how a criminal, malicious insider or act of God could cause any of the following events to occur:

— unauthorised disclosure of information via the network;

— unauthorised modification of information on the network or any device attached to it;

— denial or disruption of the network service.

Note, within the LAN environment the following risk analysis concepts should be fully understood before any analysis is undertaken:

— *Assets*; the risk analysis methodology should identify what is to be protected and its value. Assets may be classified as tangible (eg hardware, data, software) and intangible (eg Personnel, Reputation, Morale);

— *Likelihood of occurrence*; this is a measure of the probability of a loss-causing event;

— *Risk*; this is the degree of loss;

— *Safeguards*; these are physical controls, policies, mechanisms and procedures that protect assets from harm;

— *Threat*; anything that poses some danger to an asset. The occurrence of a threat may compromise the confidentiality, integrity and availability of an asset by exploiting vulnerabilities;

— *Vulnerabilities*; these are weaknesses or absence of safeguards;

— *Consequence*; refers to the undesirable result of a threat's action against the asset which results in measurable loss.

By using practical examples and experience of past occurrences it should be clear where and what vulnerabilities exist within a LAN environment. However even risk analysis cannot be totally accurate as other threats and vulnerabilities may occur after the analysis has been done.

Risk analysis should take into account all the possible areas of the business that could affect the LAN environment, for example, physical security, personnel security, information security and of course communications security. Each area should be evaluated taking into account every possible threat.

Risk analysis takes its starting point from the assumption that a risk-free local area network environment is impossible. Therefore risks must be managed. A risk is any problem or failure stemming from a perceived or known threat against perceived and known system vulnerabilities. The qualification of risks is one of the necessary activities in determining which threats should be controlled. Therefore risk analysis classifies those network risks stemming from various activities, which impact on the confidentiality, integrity and availability of the network itself. The risk analysis procedure supplies information on how to manage the risks and the most cost-effective applications of countermeasures.

The risk analysis process described in Figure 6.1 covers all the steps that must be carried out in order to accomplish the complete management of most security threats. The first step is to define and logically separate the network into different components, for example, hardware, software, communications and peripherals. This is achieved by

Risk Analysis 169

analysing the whole environment in terms of assets, safeguards and threats, as shown in Figure 6.2.

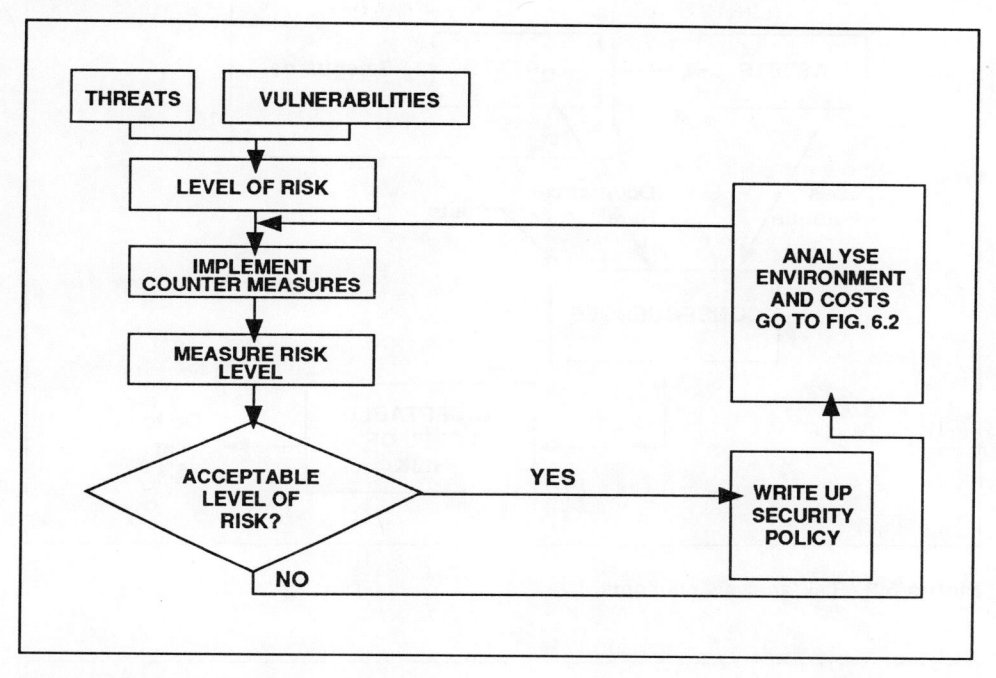

Figure 6.1 The risk analysis process

Then we define the potential threat against each network component. Note that some threats may be insignificant and if so we must assume that the threat is unimportant and accept it if it occurs. Once the threats to the local area network are identified (some are described in Figure 6.3), they can be classified in terms of its impact on the network and on the business as a whole.

As you classify the component's vulnerability to a specific threat you also determine the degree of risk associated to it. Hence if for example, you feel that having a dial-up modem connection to the LAN is a highly vulnerable area you then ascertain if this is also a high risk area. If so by combining both figures you can then determine the severity of the threat and its occurrence.

With this information you can then plan how you are going to implement the required countermeasures. The main aim is to reduce or even eliminate an identified risk. Countermeasures fall into three categories: access control (eg locks, passwords, IDs, biometric techniques), accountability (eg audit trails, monitoring line traffic, password administration) and continuity of service (back-up power supplies, contingency against natural disasters, communications contigency like alternate routeing, redundant communications paths and so on).

170 *Local Area Network Security*

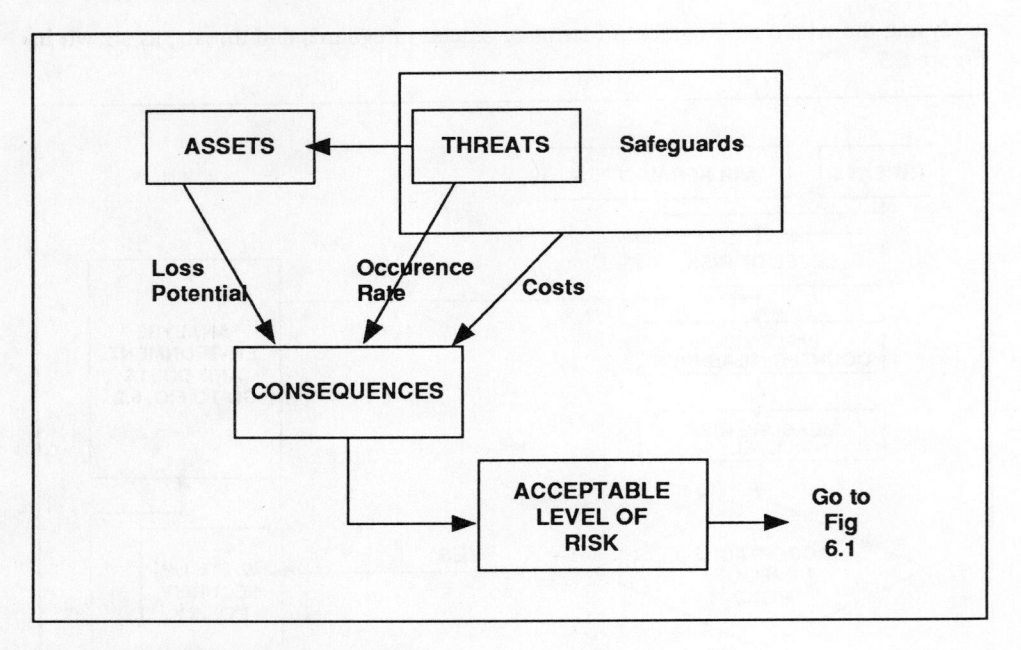

Figure 6.2 Risk analysis concerns

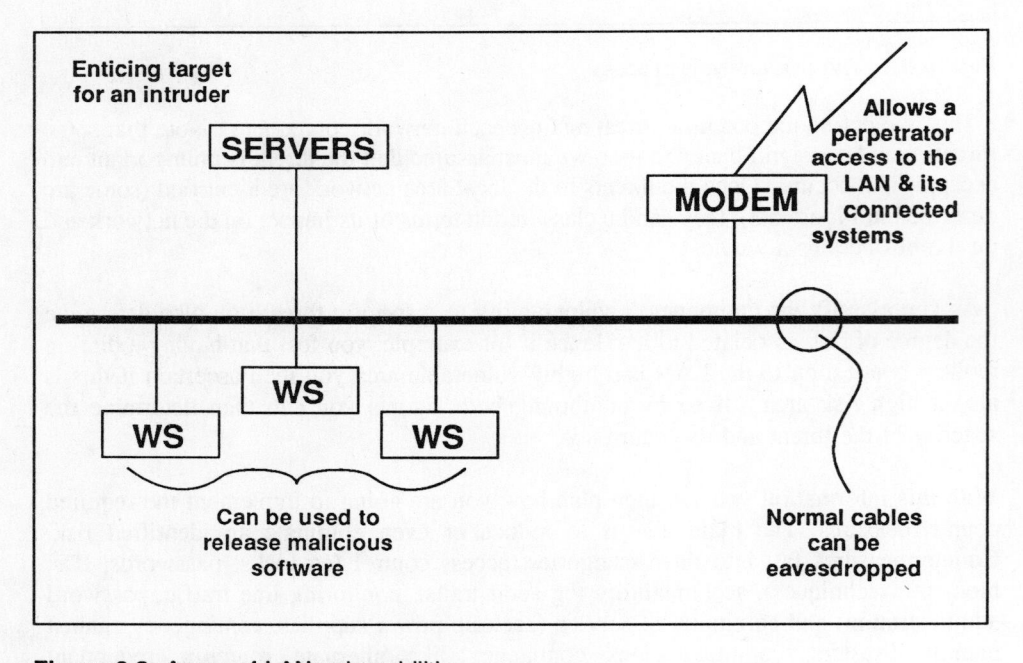

Figure 6.3 Areas of LAN vulnerabilities

CONCLUSIONS

The need for security is well known to everyone, however this does not mean that everyone is as security conscious as they should be. It is a well-known fact that human nature is usually averse to rules and regulations and therefore will always try to find a way of getting around them. The usual occurrence is to find some excuse to explain why you would break a rule, for example, it is impeding your work or would be too expensive to implement.

Security within the IT arena encompasses three main areas of vulnerability, the loss of confidentiality, integrity and availability. In order to protect these three elements *good security mechanisms* and *user awareness* are a must against any would-be malicious network hacker or network misuser. However the process of securing local area networks is not a trivial one and requires the complete commitment from management and every network user. Time, effort and money are required, although the level of each is totally dependent on each individual network and business environment.

There are some security mechanisms that can be used throughout the industry to safeguard a local area network environment against some of the threats discussed in this chapter. For example, in terms of confidentiality — encryption, routeing control and traffic padding are techniques that can be used to safeguard your data, connection and traffic flow. While in terms of integrity — encryption, digital signatures and check-sum algorithms can be used to protect data, connections and access to the system, while also facilitating a mechanism for authentication. For the larger networks, especially in terms of inter-networking into WANs, the use of a Notarisation Agent is useful to ensure non-repudiation of data sent or received.

TERMS TO REVIEW

Sage the Owl Recommends

- User Awareness
- Confidentiality
- Integrity
- Availability
- Security Policy
- Security Responsibility
- Classification of Information
- Disciplinary Measures
- Computer Misuse Act
- Risk Analysis
- Contingency
- LAN Exposures
- LAN Vulnerabilities
- LAN Threats
- Illegal use of the Network
- Passive Tapping
- Active Tapping
- Repudiation
- Denial of Service
- Viruses.

7
The Standards Situation

INTRODUCTION

Local area networks may still not appear to be one of the most promising areas to standardise. After all, one of the early attractions of local networking was the desire to provide a communications technique which was free from the constraints typical of normal telecommunications. Computing as a whole has not been a very successful area for standards. Generally the standards that have been agreed have followed many years behind the products and have therefore been modelled upon the market leader as much as possible for there to be any chance of them succeeding. Possibly with this past experience of computer standards in mind, attention was turned to standards for local area networks very soon after it was realised that products would soon be flooding on to the market.

Both the suppliers of local area networks, computer equipment and electronic office products, and their customers stood to benefit from early standards. Buyers did not want to install a local area network only to find that a limited number of items of hardware could be used with it because the suppliers of the network provided the wrong interface, or that manufacturers of the equipment which would be attached to it had not designed the necessary hardware and software. Customers have bought and will buy local area networks which have the greatest support amongst all the relevant suppliers.

Suppliers of computer and office equipment were keen to support standards for local area networks because they wished to avoid the development of a large and expensive set of interfaces to enable their products to be used with each network on the market.

The Xerox Corporation in the US was one of the first to develop both a local area networking technique (Ethernet) and some products for the office environment which use it. To help Ethernet become widely accepted, and to protect research investment, Xerox allied itself with two other companies (DEC and Intel) with different markets who were also in a position to benefit from the widespread use of local area networks. During 1980 this consortium produced Ethernet specifications which were made generally available to any other manufacturer. Shortly afterwards, the Institute of Electrical and Electronic Engineers (IEEE) in the US decided to put their weight behind a standardisation effort for local area networking. Naturally much of the input came from Xerox, DEC and Intel but other interested parties became involved.

This was known as the 802 Committee and consisted of nine working groups 802.1–9 (recently an extra group has been established which deals with LAN Security – 802.10). In 1985 the 802 Committee issued a set of four Standards (802.2, 802.3, 802.4 and 802.5) which were subsequently adopted by ANSI the American National Standard. Two of the four were later adopted by the National Bureau of Standards to constitute the Federal Information Processing Standards (FIPS 107).

When the ISO were ready to look at LAN standards, IEEE documents were mature enough to form the basis of their discussion. This discussion was concerned not only with the basic data transport mechanism but also with the applications using networks and their services which are needed to support them. In particular, one of the aims of the Open Systems Interconnection work was to ensure that a network of computer-based equipment from a number of different suppliers could be successfully put together. In this aspect the project has much in common with the aims of the designers of local area networks.

LAN STANDARD MAKING BODIES

There are two major international standards-making bodies, ISO (the International Standards Organisation) and CCITT (the International Consultative Committee for Telephones and Telegraphy). In broad terms, ISO is responsible for data processing standards and CCITT is responsible for recommending standards in public telecommunications. The CCITT does not have any direct influence in the LAN arena, although they do influence future developments into communications as a whole.

ISO (International Standards Organisation)

ISO was founded in 1947 and consists of various voluntary, non-governmental organisations and representative national standards bodies (eg the British Standards Institution (BSI) and the American National Standards Institute (ANSI)) of more than 60 countries. In addition other organisations (such as CCITT) have observer status.

The ISO Head Office address is:

> 1 rue de Varembe
> Case Postale 56
> CH-1211 Geneva 20
> Switzerland
> Tel: + 41 22 34 12 40

IEEE (Institute of Electrical and Electronic Engineers)

IEEE is a US professional publishing and standards body responsible for many of the standards governing LANs. It functions under the auspices of ANSI.

Its address is:

>10662 Los Vaqueros Circle
>Los Alamitos
>CA 90720
>USA
>Tel: + 1 714 821 8380

There are a number of advantages and disadvantages to the standard making process. Its main advantage is that it assures there will be a large market for a particular piece of hardware or software. Hence this encourages mass production leading to a reduction in price. A further advantage is that it allows products from multiple vendors (the OSI philosophy) to communicate and hence give the end-user the flexibility to choose any vendor for his network.

However a disadvantage with standards is that the technology stagnates. By the time a standard is developed, reviewed, discussed and finally accepted a more efficient technology is probably already available.

IEEE STANDARDS WORK

In February 1980 The American Institute of Electrical and Electronic Engineers (IEEE) Computer Society, formed its Local Network Standards Committee, Project 802. A document was published which set out the scope of the standards work. Figure 7.1 shows the basic form of the model used to describe a local area network and the associated parts of the system connected to it. It was intended that the standards should define the physical interfaces and services listed below:

— The service provided by the Link Layer L to the upper layers (generally defined by the OSI reference model).

— The data link protocol (L <----> L).

— The interface between the Link Layer and the Physical Layer P' in the attached device.

— The signalling protocol between the attached device and the Medium Access Unit (P'P).

176 The Standards Situation

— The physical interface P'P between the attached device and the Medium Access Unit.

— A protocol P'P.

— A signalling protocol P'P.

— The physical interface to the medium itself, ie the way the actual cable is tapped.

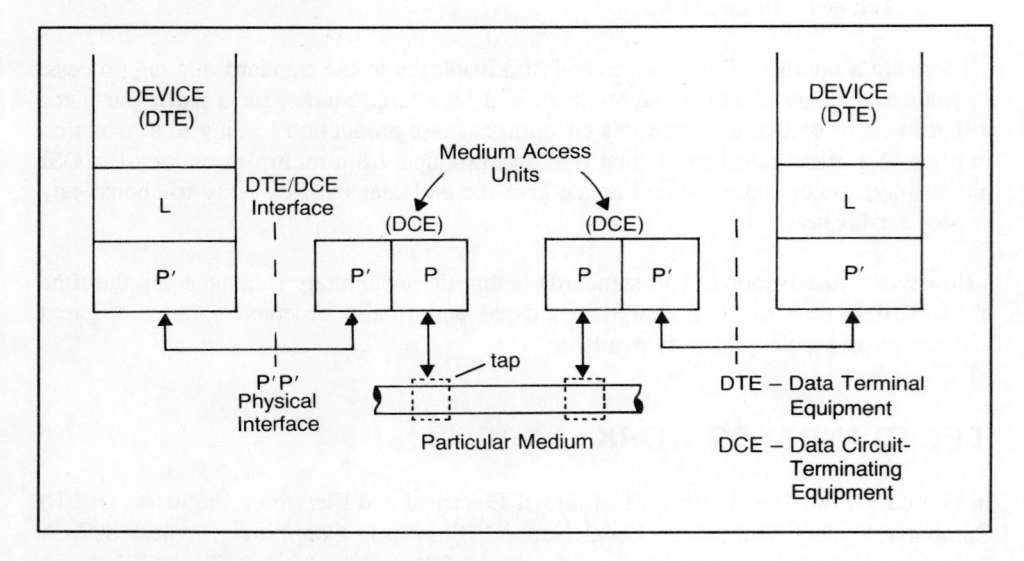

Figure 7.1 IEEE model for local area networks

The overall objective of the IEEE Local Network Standard is to promote compatibility between equipment made by different manufacturers such that data communications can take place between equipment with minimum effort on the part of the users or the builders of a system containing the equipment.

The standard is intended to be applicable to many different environments, topologies, applications and services. The standard is also intended to be used with most computer-based devices.

One important aim of the work is to insulate the end-user and the attached device from the particular characteristics (topology, access mechanism and medium) of the underlying network. How this is achieved will be discussed later.

The Committee is divided into three subcommittees:

- *Media* — the media subcommittee is concerned with the physical media used by the networks, the characteristics of the data being transported, the details of the Physical Layer and its interface to the Data Link Layer.

- *Data Link and Media Access Control (DLMAC)* — the DLMAC subcommittee is concerned with the data link protocols, the control protocols used in accessing the physical media (including addressing and framing) and the interfaces to the Physical and Network Layers.

- *High-Level Interface* — the High-Level Interface subcommittee is working on the higher level protocols used by the attached devices and is matching the particular requirements of a local area network with the five upper layers of the OSI model.

The whole set of protocols, interfaces and services correspond as far as possible with the architecture set out in the ISO Open Systems Interconnection Reference Model — *see* Figure 7.4.

The IEEE categorises LANs by the following:

- generally privately owned;
- moderate geographical coverage (anything up to 20km);
- moderate/high data rates (1 — 100 Mbps);
- low error rates (roughly 1 in 100 or 1000 in million);
- there is no restriction on the topology used;
- small transmission delays (10s of milliseconds).

Initially, the general structure used by the IEEE in defining the standards is described in Figure 7.2, and the functions of the various layers were as follows:

- *Network Layer* — this layer is primarily concerned with providing a media and access mechanism independent interface to the upper layers in the architecture of the attached device. Its other function is to decide on the route the packets of data will follow on the next stage of their journey. This is especially relevant where the device concerned is a gateway, a multiplexer or a message- or packet-switch.

- *Multi-link Sub-layer* — this layer is an optional part of the Data Link Layer and it applies to devices which support more than one link protocol, eg a switch or a gateway.

178 *The Standards Situation*

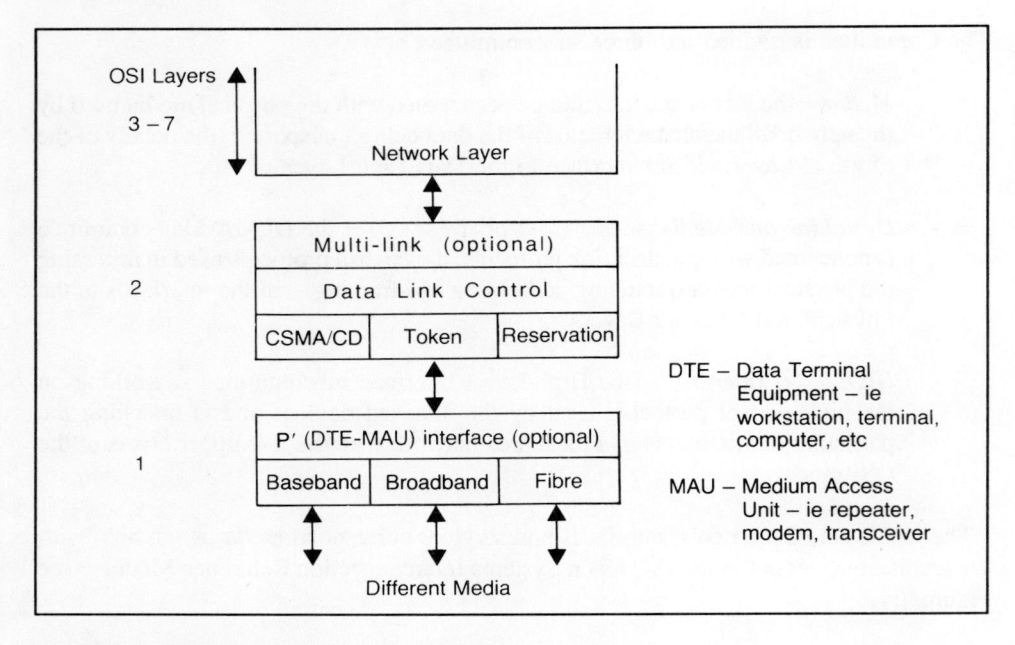

Figure 7.2 IEEE local area network structure

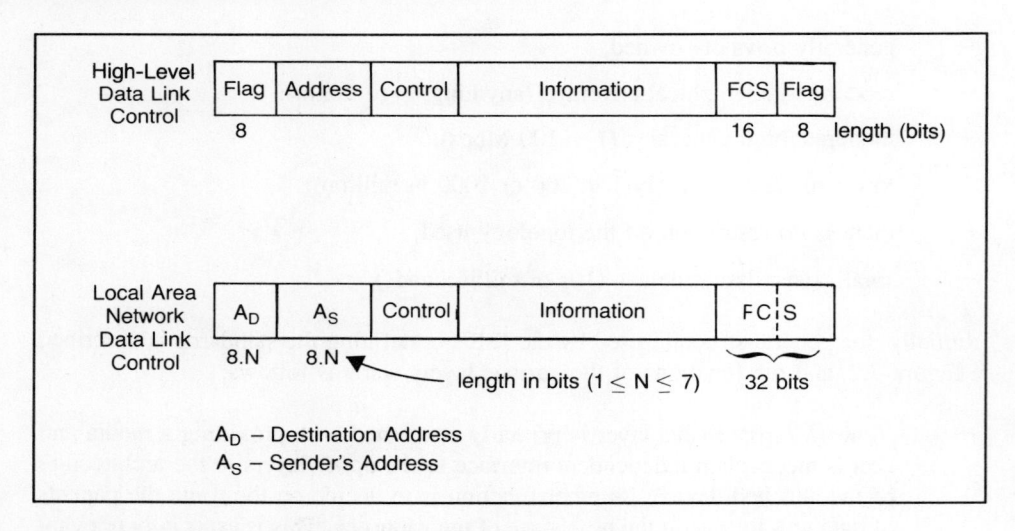

Figure 7.3 Comparison of HDLC and local network frames

— *Data Link Control Sub-Layer* — this is the part of the Data Link Layer which provides the usual data link protocol functions of framing, addressing, formatting, etc, in a form independent of the access mechanism, topology and physical medium in use.

Although HDLC was specified as the standard to aim for, it was realised that in a local network some alterations would be necessary, but the same overall function and method of operation as HDLC have been retained. Figure 7.3 shows the HDLC and the Local Network Data Link Control (LNDLC) frames. Note that LNDLC does not need to use delimiting flags since the frame preamble and carrier used on local networks are sufficient to delimit the frame. Also, because some local network access techniques require detection of collisions, the frame check (FCS) field can be twice as long to improve error detection. In addition the source and destination addresses are both needed. Further levels of addressing are possible by means of group and broadcast address bits in the ordinary address fields.

- *CSMA-CD, Token and Reservation Access Sub-Layer* — the media access sub-layer has parts which are specific to the different techniques used. CSMA/CD is applicable only to bus topology, but token access can be used on buses or rings, although work has concentrated on the bus. Both CSMA/CD and token access techniques have been described in detail elsewhere in this book.

- *P' Interface to the Medium Access Unit* — the Medium Access Unit (MAU) is the device responsible for transmitting and receiving frames of data on the medium. It generally consists of two parts: a transceiver/coupler/modem and a cable tap. This sub-layer is optional, only being needed when the transceiver is not integrated into the DTE (ie the attached device). In the case where it is integrated, no explicit external interface at this point is required.

- *P Interfaces* — of the possible media specified, interest has been concentrated on baseband coaxial cable. The methods of interfacing to the different media vary so much that one single interface is not possible.

The IEEE work began by concentrating on the CSMA/CD technique because of the very considerable experience which was available in using Ethernet, but it soon became evident that this had too little general support in the computer community for it to become a general standard. It was agreed that CSMA/CD was simple to implement and performed well under light loads, but it had the problem that no maximum time for access could be guaranteed which made it unsuitable for high-priority devices in critical situations (eg process control). This, together with the other problems of limited network size, packet length, and difficulty in pinpointing defects in the network, led to the adoption of an alternative standard, token passing.

It may seem strange that a standard should include two totally different and incompatible options, but such was the pressure from both sets of adherents that this was found to be the only possible option. It also reflects rather vividly the range of uses possible for local area networks and the inability of a single system to serve all the needs.

180 The Standards Situation

Token passing does not limit the maximum size of the packets, and it is very suitable for critical situations in which a node must be guaranteed access to the network. it is, however, much more complex to implement.

Although the CSMA/CD option of the IEEE work was based on Ethernet it has diverged from the Ethernet specification originally published.

Since this specification was defined in the early days of the IEEE model, the following four standards have been identified and approved by the 802 committee:

— *802.2 Logical Link Control* — this deals with the end-to-end protocol and is required to discipline the exchanges that take place between two communicating devices.

— *802.3 CSMA/CD Networks* — although some still call this the Ethernet Standard, there are enough differences from this industry standard to render it somewhat incompatible. The standard specifies a bus topology with CSMA/CD medium access control imposed upon each node. It also describes the physical specification of the LAN and therefore tries to provide a choice of implementation at this level. At present, the following options are available:

- 10BASE5 (original Ethernet coaxial cable)
- 10BASE2 (Cheapernet thin coaxial cable)
- 10BROAD36 (Broadband Ethernet CATV cable)
- 1BASE5 (StarLan unshielded twisted-pair cable)

— *802.4 Token Bus Networks* — this standard was mainly developed to support Manufacturing Automation Protocol (MAP). It uses broadband CATV techniques and operates from 1 to 10 Mbps.

— *802.5 Token Ring Networks* — IBM's primary thrust into the LAN market. This standard specifies a low-speed ring topology operating at 4 Mbps over twisted- pair or coaxial cable. The standard can also operate at 16 Mbps.

Work is still progressing within the other groups for future LAN standards. Figure 7.4 describes the other 802 subcommittees and their responsibilities. Figure 7.5 describes how the IEEE model fits into the OSI model which we shall discuss in the next section. It is worth noting that ISO used this model as their starting point and skeleton for their subsequent model.

OPEN SYSTEMS INTERCONNECTION

The ideal situation with regard to communications between computers and associated devices is that each should be able to send understandable messages to any other

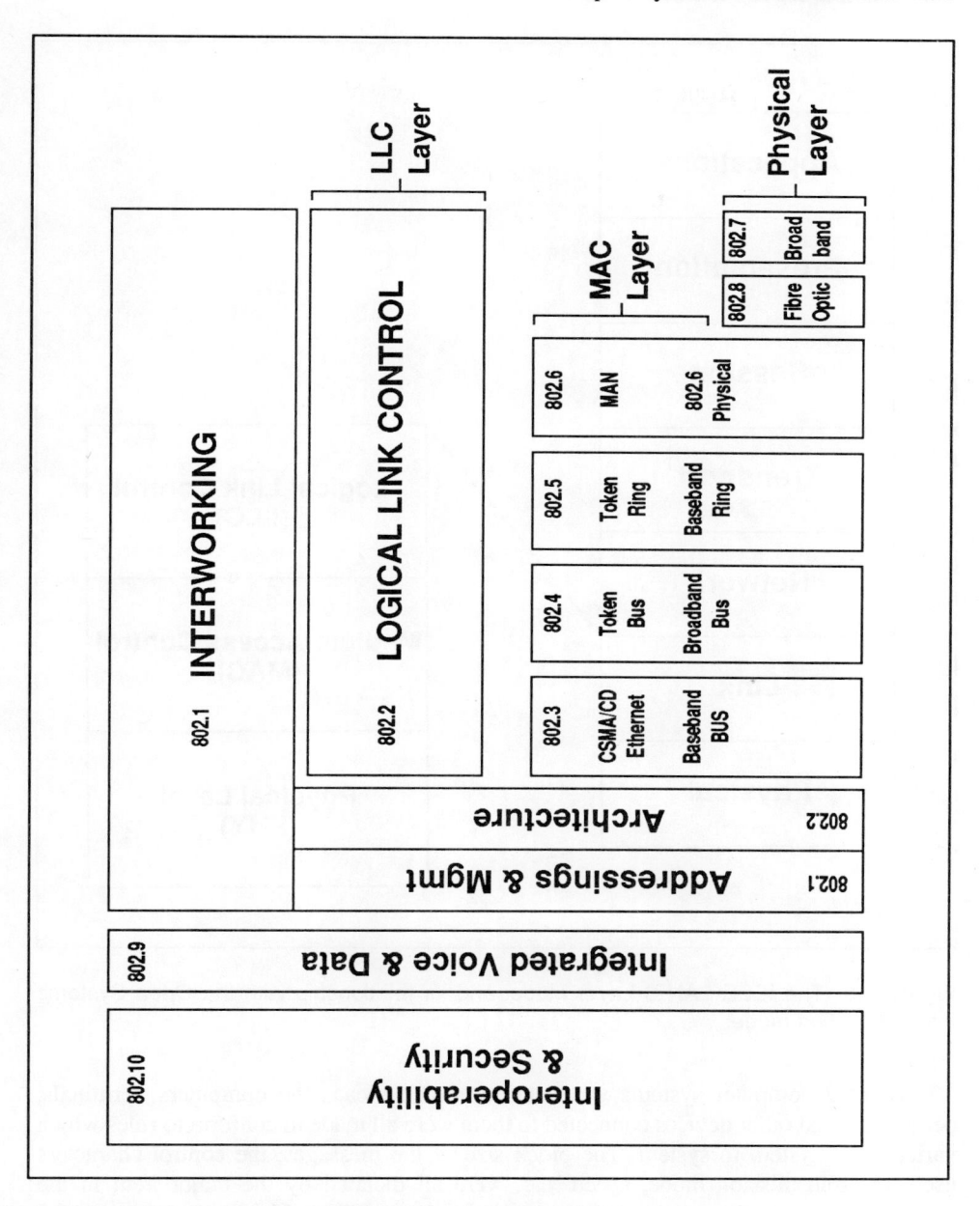

Figure 7.4 IEEE subcommittees and their responsibilities

regardless of the make or internal design of the devices involved. Until recently this has been practically impossible but the current work on open systems interconnection standards aims to rectify the situation.

182 *The Standards Situation*

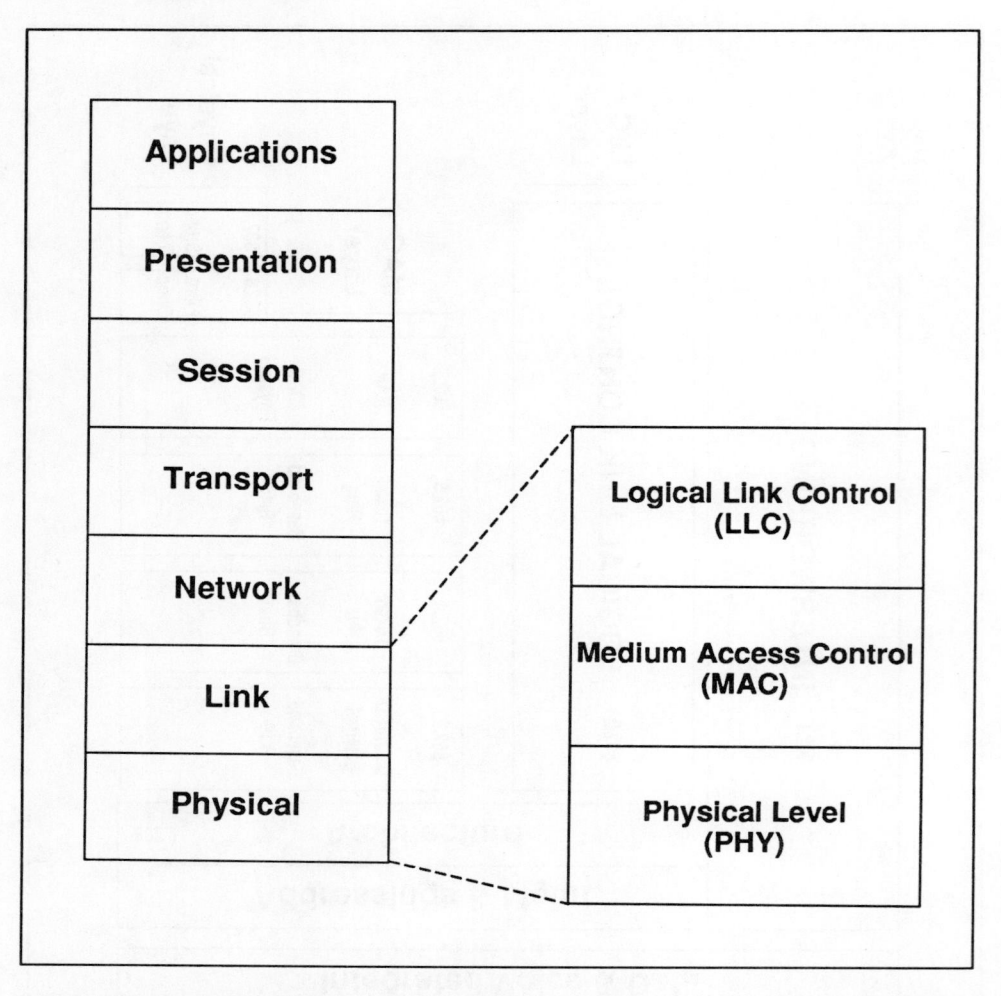

| Applications |
| Presentation |
| Session |
| Transport |
| Network |
| Link |
| Physical |

| Logical Link Control (LLC) |
| Medium Access Control (MAC) |
| Physical Level (PHY) |

Figure 7.5 The IEEE LAN 3 Layer Model and its relationship with the Open Systems Interconnection model

Traditional computer systems were closed, which means the computers, terminals, peripherals and other devices connected to them were all made to conform to rules which varied from system to system. The block size of the messages, the control characters used, the transmission mode, speed, etc, were all dictated by the major item in the system. Frequently these parameters were set by the supplier, although in a few special cases a user would design his own communications software. The situation was acceptable in the case where all the users and devices involved belonged to the same organisation, and where a limited choice of hardware was involved. Now more computing devices are being purchased by a wider range of users than ever before, many more new makes of computer are being put on the market, more office and industrial equipment incorporates computing devices than before, and interconnection of equipment is more important.

Another important factor contributing to the trend towards computing with communications is the development in the past few years of public digital networks. Thus, connections between devices on the network need not be permanent or semi-permanent. At one moment a terminal can be interacting with one computer, and at the next moment, without anyone having to physically change any wiring, the same terminal could be sending data to another computer on the network. Under these circumstances, each device on the network has the potential for being accessible (ie open) to every other using the network.

Openness implies no technical hindrances to the exchange of information, but any system is quite capable of imposing its own means of limiting access to only selected systems and users. Openness, in this sense, is new to computing although in many other areas, such as the telephone service, the concept is accepted and well understood.

If users of computing devices are going to make full use of the opportunities for interconnection then open agreements are needed, not just at the level of being able to interface to the network, but also at the level of being able to exchange information. Agreements on the symbols, formats and sequences to use for messages are needed. Thus, the essential requirement of open systems working is a set of standards for communications protocols at all levels.

This utopian communications and interworking world brings with it several advantages both to the users of IT systems and to the vendors.

The users benefit as:

— all products from different vendors conform to the same standard, hence they have a greater choice;

— no single vendor architecture will be forced upon them;

— products purchases will be based on their merit for the application rather than whether they interface with their existing equipment;

— improvements in communications can lead to increased distribution of, and access to, information.

The benefits to the vendor are:

— a widening of their potential sales market;

— fewer development risks and expenditure;

184 *The Standards Situation*

— the use of their existing research and development budget in other areas that could possibly benefit them more. If before they had to spend resources on developing interfaces they will not need to do this now as in theory their equipment should interface with other vendor's products.

Interworking

Interconnection allows two or more users to be connected together in order to exchange data, but interworking demands that these users agree to observe the same rules in order that they may understand the data and can co-operate to perform some task.

Three essential ingredients are needed for two or more computer terminals or other network users to be able to interwork:

— *A physical data transmission network to which all participating subscribers can connect* — the purpose of a data transmission network is to transmit data reliably, and preferably also cheaply and quickly, between partners. It should be easy to use and should not involve the user in complex procedures for interfacing to it. Local area networks are an example of this.

— *Compatible dialogues* — each user of the data network should be able to understand what his partner is saying. To do this, each must adopt the same conventions (protocols).

— *Applications* — within the typical office or factory it is very unlikely that all the terminals, workstations, computers, printers, etc, will be made by the same company, and yet all must be used together. In the wider context, personnel records, purchasing and planning systems, for example, may be implemented by each of the individual divisions of the organisation, but they need to be interconnected for corporate planning and other purposes.

Interworking requirements can be roughly divided or layered into processing-oriented functions and communications-oriented functions (*see* Figure 7.6). The processing-oriented functions are concerned with the ability of two systems to exchange information and to understand it. The rules required to achieve this co-operation are called high level protocols. The communications-oriented functions are concerned with the use of physical data transmission networks and the rules associated with its use are the low-level protocols.

The Open Systems Interconnection 7 Layer Reference Model

The basic model for Open Systems Interconnection has been developed by the International Organisation for Standardisation (ISO). Using it, Open Systems Interconnection (OSI) can be defined as:

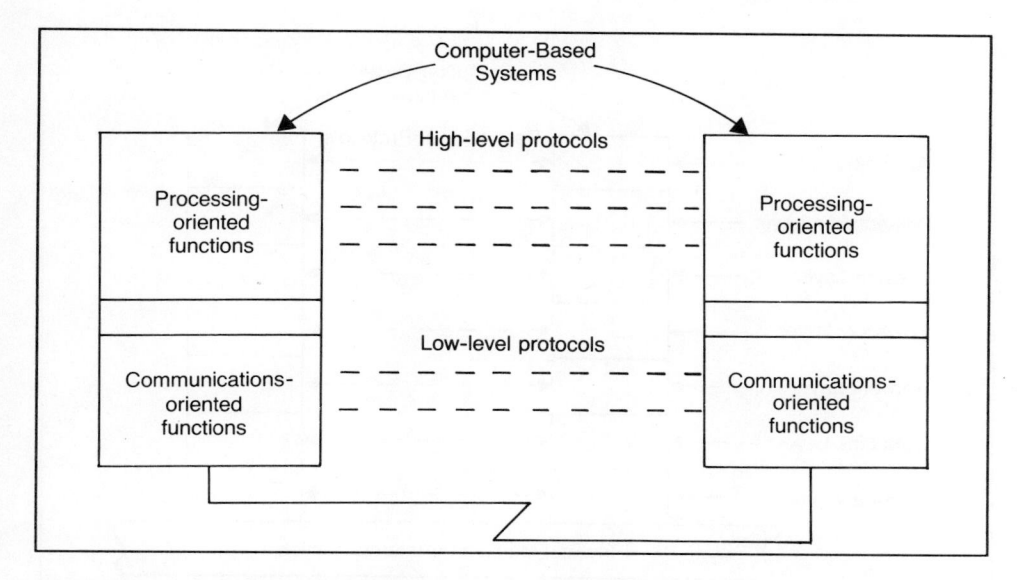

Figure 7.6 Layering computer communications systems

"standardised procedures for the exchange of information among systems which are accessible to one another for this purpose by virtue of their mutual use of these procedures".

The purpose of OSI is for any one user of a communications network to be able to communicate and work with any other. Ideally each one should not need to know the technical characteristics (eg computer types) of any other. All he really needs to know is that the others observe the same conventions.

The Reference Model of OSI was developed to provide a common basis for the coordination of standards development in the area, while allowing existing standards to be placed in perspective. It is intended that the model should provide a common reference for maintaining consistency of all related Standards. The model does not define precisely the services and protocols of the interconnection architecture but it does identify the areas where such Standards should exist.

The idea of layering was introduced in the discussion of high- and low-level protocols to divide up the interworking model into processing- and communications-oriented functions. The ISO Reference Model for OSI (shown in Figure 7.7) uses seven layers to simplify the work of defining all the protocols and services required for interworking. This allowed separate teams of experts to work independently on developing standards for each layer.

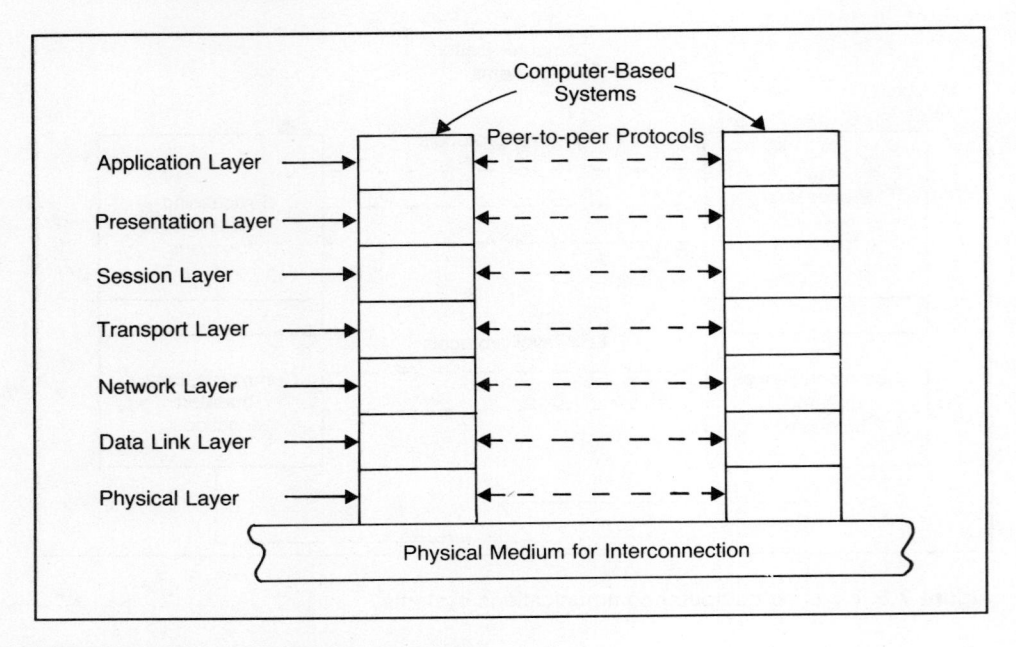

Figure 7.7 OSI 7 Layer Reference Model

Each layer is as self-contained as possible and, in defining its functions only the interfaces to the immediately adjacent layers, together with the services provided by the lower layers, need to be known.

Two users, in separate systems but in the same layer, communicate with each other using protocols appropriate to their layer (the peer-to-peer protocols). It appears to them that they are conversing directly but in fact they are using the lower layers to achieve this.

Referring again to Figure 7.7, the physical medium which joins the two systems (shown diagrammatically at the base of the figure) needs explanation. Examples are the public telephone network, leased lines or a public switched data network. The boundary in these cases is the CCITT defined boundary between the data circuit terminating equipment (a modem for example) and the data terminal equipment (the subscriber's computer or terminal). The Physical Medium could also be a local area network. Any combination of public or private network can be used to interconnect open systems.

Briefly the functions of each of the Layers are as follows.

Physical Layer

This provides the means to interface to the physical medium, and the way to control its use. Note that this Layer is entirely independent of the actual physical medium used, be it copper, coaxial, etc. Figure 7.8 below shows how this is achieved.

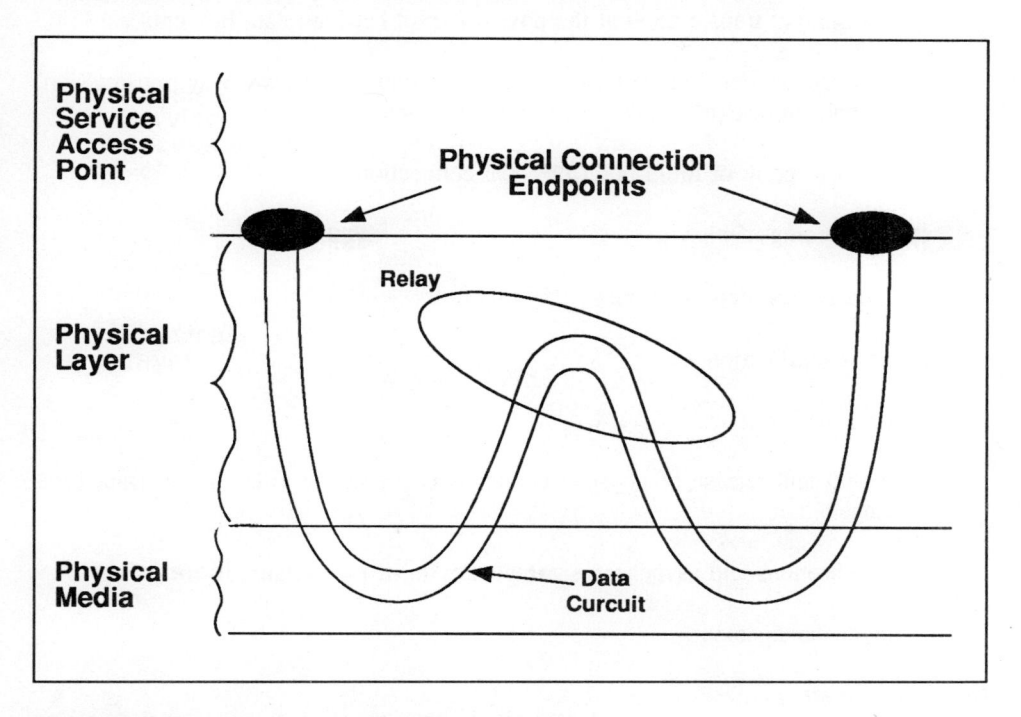

Figure 7.8 The use of relay at the Physical Layer

The Physical Layer deals with the bits received from and passed up to the Data Link Layer. It may provide a multiplexing function for multiple data links over a single physical medium.

The standards in the area pre-date the OSI model and are divided into four areas:

— Mechanical, such as type of connector, physical dimensions, allocation of pins, etc;

— Electrical, such as voltage levels, etc;

— Functional, such as the meaning of defined voltage levels on certain wires;

— Procedural, these are the rules that apply to the various functions and the sequence in which certain events may occur.

Hence in summary the Physical Layer provides the following functions.

188 *The Standards Situation*

To the layer above, the Data Link Layer:

— transparent transmission at the physical level between data link entities;

— physical service data units, ie full-duplex (simultaneous two-way transmission) or half-duplex (transmission one way at a time);

— point-to-point or multi-point physical connections;

— sequencing of bits;

— data circuit identification;

— error notification.

To itself:

— set-up and release of physical connections between entities in the Data Link Layer;

— synchronous and asynchronous transmission of bit streams;

— layer management.

Data Link Layer

In recognising that physical transmission media are subject to random faults and noises, data link protocols were introduced some time ago to enable transmission errors to be detected and corrected. High-Level Data Link Control (HDLC) is a typical example. The Data Link Layer of the ISO model is concerned with these functions. This Layer shields the higher layers from the characteristics of the physical medium, providing an error-free data link connection.

In order to achieve its objectives, the following functions are provided.

To the layer above, the Network Layer:

— one or more transparent data link connections between two entities;

— Data Link Service data units, ie the exchange of frames of data;

— sequencing of frames of data;

— error detection and notification;

— flow control (from layer above through to lower layer).

To itself:

—   set-up and release of Data Link connections;

—   Data Link Service data unit mapping;

—   Data Link connection splitting, ie divides the transmission into several physical connections;

—   synchronisation and sequence control;

—   error detection and recovery;

—   layer management.

Network Layer

This layer is required to provide a transparent means of exchanging data between systems using the network. In particular it performs the routeing, relaying and switching operations associated with establishing and operating a logical connection between networked systems. The Network Layer also performs the very valuable gateway function of linking two separate networks when these are being used to connect two end systems. Figure 7.9 shows how this is achieved. Each intermediate system may be a network in its own right and a set of one or more intermediate networked systems used for a connection is termed a sub-network.

The network service provided to the layer above, the Transport Layer, which is the user, functions as two logical queues in the connection-oriented mode of operation. Objects are placed in the queue at one end and removed from the other end. The objects include various actions, for example, status information or actual data being transmitted. The following functions are also provided to the layer above:

—   network addresses;

—   the means of transferring data between transport entities and the identification of end-points;

—   network services data units, the exchange of packets of data;

—   error detection and notification;

—   sequencing of packets of data;

—   flow control.

190 The Standards Situation

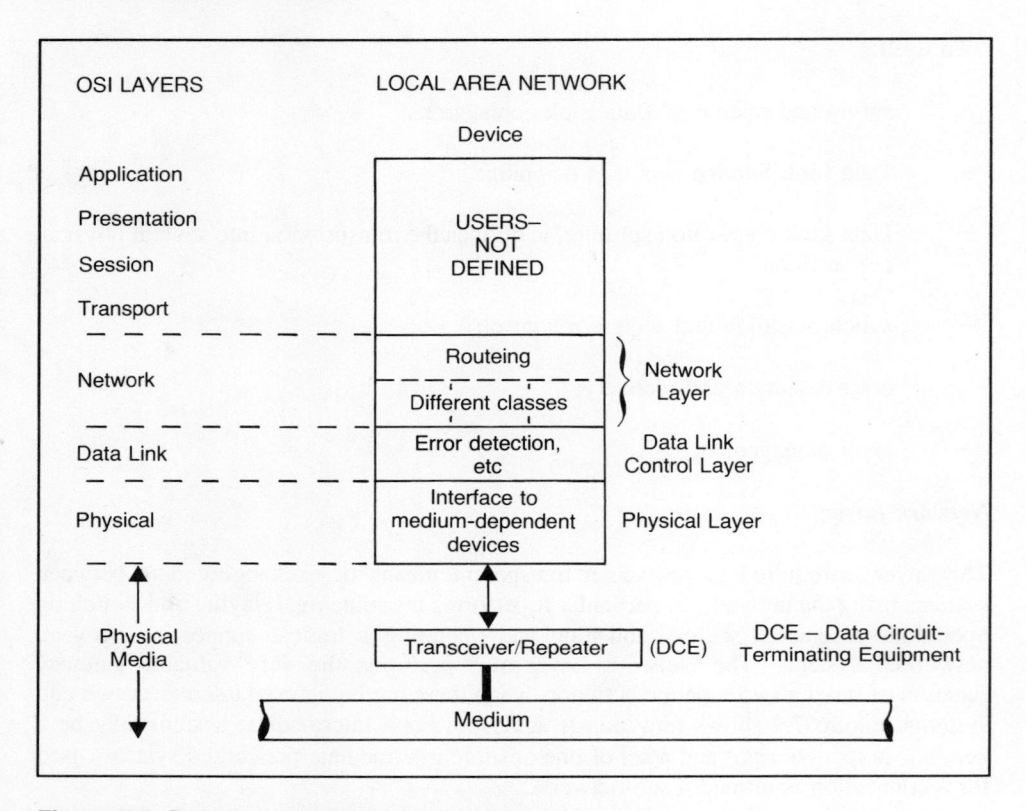

Figure 7.9 Reference model for local area networks

To itself:

— routeing and relaying;

— network connections and multiplexing;

— sequencing and blocking of data units for the purpose of facilitating the transfer;

— error detection and recovery;

— flow control and management.

Transport Layer

The Transport Layer provides, in association with the layers below it, a universal transport service which is independent of the physical medium in use. Users of the transport service request a particular class and quality of service and the Transport Layer is responsible for optimising the available resources to provide this service.

There are five classes of transport mechanisms available:

—   Class 0, this is the simple class with no enhancements to the Network Service;
—   Class 1, adds basic error recovery services;
—   Class 2, adds multiplexing capabilities;
—   Class 3, has both error recovery and multiplexing capabilities;
—   Class 4, this is the error detection and recovery class.

The quality is concerned with data transfer rate, residual errors and associated features, whilst the classes cover the various different types of traffic which diverse applications require (eg batch and transaction processing).

The following functions are provided to the layer above, the Session Layer:

—   transport connections are established between session entities identified by the transport addresses;

—   provides data transfer in accordance with agreed quality quidelines;

—   provides the facility for a session to release a transport connection.

To itself:

—   establishment of connection. It determines whether to multiplex or split the transmission, what the optimum transport protocol data unit size is and what are the transport addresses;

—   data transfer. This is a combination of distinct transmission functions like, sequencing, blocking, flow control, error detection, etc;

—   release of the data from one OSI environment to another.

Session Layer

The Session Layer (which can be thought of as the user interface into the network) establishes logical communication paths between applications wishing to exchange data. These two applications form a liaison for this purpose, called a session. The background to its name is clearly the concept of a 'terminal session' in the time-sharing environment.

The Session Layer maintains this liaison and ensures that data reaching a system is routed to the correct application. It also ensures that the information exchanged is correctly synchronised and delimited so that, for example, two applications do not try to transmit to each other simultaneously unless full-duplex working is allowed. Close

192 *The Standards Situation*

liaison with the transport layer below it, is essential at all times as Session Addresses must be converted to its equivalent transport address to enable a transport connection to be made.

The Session Layer is also responsible for managing the interaction between the presentation entities. In order to do this it provides the following functions to the layer above, the Presentation Layer:

— the creation of a session connection, so that two presentation entities can communicate between themselves;

— manages the release of a session in an orderly manner. This allows the presentation entities to release a session connection without the loss of data;

— the means of transferring data unit between presentation entities;

— flow control, managing the presentation entities in terms of whose turn it is to transmit information;

— error detection and recovery services;

— session connection synchronisation, where two presentation entities need to be synchronised in order to understand each other.

To itself:

— mapping and management of each session;

— the Transport Layer's flow control function is used for internal flow control management;

— connection recovery and release with the loss of data.

Presentation Layer

This performs a two-way function of taking information from applications and converting it into a form suitable for common understanding (ie not machine dependent), and also presenting the data exchanged between systems to the applications in a form they can understand. The layer provides services which can give independence of character representation (eg the data structure), command format and, most importantly, independence of machine characteristics.

This layer is concerned exclusively with the syntax (ie the representation of the data) and not with its semantics (ie its meaning to the Application Layer). In order to achieve this it provides the following functions to the layer above, the Application Layer:

—   transformation of syntax;

—   selection of appropriate syntax used in different application entities.

To itself:

—   acknowledges Session requests and passes on to the Application Layer;

—   searches its internal domain for the right syntax and once it has found the appropriate one it uses it to transfer the data.

Application Layer

The highest layer within the ISO Reference Model is concerned with supporting the applications which exchange information with others. Many different types of applications are relevant to OSI, from terminal to computer transaction processing to interconnected real-time process control programs. Some of the protocols associated with this layer will be concerned with particular types of application, others will be for general application support.

Since this is the highest layer in the OSI model it therefore does not provide a service to a defined layer above, however it does provide the following services to the applications themselves:

—   identifies who the communications entities are by name, address and description;

—   determines if peer partners are ready to communicate;

—   authenticates peer partners;

—   synchronises the communications between peer partners;

—   before transmission begins between two entities it defines who is reponsible for what, ie., error recovery, flow control, data integrity, syntax used, etc.

ISO WORK ON LOCAL AREA NETWORKS

The ISO has concentrated much of its effort in computer communications on Open Systems Interconnection and related protocols, including the HDLC protocol for data links. Most of the work has been in ensuring that the OSI Reference Model can accommodate the different requirements of local networking.

The OSI Reference Model was conceived as a model for computer networking primarily in the point-to-point or packet-switched situation. When applied to the local networking concept some modifications are required. One major difference between a local network and a traditional computer network is that in the former case blocks of information may be delivered to a destination from a number of different sources within a short time interval. The OSI Reference Model is generally built around the assumption that the sender and receiver of a block of information will first of all enter into an agreement about exchanging information, the format of the blocks and manner of their exchange. The exchange is generally one-to-one or one-to-many. A local area network is a many-to-many situation, and in most implementations every device on the network hears the transmissions from every other device, regardless of their destination. Some procedure must be built into the devices to extract messages addressed to them and ignore the rest.

The standard OSI Reference Model is often said to be connection-oriented, by which it is meant to imply that the end-points are bound together in an exclusive one-to-one liaison to ensure sequenced block transfer. Local area networks require a connectionless service in which there is no prior agreement or knowledge about where the next block of information is coming from. For this reason it makes sense to build a modified reference model which is particularly suited to local networking, but which can also accommodate the more established form of computer network.

Figure 7.9 shows the form such a model may take. In the OSI reference model the lowest layer, the Physical Layer, interfaces to the physical media, which can be the data circuit terminating equipment (DCE), which is the CCITT's name for a modem or device which interfaces to the transmission network. For a local area network the DCE will usually be a transceiver or repeater, which in turn is attached to the medium being used. The Physical Layer of the Local Area Network Reference Model will perform the same type of interface functions as those defined for the OSI Model. In most cases the physical medium in the local network will support only bit-serial transmission. One of the tasks of the Physical Layer will be to take the blocks of data given to it by the Data Link Layer and put these into a serial form for transmission.

The Data Link Layer has to perform the usual function of system-to-system error detection and correction. In addition a different type of flow control must be used to avoid network congestion in systems where this can be a problem. This layer may, on request, provide different qualities of service: eg sequencing, end-to-end flow control and connectionless transmission.

The Network Layer of a local area network architecture should be able to handle different classes of service: virtual circuits, datagrams, broadcasting, transaction processing, etc. Because it is unlikely that every local network will operate in complete isolation, the Network Layer must also provide the functions for handling transfers from one local network to another, or from a wide area network to a local network. It should provide a service to the upper levels which masks the features of the underlying media.

The Transport Layer is outside the parts of the Reference Model which are specific to local networking. Its purpose is to provide an end-to-end transport service to the users' applications or devices which are in the source and destination systems. The only

ISO Work on Local Area Networks   195

modification needed is that of permitting a connectionless mode of operation so that messages may be sent without sequencing or prior agreements between the applications at the source and destination.

The above description of a LAN standard model was given in the previous edition of this book, and it is still a valid working model from which ISO possibly worked. Since then ISO has taken the IEEE 802 standards and included them into their OSI model (some are still being ratified). The standards have been placed in the form of a three layer communications architecture as described below in Figure 7.10.

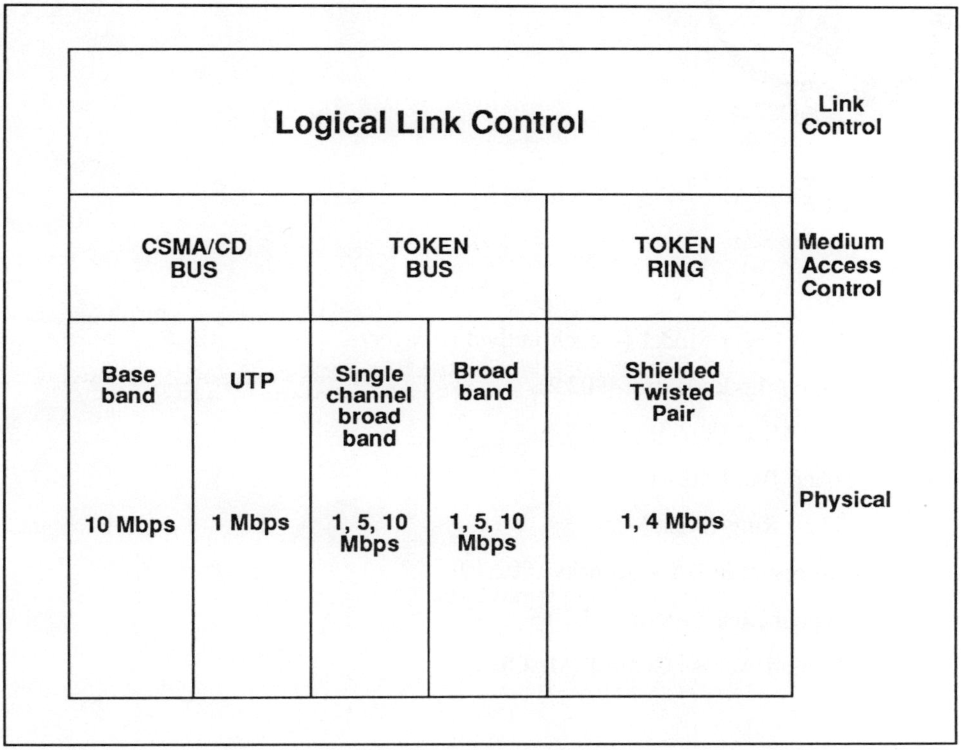

Logical Link Control					Link Control
CSMA/CD BUS		TOKEN BUS		TOKEN RING	Medium Access Control
Base band	UTP	Single channel broad band	Broad band	Shielded Twisted Pair	Physical
10 Mbps	1 Mbps	1, 5, 10 Mbps	1, 5, 10 Mbps	1, 4 Mbps	

Figure 7.10 IEEE 802 Model

TERMS TO REVIEW

Sage the Owl Recommends

- IEEE
- ISO
- OSI
- Seven Layer Model (+ each individual layer)
- Logical Link Control (802.2)
- CSMA/CD (802.3)
- Token Bus (802.4)
- Token Ring (802.5)
- Interoperable LAN Security (802.10)
- Logical Link Control (LLC)
- Medium Access Control (MAC).

8
Choosing a Local Area Network

INTRODUCTION

Most of this book is concerned with explaining the different techniques which have been used to provide a local data communications network. This chapter approaches the problem from the perspective of the potential purchaser of such a network. He or she is less concerned with how long the packets are or how they will be delivered to their destination, than with the kind of application which can be used on the network. As things stand, however, the underlying network, its topology and the way it operates have a profound effect on the quality of service offered to the end-user.

In principle, a network could be designed which would offer its users the type of service they require. This could be achieved by making the network capable of handling sufficient bandwidth to suit all present and future requirements, and by providing enough software and hardware to allow the user to interface to all other kinds of equipment and to provide all the services he or she requires. Obviously such a solution, however desirable, would be beyond the finances of most organisations, and a product of this type would not find many customers.

The problem is to find a network which is cheap enough but which has a sufficient number of facilities to make it appeal to the average company wanting to install a local network. Unfortunately no single product available is suitable for all customers. In this chapter some of the things which must be considered when choosing a network will be discussed. Only general guidelines are given.

OPTIONS FOR LOCAL NETWORKS

Before deciding on the actual local area network to buy, the potential customer should examine the existing facilities for communications within his organisation and decide which of these are relevant.

Most companies will have a private digital telephone network installed on each site, usually based on a private exchange. The network generally serves directly or indirectly every user on site and provides facilities for them to talk to each other and to other individuals outside through the use of the public telephone network. Some of these on-site networks are used to enable computer terminals to connect to a computer through the use of modems. Whilst these lines are being used in this manner they are unavailable for normal telephone conversation. However this situation is now changing with the implementation of ISDN.

The quality of the network and the exchange, and the extent to which they are used for data communications, are very important factors to take into account when considering how a local area network will be used. For example, if the existing private telephone exchange is due for replacement, the opportunity will be there to install a digital PBX which will have facilities designed particularly for digital communications between computer-related devices. Even the installation of new telephone wiring provides opportunities for the inclusion of extra cables which could ultimately be used for a local area network. The cost of putting in the wiring is considerably more than the cost of the wire. Even if the organisation was not actively considering installing a local area network, when the time comes to upgrade the system, then it should do so at that stage.

A few days employed in studying the data communications requirements could save the frustration and cost of installing a network which will be useless for data in a few years' time.

Networks which provide terminal users with facilities to access the on-site computer host are usually installed in a piecemeal fashion. When a department or office requires a new terminal then a fresh set of cables are usually installed. Even where cables usually exist it is not uncommon for them to be ignored, either because no-one knows of their existence or because they are the wrong type, or even because no-one is sure why they are there or where they should go.

New terminals are now being installed so quickly that a better scheme is required, for example, a structured wiring scheme, described in Chapter 2. The telephone network, since it is there, may be suitable, provided that the exchange can handle the traffic, and provided that the terminals are suitable for operation over this type of link. The solution which appeals to most users is the once-and-for-all installation of a local area network which can be used to link all computer-based services.

In addition to these electrical information transfer facilities there is always the internal manual postal system to be considered. A study of this can be very enlightening for the designer of a local area network, especially where it is intended to serve as the basis of an electronic office system. Knowing the traffic patterns of the messages, how many stay wholly on the site and how many are external post, is essential information for the designer of an electronic mail system.

In organisations with separate sites, the amount of post, and its character (eg letters, drawings, parcels, etc), passing between sites needs to be known, and whether the quantity justifies the existence of an inter-site electronic message system, or whether the computer network (if there is one) can be used instead.

Another aspect of the local communications problem is the need or desire to integrate voice with data handling. Does the organisation want to install, for example, a text handling system with voice annotation? Is the provision of an electronic mail facility going to noticeably affect the use of the internal telephone system? Can incoming calls be stored on computer systems if the intended recipient is unavailable, or do sufficiently good arrangements already exist to take in-coming calls? All these factors need very careful consideration. Whatever conclusions are reached it must be recognised that the rates at which voice and data handling facilities will be expanded in the future are almost certain to be different. Any solution must be flexible enough to handle this.

As new items of equipment come on to the market, the need for extra communications facilities is certain to increase. Not only will the total quantity of information being moved around increase but the individual bandwidths required for new services could well be much greater than those of ordinary computer terminals. Take, for example, the 6 MHz bandwidth required for a one-way transmission of real-time colour television. This is sufficient for hundreds of computer terminals. Broadband networks are the only really suitable systems available today to handle this quantity of information.

Summarising, the networking needs can be satisfied by using circuit-message- or packet-switched centrally controlled systems, local area networks using rings or buses, or by broadband systems. The last option has the greatest potential to handle all the on-site communications needs, but at greater cost than some other possibilities. The problems of the customer are often compounded by the limited choice of systems available which actually fulfil his or her complete requirements. One topic for consideration, therefore, is the relative urgency of the requirements. It may be advisable to wait until more products are on the market which are better oriented to the user's true needs.

PERFORMANCE

An exaustive study of network performance is beyond the scope of this book. In this section the main things to look for are presented but no firm recommendations are made.

When considering network performance a number of constraints must be taken into account:

— *Inter-frame spacing* — after each frame transmitted on the network, a gap is required to separate one frame from another. This way it may be filled with idle characters or frame preamble. Some characters are necessary before the actual frame proper starts in order that the receiver is allowed to synchronise with the signal. With the high speeds used on most local networks prior synchronisation is especially important.

- *Collision detection and reinforcement* — contention-based systems (Ethernet) rely, for their successful operation, on the ability of the station to detect that a packet has been in collision with another, and then often they reinforce the collision by 'jamming' the network with a burst of characters. The total time occupied in this transmission, ie the part of the frame transmitted before the collision is detected plus the reinforcement characters, is time wasted.

- *Station reaction time* — each device on the network needs a finite length of time to react to a transmission addressed to it. If this is long then the data which can be passed to that station is limited.

When considering the transfer of a packet of information from the source to its destination, the total time required is made up of (*see* Figure 8.1):

- *Queueing delay* — once a packet is ready to send it must be queued in the interface device behind other packets also waiting to be sent.

- *Access delay* — a packet at the head of the queue cannot generally be transmitted immediately. It has to wait for a convenient gap in the network traffic or until that station is given permission to send.

- *Transmission time* — this is the time it takes to actually transmit the whole of the packet on to the network. It is governed by the speed of the network and the operating speed of the interface unit.

- *Propagation delay* — each electrical impulse on the network travels at a high, but finite speed (approximately three quaters of the speed of light) from the sender to the destination; thus a small time has to be added for propagation on to the time already mentioned.

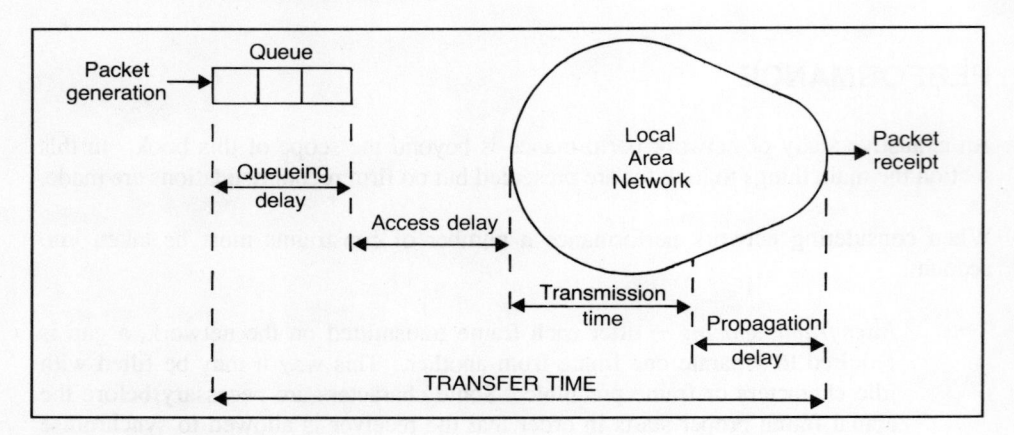

Figure 8.1 Network delays

Once that packet reaches its destination it is subject to the station and device reaction times which are typically much longer than the propagation times. The time it takes a packet to pass across a network, however, is not predictable for every technique used. The main areas of doubt are in the queueing delay and the time to access the network. The former is important when the device generating the packets is capable of doing so at high speed, or when the network is congested. The latter time is governed by the network congestion and the transmission technique used. Other factors which affect the overall network performance are:

- *Stability* — this is a measure of the time taken to successfully transmit a packet of information, If this approaches infinity under certain network operating conditions, the network is said to be unstable. Certain networking techniques are inherently more stable under all conditions than others.

- *Fairness* — fairness is the measure of the number of opportunities to transmit that each station has. If this is equal to every station then the network is fair. Fairness may not be a desirable characteristic in all circumstances. Some applications may require a limited number of stations to be always able to gain access to the network. One example is the control of a critical industrial system. Some networking techniques may be fair under normal circumstances but provision can be made for the user to allocate priorities, so that it can be made to operate in an 'unfair' manner, as far as the network is concerned, but in a more sensible manner from the user's point of view.

- *Robustness* — robustness of the network is a measure of how the network responds to failures of the media, attached devices or transceivers/repeaters. Related to this is the sensitivity or otherwise of the network whilst operating in an electrically noisy environment. This may be a very important point to consider in industrial systems in which the cable passes close to heavy machinery.

- *Failure modes* — the way a network fails can have important repercussions on the systems using it. If the failure of an attached device renders the whole network unusable this is unlikely to be acceptable to most users. Other failure modes that could be unacceptable would be an increase in delay or fewer opportunities to transmit.

- *Data transmission rate* — although the raw data transmission rate of the network may appear to be one of the most important factors determining performance, an examination of Figure 8.1 will show that this is only a proportion of the total transfer time. Most current local area networks operate at a raw transmission rate of 10 Mbps. This is beyond the input/output capabilities of all but the larger computers, but even they still need time to frame outgoing data, and analyse incoming packets.

- *Variation in delays* — experience of computer networks over many years has shown that quite considerable delays are acceptable provided they are nearly always the same. Variations between 0.5 and 2 seconds, say, can be most annoying to a terminal user. In the networks which serve human users directly, variation in delay is an important issue.

- *Framing constraints* — the size of the packet which the network can transport affects not only the size of the message which can be transported in one transmission, but also the size of the buffers required in the devices at each end.

To the above factors should be added the interaction needed between the network access mechanisms and the higher level protocols which must be used to provide the quality of service users and programs require.

In summary network performance is a subject of considerable amount of research, not just involving theoretical calculations based on typical network traffic, but under real conditions. The user's perception of the service is still the most important factor. Work needs to be done on the more human aspects of performance, that is to investigage the delays and variations which are acceptable.

PLANNING AND DESIGNING YOUR NETWORK

Meticulously planning and designing your network will probably be the most important task you will ever undertake in your local area networking implementation. We have discussed some of the options available to you and some of the performance issues that you will need to investigate before implementing any local area networking configuration. However even before this is done it is advisable to investigate your immediate and future business needs and based on this, and existing available networking options, you can proceed to the design of your own local area network. Again this section will not indicate optimum configurations, as that presupposes that all business environments are the same and have the same business requirements. However it will describe a systematic way of collecting and analysing information about your business needs so that you are better able to design an effective local area network.

The following nine steps will help you formulate a description of how your LAN should be configured and what functionality you are expecting of it.

Step 1

Determine the number of people who will use the system. If possible try and forecast what the future requirements may be.

Step 2

Interview the users. The users will provide most of the information you need to design a successful network. If you rush the user interviews, not recording every detail, you may find that you have to re-interview them later to obtain a more complete picture.

Determine who they are. List them by name and physical location. *What do they do?* Determine the type of work each user performs, especially as it may pertain to different hardware and software requirements. This information may suggest the type of network functionality required by the users.

What organisational relationships exist between them. This information will determine the functional areas needed, which applications can be shared, which resources can be shared and where you need the servers. F*inally document* the results of your interview by using a standard interview document for every user. For example:

User Interview Document

Name:	Fred Bloggs
Job Title:	Assistant Marketing Manager
Department:	Sales and Marketing
Responsibilities:	Who do they work with, Share files with, Communicate with regularly?
Security Needs:	Do they need physical security for their hardware? Do their files need to be secure? Who should have/not have access to their files?
Current Hardware:	Type of equipment, special peripherals, etc.
Current Software:	Type, for example, only Word Processing.
Proposed Additions:	Keep recommendations generic until you have designed your network. However do include the user's wish list as this will indicate the requirements of the network as a whole.
Storage requirements:	Servers and personal disks.

Step 3

Organise users into workgroups. Identify functional and logical groups. Start with a floorplan and mark the location of every user interviewed, how far apart each user is from the others, and how far apart each logical group (department) is from other groups. Note whether offices are separated by solid floor to ceiling walls or movable partitions (*See* Figure 8.2). Although organisational charts are useful in deciding the number of workgroups you require and who should go where, often the work grouping for network purposes does not match the organisational chart. You may find a more efficient network that cuts across functional and departmental lines.

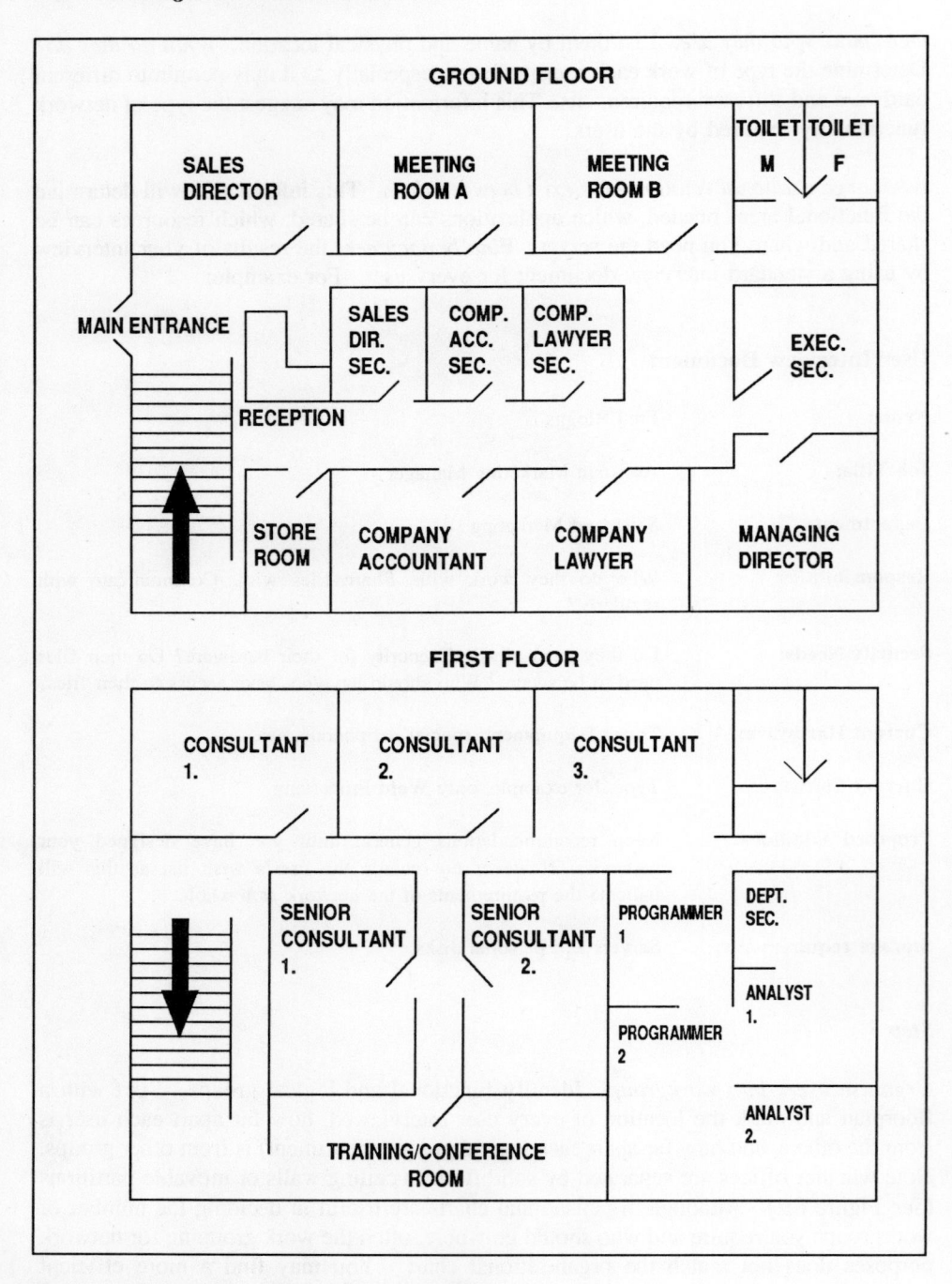

Figure 8.2 Floor chart of example company

Therefore the types of questions you will need to ask are:

— Do members of a particular department, for example, work independently or do they constantly swap information?

— Do all the members use the same tools?

— Do other members of other departments use the same tools?

— What is the level of cross-communication between different departments?

Step 4

Determine the server needs for each workgroup identified, and possibly the need for additional servers between workgroups on the same network. To do this you need to define the current or future information flow and processing requirement within every workgroup.

Disk capacity for the disk server is a function of the number and type of documents that workgroup members will be storing on the file server. Applications are normally major space utilisers and hence it is best to keep frequently used applications on a local disk. Only network-applicable applications (for example, corporate database enquiry) should be kept in shared folders on the server.

You will need to identify other types of server requirements, for example, gateways to external networks, printers, etc. You will also need to determine the performance requirements of your servers. This is a function of the amount of disk and network activity within the workgroup. By keeping the network balanced (using one or more servers per network, using bridges to isolate heavy traffic), you can minimise the need for high-performance servers.

In general the more the group shares information and uses the server, the more they will want a high-performance system. But remember that the higher the performance requirements the higher the cost of implementation.

At this stage you should also consider the back-up requirements for the complete network. These back-up requirements can differ from group to group. For example, if the traffic loads are heavy in one group and light in another, you may need a tape back-up unit for the heavy-load group, and only disk back-up for the other. It is assumed as standard, that dedicated servers should always have tape back-up facilities.

Step 5

Analyse Connections between Workgroups. By now, you should have a pretty good general model for each workgroup — its members, work flow, layout and server requirements. It is important however, to understand the whole system. Solutions that make sense for a workgroup environment may take on new meaning when viewed on a large scale. Additional equipment (for example, bridges or gateways) may be necessary to tie all the components together and have them communicate efficiently.

Bridges can be used within workgroups to isolate heavy network users (and their servers) from light networks users, while still maintaining transparent access to the entire network.

Step 6

Record the information gathered for future use. The information so far collected should give you an indication of what type of network you are going to implement. It should contain the following information:

— total number of users, workgroups, servers, printers, etc;
— security requirements;
— topology (the surface area to be covered);
— requirement for special equipment, for example, remote communications.

Remember to allow for future developments and expansion.

Step 7

Produce your initial network diagram. Draw a network diagram that shows all the proposed workgroups, networks, zones, hardware, and major system software. This diagram of existing and proposed equipment will not only give you the opportunity to list the major hardware requirements, but will also ensure that you have all of the appropriate cabling and adapters required to make the necessary connections.

Step 8

Select the requirement network products. This task is not as easy as it sounds. To find the product that best matches a user's needs, you have to know what to look for. For example, you may have decided that the network you are designing requires print spooling. If so you will need to find out what type of documents are to be spooled? How many? How often? Does it require dedicated spooling? and so on.

Step 9

Begin installation and document the whole network. This should be done with the full cooperation of all concerned. Figure 8.3 describes the final version of how a network could look. Remember that Figure 8.2 in Step 3 had identified who was going to be within the network. This is how it may look after the installation.

Planning and Designing your Network 207

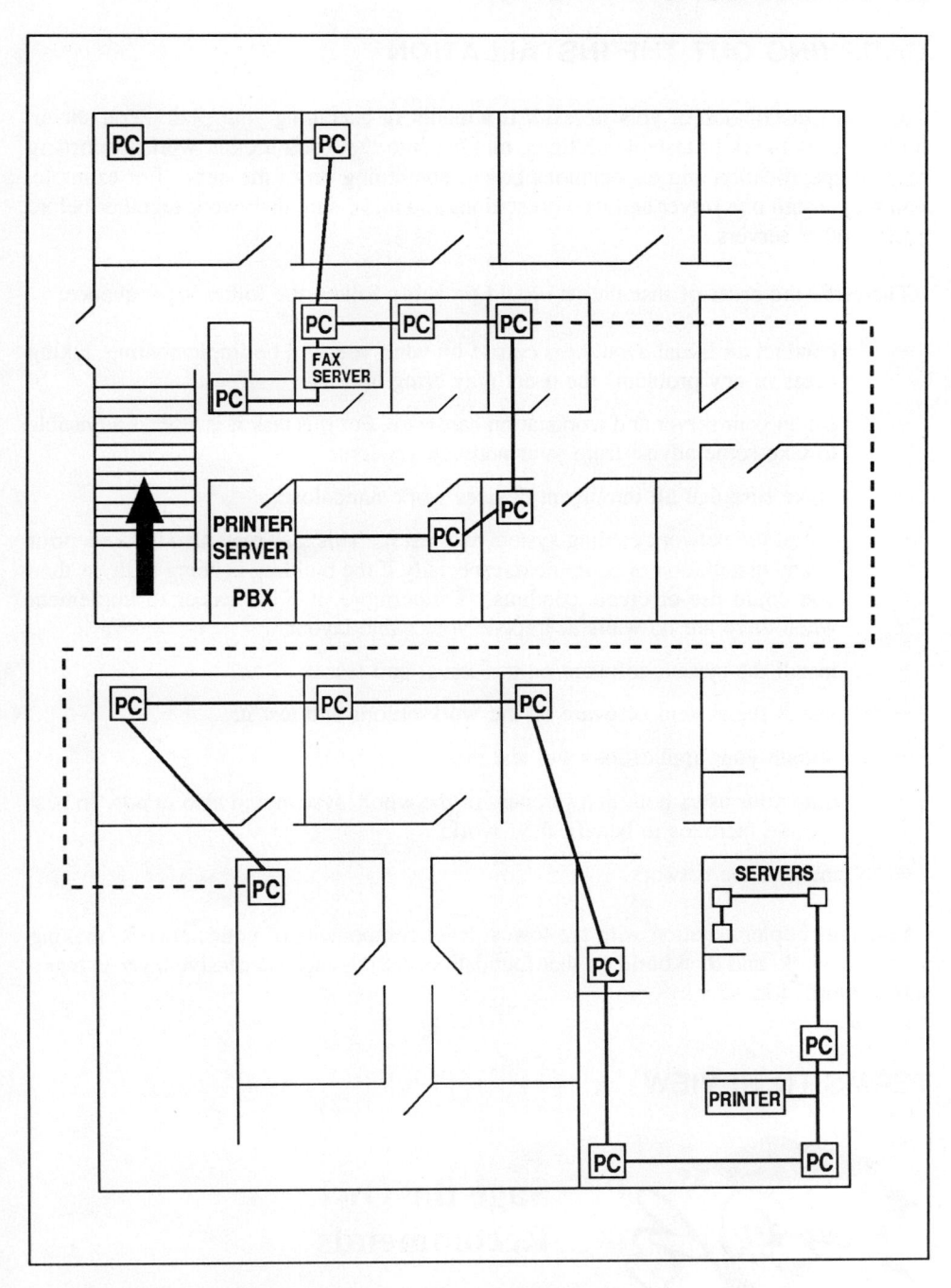

Figure 8.3 Schematic diagram of network solution

CARRYING OUT THE INSTALLATION

The actual installation of your network is a matter of executing your plan. You should build your network in testable sections, making sure that each section works according to your specification and expectations before continuing on to the next. For example, you may install one server and its workstations and make sure they work together before adding other servers.

Therefore the order of installation would probably follow the following sequence:

- conduct an initial awareness course on what you will be implementing, taking notes of any problems the users may bring up;
- set up your server and workstation hardware. For this task it is always advisable to take some advise from your network vendors;
- make sure that all intelligent devices work standalone;
- install the network cabling system and test it. This task may also be done prior to any installation of equipment, especially if the building is being built, as then you could use or create conduits. Furthermore, it is far easier to implement when there are no walls to impede your cable layout;
- install the system software on the server and test it;
- install the system software on the workstations and test it;
- initiate your applications and test them;
- train your users both in awareness of the whole system and also in how to best use the facilities to benefit their work;
- manage the network.

You start implementation with the lowest level components of your network, making sure they work, and then build on that foundation, testing each successive layer to make sure it works too.

TERMS TO REVIEW

Sage the Owl Recommends

- Inter-frame Spacing
- Collision Detection and Reinforcement
- Station Reaction Time
- Delay
- Stability
- Fairness
- Robustness
- Failure Modes
- Data Transmission Rate
- Variation in Delays
- Framing Constraints.

9
Case Study

INTRODUCTION

This chapter will briefly investigate one of the main local area networks on the market today. The network is based on the author's prior experience, and this does not mean that it is the best local area networking solution. However NetWare v3.1 does have a major share of the local area networking market.

This product summary will only describe some of its major features. It will not however, indicate all the possible additions and options that the network may possess. It will also concentrate on the latest version of the product (as at time of going to press) and therefore any prior versions or subsequent ones will be ignored. For a fuller description the reader is referred to the manufacturer or dealer.

NOVELL NETWORKING ENVIRONMENT

History

Novell Inc. set up its corporate headquarters in Utah, USA in 1983, shipping its first file server software in January of that year. It is a network systems software house developing one of the most powerful local area networking environment within the PC DOS world. The financial growth of the company reflects on a 1:1 basis the growth in the local area networking market with sales tripling each year since its inception.

Today, Novell meets its customers' present and future connectivity requirements by providing a well-tested and standard local area networking framework. This software is called *NetWare* (it is now in its ninth release), with its own networking operating system that optimises the management, sharing, translation and synchronisation of information throughout network computing.

Its product launch calendar, since 1983 describes how throughout its short history, it has released every year a new version of product offering or support for some industry standard. For example, since 1983 the following has occurred:

212 *Case Study*

- 1983, launched its first file server software;
- 1985, support for IBM's DOS 3.1 and NetBIOS;
- 1986, support for 80286 and Token Ring environment, release of fault-tolerant LAN products;
- 1987, releases its Open Protocol Technology;
- 1988, NetWare for VMS, support for OS/2 and Macintosh;
- 1989, release of NetWare Open Systems and Portable NetWare, support for 80386;
- 1990, release of SNMP-monitor.

Novell seems to be well placed for any future networking development, supporting all DOS LAN versions and OS/2. Furthermore its network operating system can work with and connect to Apple, Unix, DEC and IBM environments under open systems protocols.

NetWare Products

NetWare has evolved in the past eight years from being a small simple local area network into an open network environment that integrates servers, PCs, minicomputers and mainframe resources, its latest offering is *NetWare 386 V3.1*. This version provides transparent, controlled sharing of information among dissimilar computers. Some of its capabilities were traditionally only offered on mainframes, for example, fault-tolerance.

One of the main additions to the NetWare range of products within NetWare 386 v3.1 is the addition of a developer platform. It includes a C-Library (CLIB) Application Programming Interface (API) to support Network Loadable Modules (NLM) development, the Streams environment, Transport Level Interface (TLI) library for interprocess communications, Btrieve 386 NLM for record management and tools for the support of client/server applications.

This case study will only concentrate on this version of Novell's vast number of local area networking products. The reader is referred to *NetWare Buyer's Guide* published by Novell for a complete description of all their products.

The NetWare system as a whole comprises several components; each administers a specific area of the local area network. The components are:

NetWare 386 v3.1 Operating System

NetWare was originally developed as a server operating system for Novell's S-Net, a star network. It was later adapted for the 8088 microprocessor environment. Advanced NetWare and Version 1.2 of Advanced Netware were introduced in 1985. These versions increased the functionality of the server and were the first protected mode operating system, respectively. Since then several versions and adaptations have been released. Notably among these is support for DOS, Macintosh, Windows, OS/2 and UNIX file and print services.

The latest offering (at the time of writing) is NetWare 386 v3.1. This version includes enhancements in overall network performance and systems reliability, network administration and an improved third party development platform. This version has been designed for the 32-bit 80386 and 80486 environments. NetWare 386 is a real-time operating system that manages memory, access and all the network transactions. Added to the operating system it can also have loadable network services, for example, server-based applications. These are called Network Loadable Modules (NLM). NLMs are used by NetWare 386 to control and manage server processes and resources. This means that these services can be loaded and unloaded without bringing the server down.

The minimum RAM requirement for NetWare 386 is 4MB with a maximum of 4GB. This means that it can also support up to 32 TB(terabytes) of disk storage and up to 1,024 physical disk drives. However note (at time of going to print) these memory conditions cannot be reached with current personal computing technology. Nevertheless this feature obviously means that future technological developments can be supported. Furthermore this increased memory support means that the server can support more concurrent users (up to 100,000 concurrent files per server) applications, for example, NetWare 386 allows 250 users to run the same application from one server.

Other services offered by the operating system include Print, Resource Management, Workgroup Management, Inter-networking, Fault-tolerance and Security.

The print service allows the users to share up to 16 printers on the network per print server, and multiple print servers can be run on a single network. The printers can be situated anywhere on the network, for example either attached to a server or to any workstation. However wherever the printer is attached, specific software is required for it, ie if attached to a workstation Terminate and Stay Resident software is loaded on the workstation itself.

Resource management features allow the network administrator to check the status of each node running on the network and hence find out what resources are being used. This is done by using the Monitor utility.

Workstation management is achieved via the Workgroup administration tool. This permits the workgroup manager (which could be the network administrator himself or several assigned responsible individuals) the management of security and network performance.

Fault-tolerance has been one of the foundation stones of NetWare from the beginning. This is a software driven methodology where the network administrator can add specific

214 *Case Study*

fault-tolerant features, like duplicate directories, file allocation tables, etc as he needs them. The main fault-tolerant feature is disk mirroring. This protects the system against loss of data due to defective disk drives. Disk mirroring means that every transaction is duplicated on the disk drives, therefore if there is a disk failure the software automatically switches over to the back-up disk with no loss of data.

Inter-networking is achieved on NetWare 386 by the integration of different networking hardware within a single logical network. Figure 9.1 describes a typical configuration for a NetWare file server. The sub-networks can all use the same media and topology, or each can use different media and topology.

Finally, security is provided in layers that can protect individual files, groups of files, users and passwords. A user can be limited to operate within specific files, directories, workstations, or during certain hours of the day. Passwords are encrypted (both at the server and while in transit across the cable).

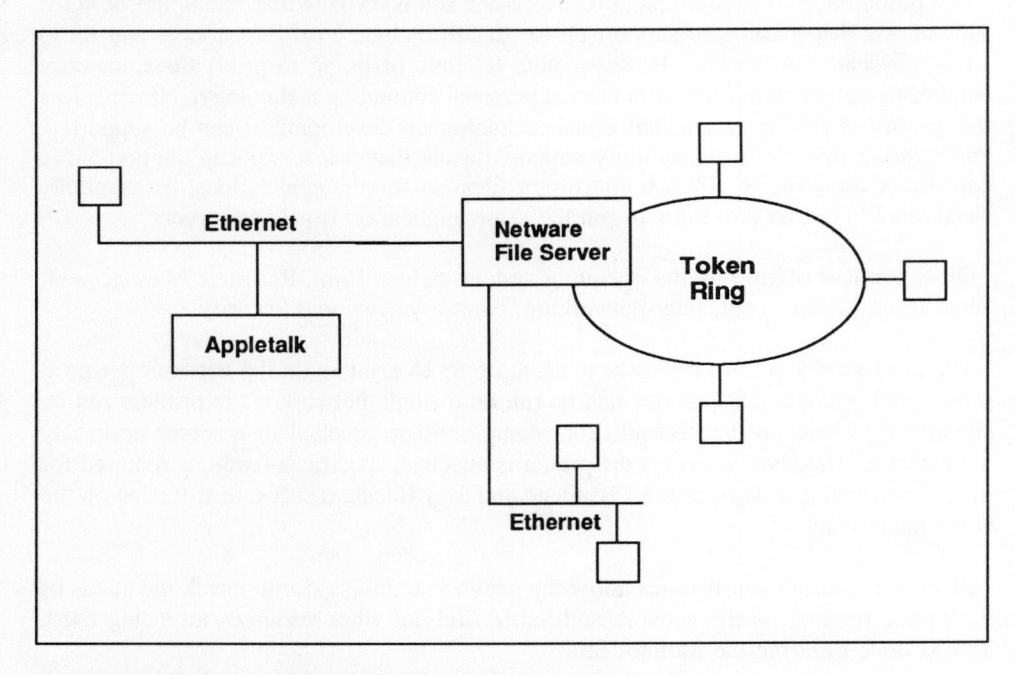

Figure 9.1 NetWare inter-networking capability

Installation of NetWare 386 v3.1

The installation of any local area networking product requires patience and an uninterruptible environment. The following brief description is only given as an example of what is required when installing NetWare 386. It is always recommended to read the

Novell Networking Environment

installation procedures described in the manuals before proceeding with any installation. Furthermore, if after doing this the installer still does not understand most of the points explained in the manual, he/she should go back to the supplier for help. Remember they sold you the software and hence should support it.

First start with a clean hard disk (by performing a low-level format). Then run Novell's proprietary utility *COMPSURF* which makes the hard disk NetWare ready. Create a *DOS* partition so that you can install the NetWare 386 software in it, for example a 3MB partition. Copy the system files onto this partition and create an *AUTOEXEC.BAT* with one entry *SERVER*. This is your fileserver boot file when installation is complete.

You then have to select and load your disk driver and run the install program. The install program is menu-driven and is used to create NetWare partitions and volumes, and mirror hard disks. It also loads the *SYSTEM* and *PUBLIC* files onto the network.

Once you have finished installing the file server you then install the print servers and setup the workstations. The workstations are installed by running *SHGEN.EXE* that creates *IPX.COM*, the network protocol file (note, follow the options on the screen).

You can now, as network administrator, begin to set up your network in terms of workgroups and working directories. Follow the instructions in the manuals in order to get the optimum configuration in terms of directory and workgroup sizes.

The next important step is to set up security levels for all the users. Passwords should be time-dated, forcing people to change them every so often. Additionally you can also set up lengths of time users can spend on the network and time periods between which they cannot log-on.

You can finally load any of the *NLMs* or network applications supplied in your installation kit, for example, if you wish to allow the storage of different file-types, OS/2, Macintosh etc, you must run *ADD NAME SPACE* to configure the volumes to enable this.

Hardware and Software requirements

NetWare 386 v3.1 requires a network server machine, workstation and network adapters. The server requires a minimum of 4MB of RAM and high-capacity disk drives. There are more than 50 microcomputers that have been certified as NetWare 386 servers, for example IBM PS/2 Model 70 or Compaq 386. The workstations that can be used are varied for example, MSDOS XT machines, Macintosh and IBM PS/2.

The type of network adapter used depends on the type of machine used as a server and workstation, for example for IBM machines, IBM Token Ring Micro Channel Bus Adapter.

216 *Case Study*

In terms of the software required, NetWare 386 contains all the software necessary to install and operate the network server and connect up to 250 active workstations on the network. The NetWare package contains the following:

— NetWare 386 v3.1 operating system and documentation;

— DOS workstation software and documentation;

— OS/2 workstation software and documentation;

— LAN drivers;

— NetWare print server v1.2 NLM and documentation;

— Btrieve 386 NLM and documentation;

— NetWare 286 external bridge kit.

TERMS TO REVIEW

Sage the Owl Recommends

— NetWare v3.1

— CLIB — C-Library

— API (Application Programming Interface)

— NLM (Network Loadable Modules)

— TLI (Transport Level Interface).

10
The Future

INTRODUCTION

Since the last publication of this book in 1982 the local area networking world has grown up and has become totally integrated into the information technology world. Then, many still felt that the personal computer was still a toy that would never have any real applicability in the business world. However, as we all have seen the phenomenal growth in and dependency on the use of personal computers has meant that local area networking has also grown.

There are still many local area networking areas that will need investigation and new technology, for example, the use of digital multi-media local networking. However local area networking is here to stay and no doubt will develop further in the years to come. The trend in communications, like in any other environment, is towards building complete, efficient and effective applications and systems. Businesses do not design networks as such, they design applications. This means that the whole environment is looked at and the network is just one part of the whole.

Higher performance requirements and the use of new technology means that the way ahead for local area networking is becoming confusing. Many are asking now whether the end of the local area network is near as greater communications requirements are needed in business. The move is towards the use of wide area network environments. Fibre optics is contributing heavily to the changes taking place in the communications industry and in this chapter we look at Fibre Distributed Data Interface (FDDI) and how the local area network will cope with this development.

Other developments to come include the use of infrared technology. This could be a cost-effective method of allowing computers and computer peripherals to interconnect without the need for wires. This is discussed in more detail later.

Since the tendency in the communications world is towards transmitting high-quality and high volumes of information as quickly as possible, the development of public digital transmission such as Integrated Services Digital Network Services (ISDN) will impact the use of local area networks. By providing users with digital transmission of

64Kbps and higher, ISDN reduces the need to use alternative public technology for accessing wideband facilities. In addition, ISDN makes it possible to use network channels more efficiently for non-voice traffic.

The future looks very promising for the network planner and implementor. However, the usual dilemma will always be paramount, that of what if you implement some technology that will change or disappear in the near future. For this reason it is always advisable to justify your network requirements in terms of corporate goals. The use of communications technology within most companies is normally viewed in terms of a cost saving or in terms of how it will position the company for the future. The first aim is tactical, the latter is strategic. The question that needs to be asked then is which objective applies to your environment?

Future developments can only be predicted in the most general sense and so should not be an obstacle to your implementation. Therefore you should always meet your immediate needs, once this is done the future can be considered in terms of risk analysis. Any alternative technology is always going to be risky and some applications will increase the level of risks associated with the use of different technology. For example, a microwave system in a growing urban area will always have a high risk level, and hence must be fully investigated.

FDDI AND LANS

Fibre Distributed Data Interface (FDDI) is a 100 Mbps token passing, fibre optic ring. It is a set of standards developed by ANSI. It was developed in response to the growing need for high-speed, high-bandwidth transmission over a reasonable distance. FDDI is intended to fill the middle ground between LANs and WANs. A typical FDDI backbone network could be (*see* Figure 10.1) the interconnection of multiple slower LANs, and also into, for example, an X.25 WAN. On top of the backbone FDDI configuration, it can also be used to connect high speed peripherals to mainframes over large distances.

The main advantage to FDDI is the use of fibre optic cabling. The reasons for fibre are obvious: it can be used over large distances as the signal degrades slowly; it is ideal for high-speed transmissions due to its high bandwidth; electrically noisy environments are no problem and it generates no radiation itself.

A simple FDDI configuration could look like the one shown in Figure 10.2. Here a two cable configuration would be used to implement two rings, a primary and secondary ring. These rings are counter-rotating, ie the data flows in one direction around the primary ring and in the reverse direction in the secondary ring.

In Figure 10.2 you will notice that all the nodes are connected to both rings. This type of node is known as a dual attached station. The advantage of this type of configuration is that if any ring fails, then the nodes will remain on the FDDI ring after it has healed itself. The disadvantage is the costs of implementing and maintaining it.

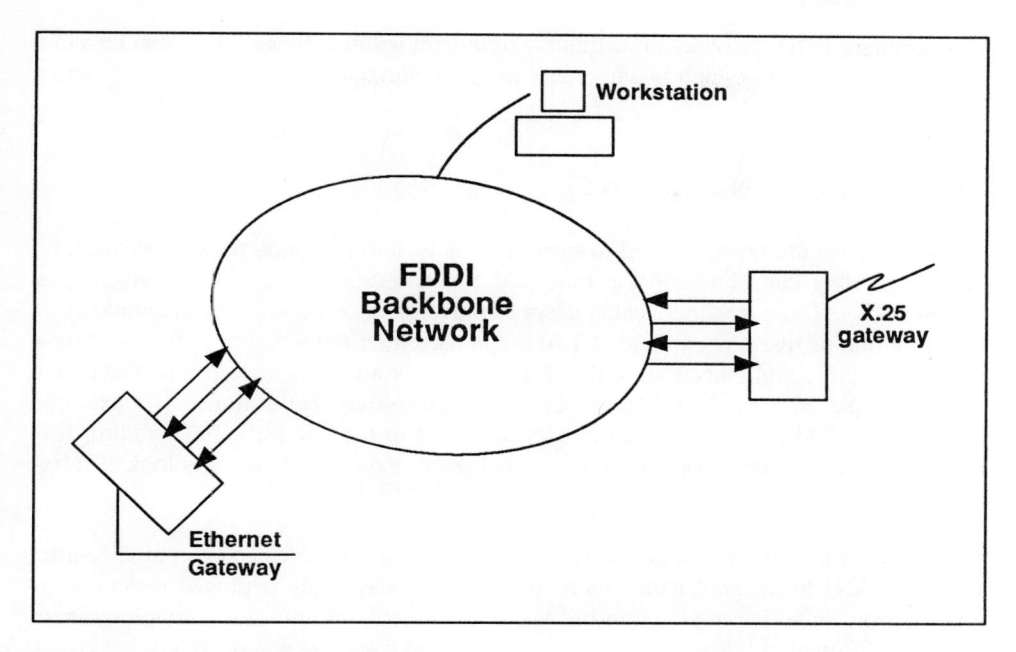

Figure 10.1 FDDI backbone network

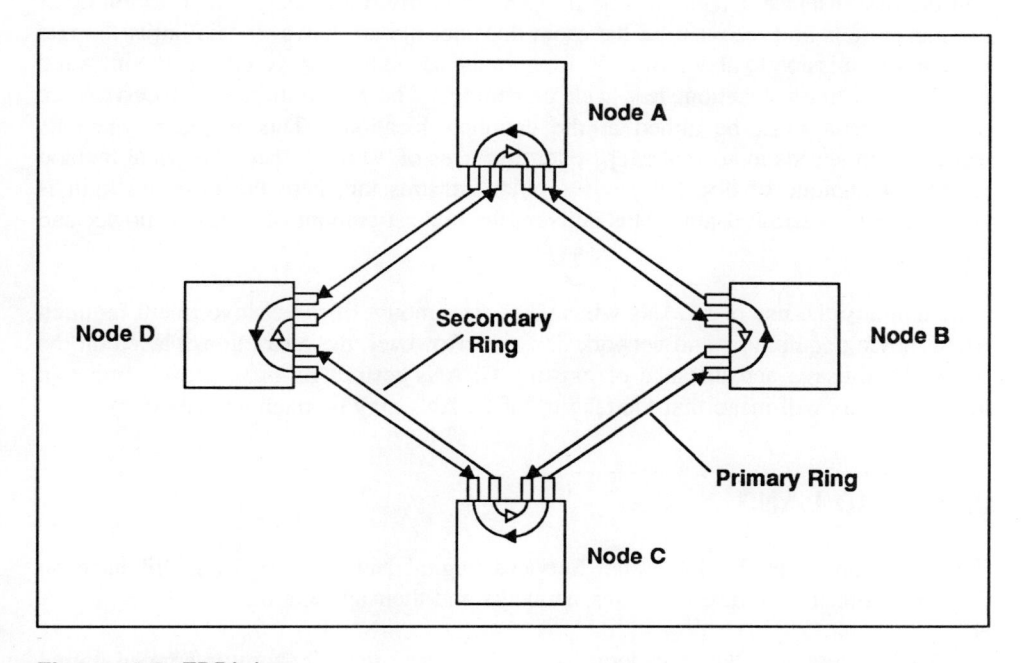

Figure 10.2 FDDI ring

In summary FDDI provides an extremely high-bandwidth network which can cover an area of about 200km, which is why many people believe it is in-between a LAN and a WAN.

CORDLESS LANS (CLANS)

Cordless LANs are being viewed in many circles as the local area network of the 21st century as they can eliminate the time and expense required to install conventional cabled LANs. These systems enable users to move or re-configure their networks with the minimum of fuss and expense. CLANs can use either radio waves or infra-red light to provide the communications link. Radio CLANs are well known but due to the constraints placed upon them in terms of which transmission bands to use, (for example the use of 915 Mhz clashes with the spectrum used in the UK for cellular radio), it is likely to be some time before any standard is agreed upon. Therefore lets look at infra-red.

Infra-red technology (available since the 1960s) is the technology that is mainly used within CLANs to transmit data - its a cost effective and easily deployed technique of transmission (note: it can also transmit voice and video). Within this technology there are three different applications.

In the first instance, a room can be flooded with infra-red energy. The positioning of the transmitters and receviers in the room does not matter, however this limits the rate of data transmission to about 10 to 20 feet. In the second option you direct the infra-red light to a common location, ie a wall or ceiling. The transmitters and receivers are directional and must be aimed at the common location. This increases the data transmission speeds to several Mbps over distances of 30 to 40 feet. The final method uses the technique of directed point-to-point transmission, here the infra-red light is focused into a narrow beam. This delivers the highest amount of infra-red power and distance.

In summary the use of CLANs will reduce the amount of direct investment required when moving equipment and network devices. However, the restrictions placed on the speed, band-usage and distance of existing CLANs restrict its use. Development in improving this will mean that the take up of CLANs may be phenomenal.

ISDN AND LANS

The provision of public Integrated Services Digital Networks (ISDN) will have an immense impact on future local area networks and their applications.

ISDN is a network, that in general has evolved from the telephony integrated digital network, that provides end-to-end digital connections to support a wide range of services,

ISDN and LANs 221

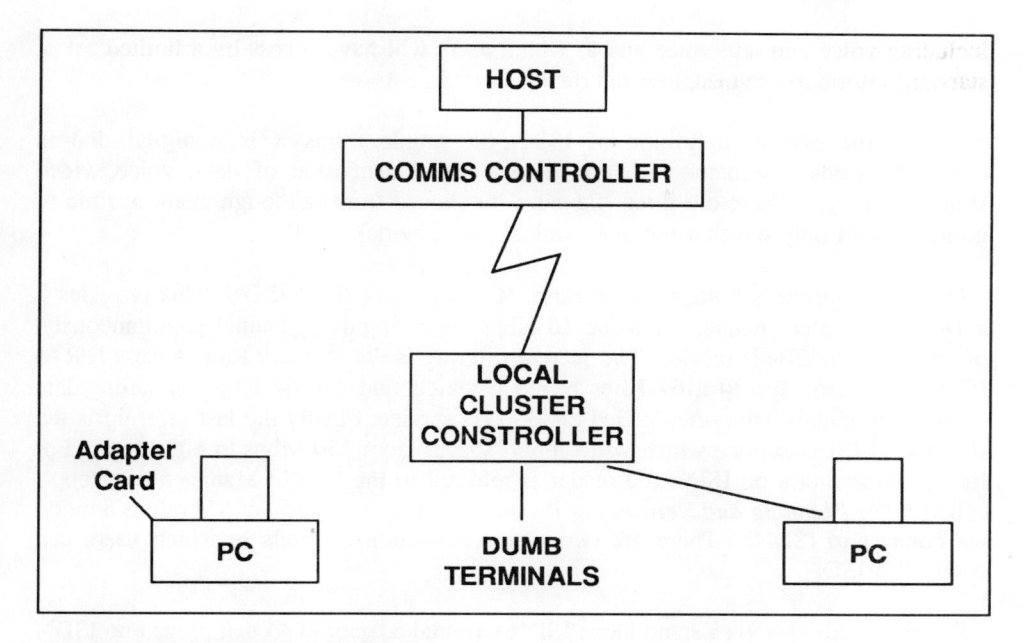

Figure 10.3 Typical host application

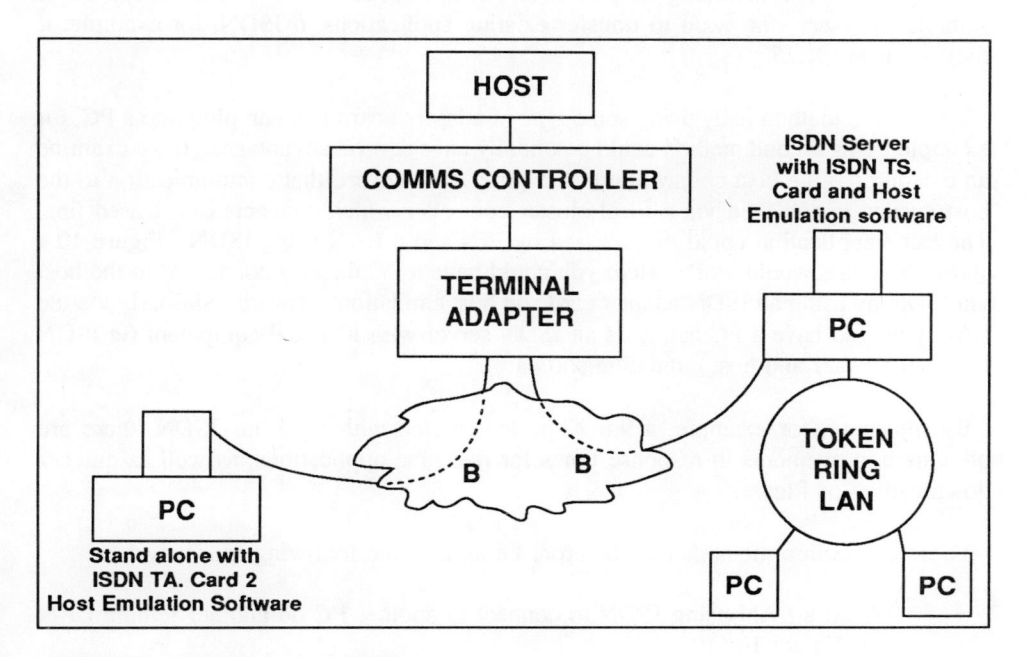

Figure 10.4 Host access via ISDN

222 The Future

including voice and non-voice and to which users will have access by a limited set of standard multipurpose customer interfaces.

This is the official definition of ISDN, in simple terms it is a digital dial-up communications environment that facilitates the transmission of data, voice, video simultaneously. There are three 'flavours' to choose from (although again at time of going to print only the first two are available worldwide).

The first offering is a narrowband Basic Rate Access (BRA) ISDN. This provides 2 x 64 Kbps bearer channels and one 16 Kbps signalling/data channel simultaneously, often called the 2B+D service. The second offering is the Primary Rate Access (PRA) ISDN. This provides 30 x 64 Kbps bearer channels and one 64 Kbps signalling/data channel simultaneously, often called the 30B+D service. Finally the last offering is the Broadband-ISDN service which will support speeds from 150 Mbps to 600 Mbps. For further information on ISDN the reader is referred to the Insight Management Report called *ISDN Planning and Networking Products* by the same author. Therefore how do we connect to ISDN? There are two main connection methods in which users can connect to ISDN.

The first method is via a stand-alone ISDN terminal adapter (TA) that plugs into ISDN network termination equipment. TAs typically offer a range of interfaces for connecting existing equipment, including telephones and computers to ISDN. A stand-alone TA is suitable for users who want to transfer existing applications to ISDN, for example, if they are using X.25.

The second method is by using some type of adapter board that can plug into a PC, for example. This second method could potentially have several advantages. If we examine an existing remote host connection (*see* Figure 10.3) we see that communication to the host system is achieved via a local cluster controller which connects to a leased line. The same application could be accessed by PCs and a LAN using ISDN. Figure 10.4 shows how this would work. Here you could have a PC directly connected to the host via ISDN by using an ISDN adapter card and host emulation software. Similarly via the LAN you cold have a PC acting as an ISDN server with identical equipment (ie ISDN terminal adapter and host emulation software).

By replacing, for example, a 9.6 Kbps leased line with 64 Kbps ISDN, there are obvious improvements in response times for real-time applications, as well as quicker downloading of files.

These connection methods can therefore be used in the following four ways:

— PC on a LAN using ISDN to connect to another PC on another remote LAN (*see* Figure 10.5);

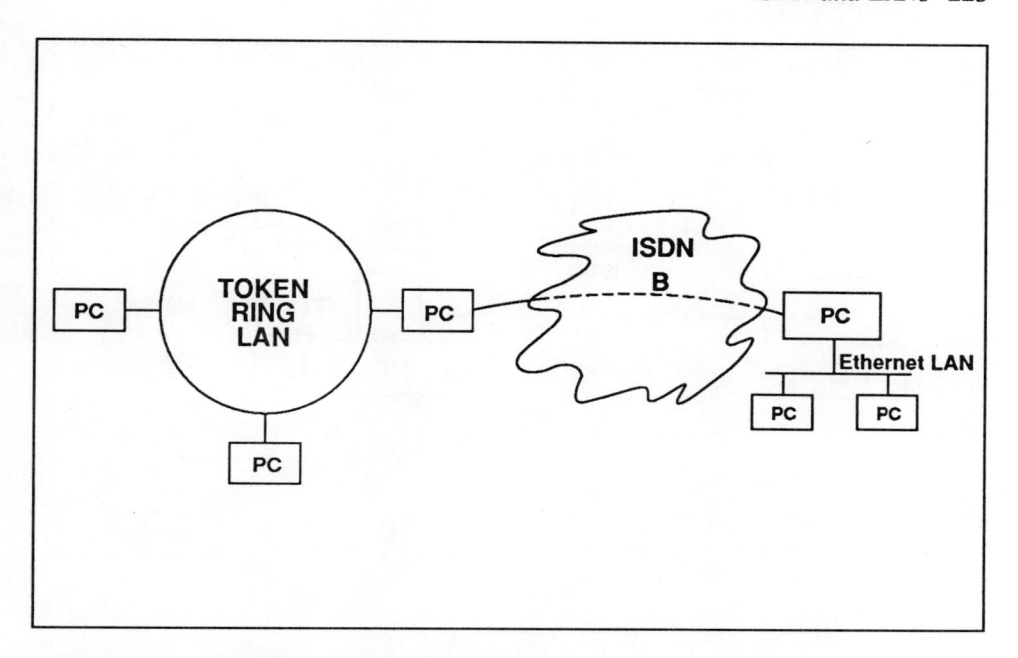

Figure 10.5 LAN interconnection using ISDN

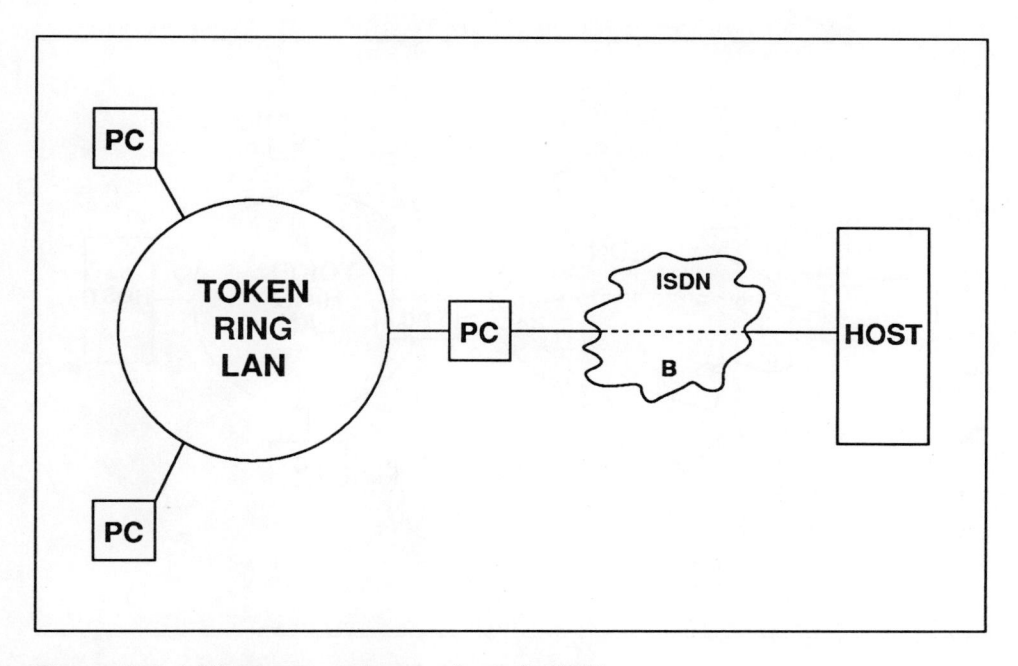

Figure 10.6 LAN interconnection to a host via ISDN

224 *The Future*

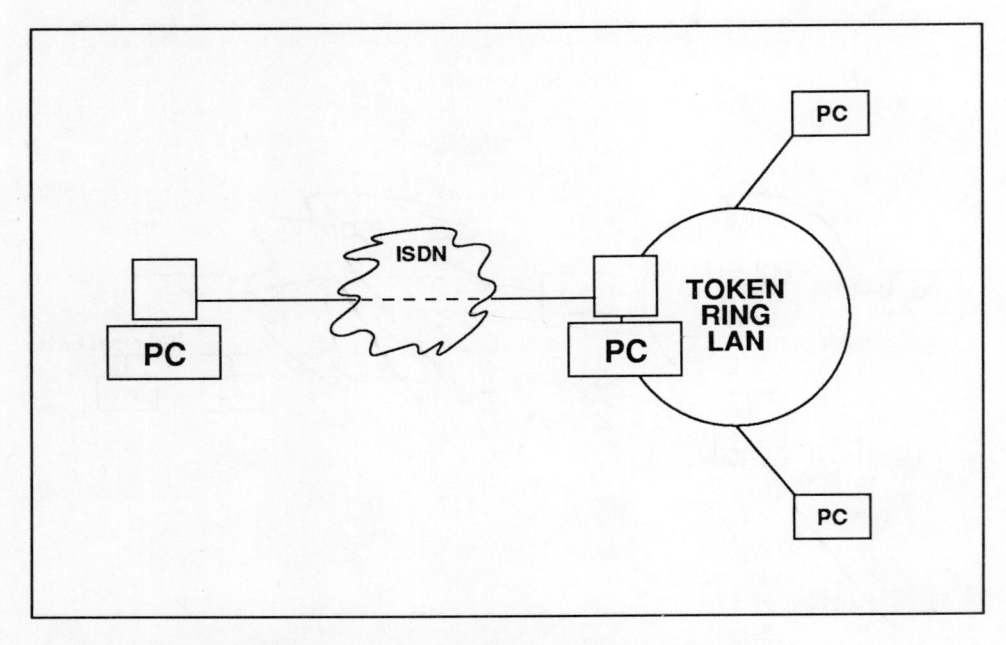

Figure 10.7 Stand-alone PC interconnection to a LAN using ISDN

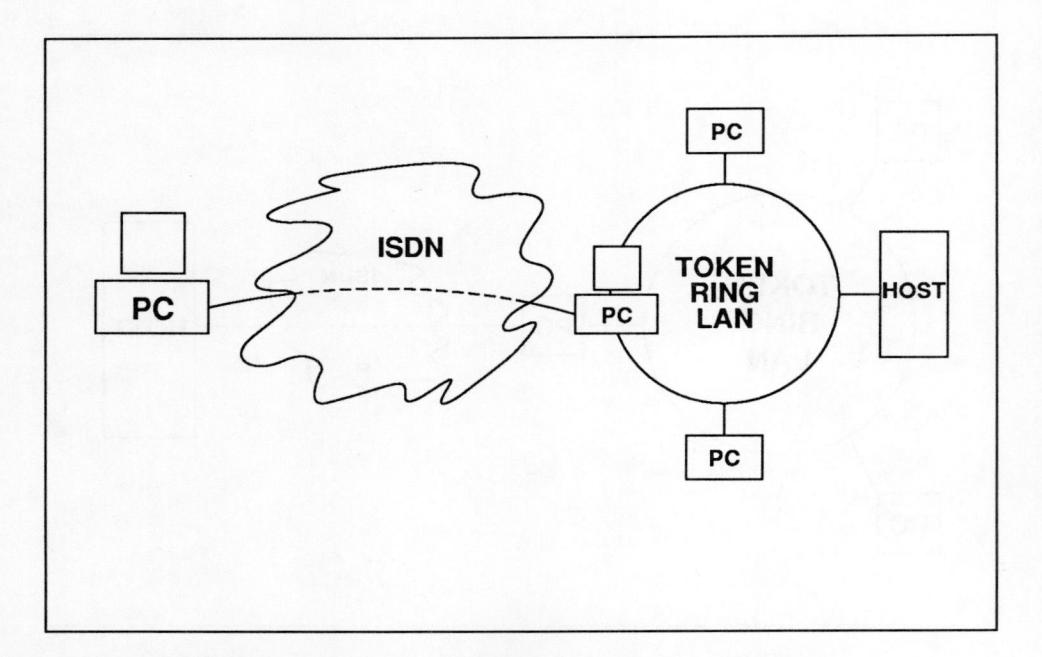

Figure 10.8 Stand-alone PC interconnection to a host via a LAN and ISDN

- PC on a LAN using ISDN to connect to a remote host system (*see* Figure 10.6);

- stand-alone PC using ISDN to connect to a PC on a remote LAN (*see* Figure 10.7);

- stand-alone PC using ISDN and a remote LAN to connect to a host (*see* Figure 10.8);

These interconnection configurations using ISDN will only be of economic use to a user if ease-of-use and cost-effectiveness are two of the main advantages. In the long run the quality of service and communications cost at the user interface will determine the success of these techniques in a competitive environment.

TERMS TO REVIEW

Sage the Owl Recommends

- FDDI
- CLANs
- ISDN.

Glossary

Administrator The individual responsible for managing the network. This person configures the network, manages its resources and security.

Alternate routeing A technique used so that transmission can continue on an alternative path in the event of a node failure or congestion.

ANSI American National Standards Institute; A US group that defines standards for the information processing industry.

Application Layer Level seven of the ISO OSI Model that provides the application interface.

API (Application Programming Interface). A set of software specifications covering service, management and exchange rules. It is a method by which application software talks to communications software.

Architecture A framework for a computer or communications system which defines its functions, interfaces and procedures.

Asynchronous communications Data transmission mode where each transmitted character has integral start and finish bits. This means that the character can be sent at an arbitrary time, and separate from any other character.

Back-end The server part of a client/server configuration that facilitates a service across the network that has been requested by the client.

Backbone network	A high capacity network that links together other networks of lower capacity.
Balun	A transformer for levelling out impedance differences so that a signal generated onto a coaxial cable can transfer on to twisted-pair.
Bandwidth	The capacity of a communications channel to carry data.
Baseband	A means of data transmission where the information is modulated on to a single carrier frequency, eg Ethernet.
Basic Rate Access (BRA)	ISDN's 2B+D offering.
Baud	Unit of signalling speed that is expressed in terms of the number of discrete conditions or signal events per second.
Bit	A binary unit of data that can have two values, true or false, ie 0 or 1.
Bits per second (bps)	The rate at which individual bits are transmitted across a communications link.
Bridge	A network interconnection device that connects two distinct LANs.
Broadband	A method of using a transmission medium having a wide frequency bandwidth. In it several signals can be carried simultaneously by allocating different channels to separate frequency bands.
Broadcast	The simultaneous transmission of data via a network.
Brouter	Network interconnection device that is usually defined as a bridge that supports more than two LAN connections.
Bus topology	A type of network in which all the devices are connected in a line to a single cable.
Byte	Eight bits forming a unit of data.

CATV	(Community Antenna Television). The distribution of television signals from a central point by means of cables.
CCITT	Comité Consultatif International Télégraphique et Téléphonique. An international body through which the national telecommunications bodies coordinate their activities.
Circuit switching	A method of connecting together two users of a transmission service which allocates a circuit for their exclusive use for the duration of the call.
Client/Server computing	The division of labour between two intelligent computing devices.
Channel	A means of transporting information signals. Several channels can share the same physical circuit.
Coaxial cable	A cable consisting of an insulated central wire surrounded by a second casing of fine wire.
Collision	When two information signals attempt to use the same channel simultaneously.
Communications server	A specialised device that provides access to external networks and hosts that cannot be directly connected to a LAN.
Concentration	The function of channelling information from a number of users on to a smaller number of higher-capacity links. A concentrator is the device which performs this function and it is generally programmable.
Connectivity	The ability to establish a communications link between two systems so that information can be transferred between them.
Connection	A circuit consisting of means of conveying information from one place to another.
Contention	When more than one user attempts to use the same channel simultaneously.

CSMA (Carrier Sense Multiple Access). A method of sharing a channel. Before transmitting any information, the sender looks for the presence of a carrier signal, indicating that the channel is already being used. If a carrier signal is not present, the sender can transmit.

Database An organised collection of information in which data is available to all systems, instead of each specific application having its own individual collection.

Datagram A single packet, in a packet-switched network, which is routed without reference by the network to any other datagram being sent.

DCE (Data Circuit-Terminating Equipment). A CCITT term that denotes a communications device installed in a user's premises that is responsible for establishing, maintaining and terminating a connection. A modem is an example.

Data Link A direct serial data communications path between two devices.

Data Link Layer Level two of the ISO OSI Model which is responsible for synchronisation and the handling of errors so that transmission can take place over the physical link.

DTE (Data Terminal Equipment). A CCITT term for a piece of equipment where a communications path ends, for example a PC.

DECnet Proprietary peer-to-peer network technology originally developed for use as a WAN by Digital Equipment Corp. LANs have adapted its philosophy in terms of Ethernet protocols.

Disk Server A storage device that allows users access to a central storage area. Normally used to share large databases.

Distributed Database One organised collection of data which has been subdivided or copied, and distributed amongst several different locations in a distributed system.

Glossary

Distributed Processing	The distribution of information processing functions amongst several different locations in a distributed system.
Distributed System	An information processing system in which a number of individual processors at different locations are linked together so that they can cooperate.
Drop Cable	A cable that links a network adapter to an external transceiver attached to a coaxial LAN.
Duplex	Simultaneous, two-way independent transmission of data.
Dynamic Routeing	A process for selecting the most appropriate path for a packet to travel across a network.
Error Control	A means of ensuring that information received across a transmission link is correct.
Error Correction	A technique to restore data integrity in received data that has been corrupted during transmission.
Error Detection	A set of techniques used to detect errors in received data, for example, parity checks.
Ethernet	A 10 Mbps bus network using CSMA/CD over either coaxial or unshielded twisted-pair cables. Originally developed by Xerox, Intel and DEC.
End-User	A person who uses an information processing system.
FDDI	(Fibre Distributed Data Interface). A fibre optic based token passing ring LAN with dual counter-rotating rings. Each ring can carry data at a rate of 100 Mbps using a 125 MHz transmission frequency.
File	An organised collection of data records which can be accessed by name.
File Server	A computer attached to a LAN that allows the sharing of files to its users.
Frame	A group of bits sent over a link.

232 Glossary

Front-end The client part of a client/server application that requests a service from a server.

Full Duplex A channel capable of transmitting in both directions at the same time.

Gateway A computer system or exchange in one network which allows access to and from another network.

GUI (Graphical User Interface). The user interface that makes use of Windows, Icons, Menus and Pointers (WIMP).

Half Duplex A two-way means of transmission, but data can only travel in one direction at a time.

HDLC (High Level Data Link Control). A protocol designed for data transmission which does not use control characters and is data-independent.

Host A computer system on which applications can be executed and which also provides a service to users of a computer network.

Hub The centre of a star network.

Interface A boundary between two devices or two pieces of software across which the form and functions of the signals which pass it are specified.

ISDN (Integrated Services Digital Network). An approach to switched digital networking that can handle a range of digital voice, data and video.

ISO (International Organisation for Standardisation). The body which exists to promote the development of standards in the IT world. Membership consists of national organisations which are most representative of standardisation in their countries.

Layer A set of logically related functions which are grouped together. Interfaces to and from the layer can be standardised but not the ways the internal functions are performed.

Logical Connection	A connection in which the means of information transfer may not exist as a real physical entity for the duration of the call.
MAN	(Metropolitan Area Network). A high speed network designed to link together sites in a metropolitan area.
Manchester encoding	A technique for sending information bit-serially, in which the data and clock signals are combined.
Message	A logically related collection of data to be moved.
Modem	A piece of equipment which converts digital signals into analogue and vice versa.
Multiplexing	The use of a single physical link for two or more simultaneous separate transmission.
NetWare	LAN Network Operating System developed by Novell. There are two main product lines — NetWare 2.x designed to run on an Intel 80286 platform and above, and NetWare 3.xm designed to run on an Intel 80386 platform and above.
Network address	A group of characters that uniquely identifies the location of a node on a network.
Network architecture	The communications equipment, protocols and transmission links that constitute a nework, and the methods by which they are arranged to implement the network.
Network Layer	Level three of the ISO OSI Model which is responsible for establishing, maintaining and terminating the switched connection between end systems.
Network Topology	The different configurations that can be adopted in building networks, eg, ring, bus, star, etc.
Network Management	All aspects dealing with operation, monitoring, accounting and supervision of networks.
Node	A point at which two or more communications lines meet. Usually applied to a computer or switching device situated at this position.

Glossary

OSI
(Open Systems Interconnection). Standardised procedures for the exchange of information between terminals, computers, people, networks, etc which are accessible to one another by virtue of their mutual use of these procedures.

OSI Reference Model
An architectural model that describes how open communications can be achieved between computer systems through the use of a layered protocol stack. It has seven layers.

Packet
A block of data with a defined format containing control and data fields.

Packet-switching
A term used in data transmission network which is designed to carry the data in the form of packets. The data, in packets, is passed to the network, and devices within it use the control information to transmit the packet to the correct destination.

Parity bit
An extra bit added to a group of bits, usually to seven bits to make up a byte. The parity bit can be of 0 or 1 value so that every byte will then add up to an odd or even number, depending on whether odd or even parity is chosen.

Peer-to-peer
Communications between two devices on an equal footing.

Physical connection
A transmission means between two or more users which usually consists of electrical conductors along which signals are transmitted.

Physical Layer
Level one of the ISO OSI Model which is responsible for the mechanical and electrical interface to the communications medium.

Polling
A process whereby terminals are invited one at a time to transmit information.

PTT
(Postal, Telephone and Telegraph Administration). A general term used to denote a supplier of telecommunications services.

Glossary

Presentation Layer	Level six of the OSI ISO Model which provides the means to represent the format of the information exchange, without changing its meaning.
Primary Rate Access (PRA)	An ISDN access method that uses the maximum data rates of 2.048 Mbps split into 30B+D channels.
Print server	A computer and/or software that provides users with shared access the network printer(s).
Protocol	A set of rules to ensure a meaningful communication between cooperating partners.
Protocol converter	A device (hardware and/or software) that translates between two protocols to facilitate communications between different systems.
Public Data Network	A communications system whhich is intended for transmission of digital data, and which is available to anyone wishing to subscribe to it.
Real-time	Normally used to describe the situation where a computer is used to control and monitor directly a manufacturing process.
Repeater	A device used to re-generate, amplify and re-transmit signals.
Ring Topology	A layout scheme in which the network takes the form of a closed loop with the devices attached to the ring.
Routeing	The function of selecting the path for transmission of data within a network.
Router	Hardware and software that enables users to interconnect LANs at the Network Layer, providing bridging services across the network.
Satellite processor	A computer system which has a subsidiary role in a distributed system.
Server	A node that permits other nodes on the LAN to access its resources.

Glossary

Session — When two pieces of software, two users, resources, or other components in a network, are connected together for the purpose of exchanging information, they are said to be in session.

Session Layer — Level five of the ISO OSI Model which is responsible for establishing communications sessions with other systems.

Simplex — A communications system that can only carry a signal in one direction at a time.

Star topology — A network scheme where each node is connected to a central hub.

Station — A single addressable unit on a network. A station may represent a single device or a group of devices attached through another (eg a concentrator).

STDM — (Statistical Time Division Multiplexing). A technique whereby a multiplexer apportions time on a dynamic basis only to those channels which are active.

SQL — (Structured Query Language). A standardised query language that can be used for querying databases across a network in a client/server environment.

Switching — In a computer or communications network, switching is the process by which services or data are directed to the appropriate user.

Synchronous transmission — A method of communication in which data is sent in blocks, without the need for start and stop bits between each byte.

System — A collection of computers, associated software, peripherals, terminals, human users, etc, that form an autonomous whole capable of information processing.

Terminal — A device which allows an end-user to input data to and receive it from a computer system.

Terminal emulation — Software that allows a PC to mimic the attributes of a dumb host terminal.

Terminal Server	A device attached to a LAN that allows a number of attached asynchronous dumb terminals to communicate with a host.
TDM	(Time-Division Multiplexing). A method of dividing up digital channels to make maximum use of their bandwidth, by taking input from each source in turn.
Token bus	A LAN with a bus topology that uses token passing as its access method.
Token passing	A technique for restricting access to a network to a single node at a time. A token is passed around the network, granting permission to transmit data. The sender attaches its message to the token as it passes.
Token ring	A ring network topology which uses token passing to control access to the network.
Token	A unit of information in the form of a packet which acknowledges that control of the network is to be relinquished upon receipt of the packet. An empty packet containing a token is forwarded to the next node on the line.
Transaction Processing	The entering of records of events into information processing systems as each event occurs.
Transceiver	A transmitter/receiver through which devices can access the network.
Transparent	A communications link is said to be transparent when it does not alter in any way the contents of the messages it transmits. A computer system or program used as an interface to another system is transparent when the user is aware only of the final system.
Transport Layer	Level four of the ISO OSI Model which is responsible for providing end-to-end control and information interchange.
Tree topology	A network scheme where there is only one route between any two nodes.

Unshielded twisted-pair	A standard cabling used for telephone lines.

Virtual circuit	A link that seems and behaves like a dedicated point-to-point link or a system that delivers packets in sequence.

V-Series (CCITT)	The CCITT Recommendations for data transmission over telephone networks.

X-Series (CCITT)	The CCITT Recommendations for data transmission over digital data networks.

Index

Accountability   160, 161, 170
Administrator   213-215, 227
ALOHA   12, 14, 41, 81-84, 87, 109, 114
ANSI   142, 147, 174, 175, 218, 227
Application Layer   193, 227
Architecture   13, 111, 118, 138, 177, 183, 185,
                         194, 195, 227, 233

Assurance   160
Authentication   160, 165, 171
Authorisation   160
Availability   6, 26, 29, 56, 61, 70, 137, 147,
                         149, 159, 160, 162, 164, 168,
                         170, 172

Backbone   2, 37, 113, 114, 143, 218, 219,
                         228
Bandwidth   23, 28, 31, 33, 41, 42, 54-57, 59,
                         70, 74, 76, 82, 84, 85, 90, 92,
                         101, 107, 141, 143, 144, 197,
                         199, 218, 219, 228, 237
Baseband   27, 30-32, 48, 49, 52, 53, 52, 54,
                         71, 112, 179, 228

Basic Rate Access (BRA) 222, 228
Baud   59, 228
Bit   12, 29, 31, 52, 114, 134, 140,
                         149, 188, 194, 213, 228, 233,
                         234

Bridge   62-65, 64, 65, 67, 216, 228
Broadband   19, 31, 32, 49, 52-55, 54, 55, 54,
                         55, 57, 56, 58, 71, 142, 144, 180,
                         199, 222, 228

Brouter   67, 228
Buffer insertion   94

240 Index

Bus	11, 16, 22, 28, 30, 35, 49, 50, 49, 51, 55, 57, 58, 71, 78, 79, 81, 85, 86, 91, 98, 107, 114, 120, 122, 130, 137, 166, 179, 180, 196, 215, 228, 231, 233, 237
Byte	228, 234, 236
Cambridge Ring	94, 125
Capacity	2, 5, 16, 22, 37, 38, 46, 47, 49, 70, 75, 78, 79, 95, 98, 109, 119, 124, 127, 130, 138, 140, 144-146, 152, 156, 204, 215, 228, 229
Carrier Sense Multiple Access (CSMA)	87, 114
Carrier Sense Multiple Access/Collision Detect (CSMA/CD)	109
CATV	30, 32, 54, 180, 229
CCITT	10, 174, 186, 194, 229, 230, 238
Channel	5, 12, 16, 41, 49, 53, 55, 56, 61, 75, 76, 78, 88, 89, 91, 92, 107, 110, 141, 144, 215, 222, 228-230, 232
CIA	147, 159, 160, 162
Circuit Switching	229
Client	13, 118, 124, 151-157, 212, 227, 229, 232, 236
Cluster	11, 74, 223
Coaxial	9, 19, 22, 26, 28, 30, 31, 30-32, 35, 41, 42, 44, 48, 57, 58, 70, 104, 109, 139, 144, 179, 180, 187, 228, 229, 231
Collision	49, 79, 82, 87-90, 109, 110, 114, 115, 200, 209, 229
Concentration	37, 229
Conferencing	105, 117, 133, 140, 144, 145, 150
Confidentiality	147, 159, 162, 163, 165, 168, 170-172
Connectivity	24, 70, 211, 229
Contention	3, 22, 58, 75, 79, 86, 87, 114, 200, 229
Cost	1, 3, 10, 16, 23, 26, 29, 31, 32, 37, 39, 49-52, 58, 65, 67, 70, 74, 98, 106, 111, 116, 117, 122, 129, 132, 133, 142, 143, 146-149,

	155, 159, 160, 167, 169, 198, 199, 204, 217, 218, 220, 225
Data Link	62, 68, 175, 177-179, 187-189, 194, 230, 232
Database	11, 61, 118, 124, 132, 138, 145, 150, 153-157, 204, 230
Datagram	6, 230
DEC	67, 68, 88, 173, 174, 212, 231
Distortion	25, 28, 32, 140, 141
Distributed	11, 12, 17, 18, 20, 42, 75, 116-118, 124, 125, 127, 138, 142, 151, 159, 164, 165, 217, 218, 230, 231, 235
Drop cable	231
Duplex	31, 54, 188, 192, 231, 232
Electronic mail	11, 18, 61, 117, 118, 132, 134, 135, 137, 150, 198, 199
Empty slot	93, 94, 96
End-User	79, 127, 175, 177, 197, 231, 236
Error	7, 8, 17, 23, 26, 48-50, 62, 70, 80, 90, 92-95, 109, 111, 163, 177, 179, 188, 189-194, 231
Ethernet	12, 13, 41, 49, 52, 88, 90, 108-110, 109-111, 115, 133, 173, 179, 180, 200, 228, 230, 231
Facsimile	17, 132-134, 139, 143, 150
FDDI	143, 164, 217-220, 219, 226, 231
Fibre optic	9, 26, 32, 34, 33, 35, 43, 48, 70, 78, 104, 143, 165, 218, 231
File	11, 60, 61, 71, 115, 123, 125, 131, 134, 138, 142, 145, 146, 150, 155, 156, 204, 211-215, 231
File sharing	146
File transfer	11, 115, 123, 145, 146, 150, 156
Files	13, 61, 122-125, 131-134, 138, 145, 146, 203, 213-215, 223, 231
Frame	37, 59, 64, 79, 82, 87, 112, 179, 199, 200, 202, 209, 231
Frequency Division Multiplexing (FDM)	30

242 Index

Gateway	59, 60, 68, 71, 103, 126, 130, 137-139, 146, 148, 149, 177, 178, 189, 232
Graphics	8, 11, 127, 139, 143, 144, 152
Headend	54
High-level Data Link Control (HDLC)	188
Highway	49, 122, 133
Host	4, 5, 20, 53, 59, 60, 74, 122, 134, 139, 198, 221-225, 232, 236, 237
Hub	18, 45, 46, 99, 103, 104, 106, 107, 232, 236
IBM	13, 42-44, 59, 64, 68, 111, 117, 138, 156, 180, 212, 215
IEEE	11, 27, 64, 88, 174-182, 195, 196
Infra-red	22, 40, 42, 70, 219, 220
Integrity	112, 124, 137, 147, 159, 162, 166, 168, 170-172, 193, 231
Interface	6, 10, 16, 29, 37, 41, 54, 118, 125, 126, 143, 145, 146, 154, 164, 173, 175-177, 179, 183, 184, 187, 191, 194, 197, 200, 212, 216, 217, 218, 225, 227, 231, 232, 234, 237
Interference	24, 25, 28-30, 33, 41, 54, 58
Layer	6, 27, 30, 67, 68, 175, 177-179, 182, 185-196, 207, 227, 230, 232-237
Logical	6, 63, 85, 86, 160, 166, 180, 189, 191, 196, 203, 214, 233
Loop	22, 35, 46, 91, 120, 122, 130, 235
Mainframe	16, 45, 56, 68, 124, 138, 149, 151, 152, 156, 163, 212
Manchester Encoding	52, 53, 71, 233
Mesh	22, 30, 31, 52, 119, 120, 150
Message	6, 14, 16, 24, 47, 48, 75, 77-81, 85-88, 91, 92, 94, 99, 103, 109, 120, 121, 130, 131, 135, 137, 141, 142, 145, 148, 165, 166, 177, 199, 202, 233, 237
Metropolitan Area Network (MAN)	11

Modem	12, 54, 56, 57, 102, 169, 179, 186, 194, 230, 233
Modulation	26, 31, 32, 41, 52, 57, 141
Monitor	48, 92-94, 97, 98, 119, 163, 212, 213, 235
Multiplexer	4, 74, 75, 103, 125, 177, 236
Multiplexing	4, 5, 14, 22, 30, 54, 56, 73-76, 84, 90, 92, 93, 104, 109, 114, 187, 190, 191, 233, 236, 237
NetWare	13, 211-216, 233
Network Address	233
Network Architecture	138, 194, 233
Network Layer	67, 68, 177, 188, 189, 194, 233, 235
Node	6, 46-50, 67, 75, 77, 80-82, 84-94, 96-98, 103, 112, 114, 120, 121, 125, 138, 141, 142, 150, 153, 180, 213, 219, 227, 233, 235-237
Noise	24, 25, 27, 41, 54, 70, 82, 89, 101, 162
Packet	6, 7, 11, 12, 14, 22, 26, 41, 47, 48, 54, 56, 58, 62, 63, 79-83, 85, 86, 87-98, 103, 106, 109, 110, 112, 122, 141, 146, 147, 177, 179, 194, 199, 200, 202, 230, 231, 234, 237
Parity	93, 94, 231, 234
Peer	186, 193, 230, 234
Personal Computer (PC)	1, 2, 58, 108, 117, 130-132, 137, 138, 146, 148, 154, 163, 167, 203, 213, 217
Physical Connection	3, 5, 10, 17, 18, 20, 22, 24-26, 32, 38, 39, 54, 62, 63, 78, 92, 140-143, 147, 160, 168, 175-177, 179, 180, 184, 186-189, 191, 194, 203, 213, 229, 230, 233, 234
Polling	3, 45, 76-78, 84, 91, 99, 109, 114, 234
Presentation Layer	192, 235
Primary Rate Access (PRA)	222, 235

244 Index

Printer	1, 58, 61, 71, 117, 131, 145, 163, 213, 235
Protocol	6, 11, 59, 64, 67, 68, 75, 77, 88-91, 103, 109, 118, 123, 125, 138, 175, 176, 178-180, 191, 193, 212, 215, 232, 234, 235
Radio	4, 12, 22, 40, 41, 54, 56, 70, 78, 81, 219
Reference Model	13, 175, 177, 185, 186, 190, 193-195, 234
Reliability	17, 23, 24, 30, 48, 49, 58, 70, 82, 106, 109, 111, 137, 213
Repeater	46, 48, 91-94, 97, 125, 194, 235
Reservation	84, 114, 179
Resource Sharing	1, 17, 22, 45, 58, 74, 84, 87, 124, 125, 133, 150, 159, 160, 163, 213
Ring	13, 22, 30, 35, 42, 46-51, 64, 67, 71, 75, 85, 86, 91-95, 97, 98, 107, 110, 111, 112-115, 120, 122, 125, 130, 137, 143, 166, 180, 196, 212, 215, 218-220, 231, 233, 235-237
Risk Analysis	161, 167-170, 172, 218
Routeing	6, 38, 62-64, 67, 120-122, 142, 150, 166, 170, 171, 189, 190, 227, 231, 235
Security	25, 32, 41, 45, 51, 59, 61, 65, 70, 104, 106, 138, 147, 152, 156, 159, 160, 161-165, 167-172, 174, 196, 203, 206, 213-215, 227
Server	13, 18, 45, 46, 49, 58-60, 59-61, 118, 124, 134, 137, 145, 148, 151, 152, 153-157, 163, 165, 204, 206, 207, 211-216, 223, 227, 229-232, 235-237
Session Layer	191, 192, 236
Simplex	236
Slot	49, 74, 75, 82, 84, 87, 90-94, 96
Star	11, 22, 45, 46, 50, 51, 71, 77, 78, 99, 100, 99, 101, 103, 106, 111, 115, 119, 137, 141, 150, 213, 232, 233, 236

Station	24, 48, 64, 75, 89, 90, 92-94, 97, 98, 166, 200, 201, 209, 219, 236
Statistical Time Division Multiplexing (STDM)	75
Switching	5-7, 11, 12, 14, 19, 22, 45, 94, 99, 101, 103, 140, 142, 189, 229, 233, 234, 236
Synchronous	4, 59, 74, 188, 236
System	2, 8, 12, 15, 16, 18, 20, 23-26, 29, 31, 32, 35, 37, 39, 41-47, 49, 52, 54, 57, 56, 58, 59, 64, 74, 75, 77, 78, 81-83, 86-88, 91, 92, 94, 97, 99, 102, 103, 106, 108-111, 117-119, 122-127, 129, 130, 131-134, 137-141, 143, 145, 146, 149, 154, 156, 157, 159, 160, 161, 163, 165, 167, 168, 171, 175, 176, 180, 182, 183, 189, 192, 194, 198, 199, 201, 202, 204, 206, 207, 211, 212, 213-216, 218, 223, 225, 227, 230-233, 235-238
Terminal Emulation	2, 3, 6, 27, 30, 37, 43, 59, 67, 71, 77, 81, 99, 101-103, 115, 117, 118, 122, 124, 126, 127, 129-131, 136, 138, 140, 143, 144, 146, 148, 149, 183, 186, 191, 193, 198, 202, 222, 223, 230, 236, 237
Token	13, 42, 47, 85, 86, 93, 96-98, 111-115, 143, 179, 180, 196, 212, 215, 218, 231, 237
Token Passing	85, 86, 93, 96-98, 114, 143, 179, 180, 218, 231, 237
Token Ring	13, 42, 47, 111, 113-115, 180, 196, 212, 215, 237
Topology	10, 11, 14, 22, 24, 25, 36, 44-47, 49-51, 64, 70, 73, 75, 99, 101, 108, 109-112, 114, 119, 120, 137, 177, 179, 180, 197, 206, 214, 228, 233, 235-237
Transaction Processing	191, 193, 194, 237
Transceiver	91, 179, 194, 231, 237
Transparent	5, 59, 61, 62, 64, 65, 68, 122, 148, 188, 189, 206, 212, 237

Transport Layer 189-192, 195, 237
Tree 11, 22, 49, 51, 64, 109, 237
Twisted-pair 22, 26-30, 32, 35, 42, 48, 50, 70, 104, 180, 228, 231, 238

University of Hawaii 12, 81, 87, 109
Unshielded Twisted-Pair 28, 180, 231, 238

Video 11, 17, 30, 42, 53, 58, 117, 133, 143-145, 148, 150, 220, 222, 232

Virtual 6, 59, 138, 194, 238
Voice 4, 17, 20, 30, 37, 42, 53, 98, 106, 115, 117, 132, 133, 140-143, 145, 148, 150, 199, 218, 220, 222, 232

Workstation 45, 60, 67, 108, 117, 131-134, 137, 138, 146, 150, 156, 163, 165, 166, 207, 213, 215, 216